PLURAL LANGUAGES,
PLURAL CULTURES

Plural Languages, Plural Cultures

Communication, Identity, and Sociopolitical Change in Contemporary India

LACHMAN M. KHUBCHANDANI

An East-West Center Book
from the East-West Culture Learning Institute
*Published for the East-West Center
by University of Hawaii Press*

Copyright © 1983 by The East-West Center
All rights reserved
Manufactured in the United States of America

Library of Congress Cataloging in Publication Data

Khubchandani, Lachman Mulchand.
  Plural languages, plural cultures.

  Bibliography: p.
  Includes index.
  1. Sociolinguistics—India. I. East-West Center.
II. Title.
P40.45.I4K5   1983   401'.9   82-20973
ISBN 0-8248-0639-5 (pbk.)

Respectfully Dedicated
to the Memory of
SUNITI KUMAR CHATTERJEE
(1890-1977)

Contents

List of Tables	ix
Acknowledgments	xi
Introduction	xiii

PART ONE: SOCIOLINGUISTIC REALITIES

1. *Language in a Plural Society* — 3
   - Linguistic Regions — 4
   - Language Plurality — 5
   - Bilingualism — 12

2. *Language Modernization* — 19
   - "Center-Periphery" Hypothesis — 19
   - Assumptions of Language Development — 22
   - Functional Heterogeneity — 25
   - Language Standardization — 27
   - Language Cultivation — 30
   - Contemporary Trends — 37

3. *Language Manipulation* — 40
   - Contours of Speech Behavior — 40
   - Language Claims — 41
   - Mother-Tongue Identity — 45
   - Bilingual Identity — 51
   - Politicization of Language Data — 54
   - Language Manipulation as a Tool for Social Planning — 61

4. *Language-Promotion Activities* — 65
   - Language Politics — 65
   - Language and Education — 69
   - Language Elaboration — 75
   - The Role of English — 77
   - Language-planning Agencies — 81

PART TWO: CHALLENGES OF CHANGE

5. **Plural Speech Communities** — 89
   - Identity Pressures — 90
   - Stable and Fluid Zones — 105
   - Homogeneity in Communication — 107
   - The Hindi-Urdu Amalgam — 112
   - Domain of a Language — 114

6. **Language Ideology in Education** — 117
   - The Education System before the British — 117
   - Language in Colonial Education — 119
   - The Mother Tongue as Instructional Medium — 124
   - Plural Media — 126
   - Identity versus Communication — 129

7. **Pressures from Language Elites** — 134
   - Group Dynamics — 134
   - Privileges of Language Study — 137
   - Struggle over the University Language Medium — 139
   - Linguistic Minorities — 144
   - Polarization of Issues — 145

8. **Directions of Language Planning** — 149
   - Human Sensitivities — 150
   - Situation-bound Planning — 152
   - Grass-roots Approach — 156
   - Deliberate Behavioral Change — 157

   Epilogue — 163
   - Concept of Language — 163
   - Language and Communication — 166
   - Patterns of Plurality — 167
   - Pangs of Transition — 171

   Appendix: Languages Used as Media — 177
   Bibliography — 183
   Language Index — 193
   Subject Index — 199

Tables

Chapter 1

1. Major National and Administrative Languages — 6
2. Communication Environments in Indian States and Union Territories, 1961 — 10
3. Percentage Distribution of the Press in India by Language, 1977 — 15
4. Classification of Periodicals according to Contents, 1977 — 16

Chapter 2

5. Dimensions of Language Development — 21
6. Speech as Living Phenomena — 32

Chapter 3

7. Claims of Hindi-Urdu in the 1961 Census — 55

Chapter 4

8. Speech Behavior and Language Education — 72

Chapter 5

9. Speakers Claiming Hindustani, Urdu, and Hindi as Mother Tongue, 1931–1961 — 91
10. Census Claims of Main Bihari Languages in Bihar, 1951–1961 — 92
11. Census Claims of Bihari Languages throughout India, 1961–1971 — 94
12. Census Claims of Rajasthani Languages and Other Vernaculars of the HUP Region, 1961–1971 — 96

13. Percentages of Muslims and Urdu Speakers to Total Population in Various States, 1951–1971 … 97
14. Increase (or Decrease) of Percentages in Hindi and Urdu Populations, 1951–1961 … 98
15. Profile of Urdu as Mother Tongue, 1961–1971 … 100
16. Profile of Hindi as Mother Tongue, 1961–1971 … 101
17. Growth Percentages of Dominant Languages Other than Hindi-Urdu, 1951–1961 … 106

Chapter 6

18. Bilingual Media … 127

Chapter 7

19. Time Allotted to Language Instruction in Different States, Class X (1974) … 140
20. Polarities in the Language-Medium Controversy … 146

Epilogue

21. Major Types of Pluralism … 172

Appendix

Languages Used as Media … 178

Acknowledgments

SOME OF THE MATERIAL presented in this book first came up during seminars at Zagreb University in 1969-1970, when I was conducting a course on "India as a sociolinguistic area" for the students of linguistics and Indology. There followed a series of lectures on the same theme at the Süd-Asien Institut, University of Heidelberg, during the summer of 1970. Later I pursued this study at University College, London, with the sponsorship of the Commonwealth Universities Association (1970-1971), and at the Indian Institute of Advanced Study at Simla (1972-1974).

The volume was written during my stay at the East-West Center as Senior Fellow of the Culture Learning Institute (1974-1975). An epilogue has been added in 1981, in midst of my preoccupation with setting up training programs for the Centre for Communication Studies at Poona.

In a way, the study is an expression of the stimulation I have received from my cross-cultural experiences since 1947, when I became a refugee as a result of the partition of the country. My varied assignments as a schoolteacher, moving on to journalism and then to linguistics and communications, and working in such diverse settings as Delhi, Philadelphia, Poona, Zagreb, London, Simla, Singapore, Khartoum, and Honolulu, have sharpened my sensitivity to some of the intricacies of plural societies.

During the early phase, I was greatly inspired by my teacher Professor Suniti Kumar Chatterjee (1890-1977), the great doyen of Indian linguistics, whose views on language and society have helped shape my thinking, and I now dedicate the book to his memory. I am deeply indebted to Professor S. M. Katre of the Deccan College Postgraduate Research Institute, who has been a constant source of inspiration, and also to Professor Prabodh Pandit (1923-1975) of Delhi University, with whom I always enjoyed discussing issues of language development in the context of Asian pluralism.

In a direct sense, the study owes much to the forward thrust of the East-West Center in providing the nucleus for cross-cultural understanding and viewing the issues of language modernization in that context. I am particularly indebted to Verner Bickley and Mark Lester at the Culture Learning Institute for stimulating interchanges. I have also enjoyed discussing various issues concerning this study with Everett Kleinjans and John Brownell.

This volume owes its existence to the initiative of the University of Hawaii Press. I deeply appreciate the exacting and helpful approach of the copyeditors in giving final shape to the manuscript.

I also express my profound gratitude to many of my colleagues at different institutions who have shown personal interest in my academic pursuits. It will not be possible to name them individually; hence they remain anonymous.

Poona   LACHMAN M. KHUBCHANDANI
1 January 1982

Introduction

SOUTH ASIA is often described as a "linguistic madhouse," a "museum of languages," or as a "sociolinguistic giant"—posing a serious challenge to agencies concerned with social planning. Many social scientists have reacted with bafflement at the relatively fluid segmentation patterns in social and language behavior and at the diversification of language use prevailing in the traditional sociopolitical order in large parts of the subcontinent.

Many political and sociolinguistic studies of the 1950s and 1960s have reminded us of the upsurge of modern European languages in the wake of the Renaissance, which brought to the fore questions relating to linguistic and national boundaries of the newly independent nations—a powerful factor in shaping many European nation-states. In this context, the multiplicity of languages in the developing world was often regarded as a serious challenge to sociopolitical development.

The challenges of language transition faced by many "new" nations in Asia and Africa, along with the pressures of universal literacy, the extension of mass communication through massive technology, and the manipulation of language for political and socioeconomic gains, lead us to look at language in a new paradigm. Some of these concerns characterize the period since the end of World War II as an era of "new awareness" of language. Such awareness has given birth to decision-making processes, several of them unique to individual countries, attempting to resolve the dilemma. In turn, this development has led many social scientists to reconsider the earlier dictum of "one nation—one language," so pervasive until the 1950s, and to examine critically the implications of multilingualism in a society.

At this juncture, therefore, it becomes appropriate to search for answers to such questions as: Is plurality of languages in an area a handicap or an asset in social development? If it is regarded as a handicap in integrating a nation, should we try to cope with it through some kind of selective bilingualism (or multilingualism) to bring some order out of chaotic diversity? If it is regarded as an asset, what exactly needs to be done to use the potential of this heritage and to gain insights into the dynamics of pluralistic societies generally?

Recent studies in linguistics, and particularly in sociolinguistics, project the entire variability phenomenon in language activity as a "natural" process of verbal behavior. In this light, the primacy of the pursuit of uniformity and homogeneity in a language or language area, so far universally assumed as an article of faith, needs to be supported by valid propositions. If our response to the fast-changing socioeconomic scene is to be adequate, a deeper understanding of the realities of speech behavior in these regions is essential.

This study treats of the language scene in South Asia. In particular, it reviews the tribulations of the Indian polity over various issues pertaining to language in the context of cultural pluralism during the past three decades. The study is presented in two parts: "Sociolinguistic Realities" and "Challenges of Change."

Part One stresses the "organic" features of communication and identity in plurilingual societies. In providing a backdrop of the speech communication patterns in the subcontinent, Chapter 1 is concerned with some of the spatial factors of linguistic heterogeneity. Chapter 2 critically reviews the premises assumed by elites and development experts in modernizing language. Chapter 3 discusses the subjective traits of language identity that make it susceptible to manipulation by an individual, a group, or a state. Chapter 4 surveys the sociopolitical and educational scene concerning the study and development of languages in India.

Part Two probes certain specific issues which plural speech communities face in meeting the demands of contemporary ideologies, institutions, and technology. Chapter 5 brings into focus the "fluid" characteristics of language identity in the vast Hindi-Urdu-Panjabi region. Chapter 6 traces the impact of the politicization of the language issue in education from the colonial period to the contemporary language ideologies among conflicting language elites. Chapter 7 discusses the dynamics of rival pressure groups over language privileges. Chapter 8 draws attention to the limitations of effecting deliberate language change through "intellectual" fostering of language standards.

The epilogue, in summing up, poses a few questions concerning the concept of language itself, in the context of a growing acceptance of cultural pluralism throughout the world.

Part One

SOCIOLINGUISTIC REALITIES

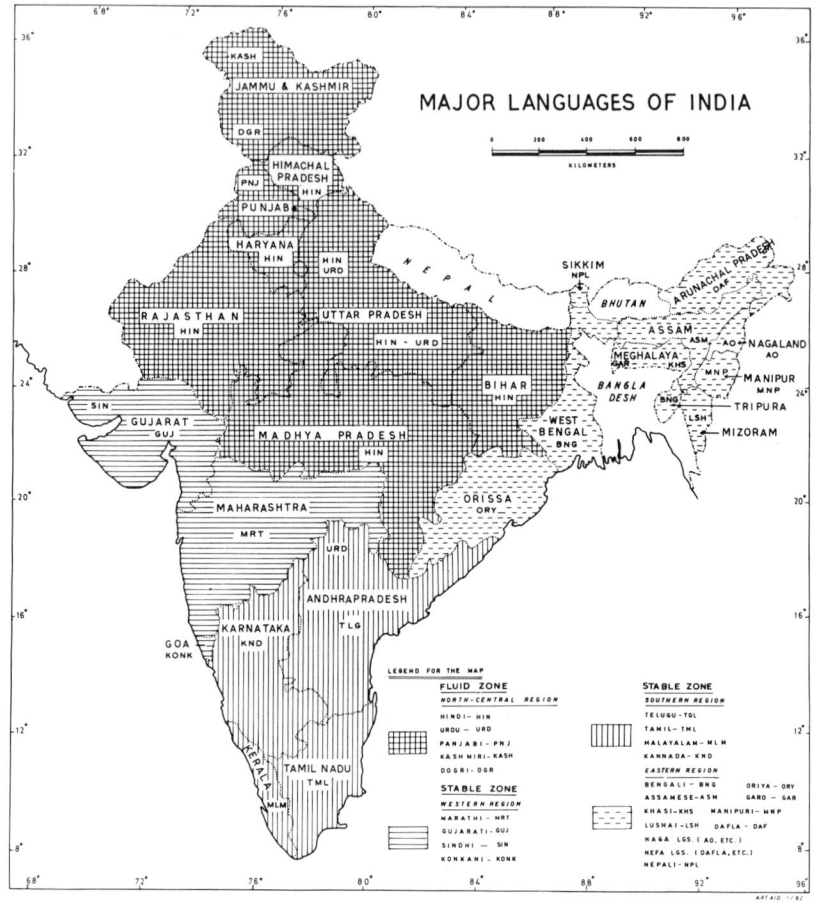

Major Languages of India and Numbers of Speakers in 1971 (in millions)

FLUID ZONE

North Central Region: Hindi, 208.5 million; Urdu, 28.6; Panjabi, 14.1; Kashmiri, 2.5; Dogri, 1.3.

STABLE ZONE

Western Region: Marathi, 41.8 million; Gujarati, 25.9; Sindhi, 1.7; Konkani, 1.5.

Southern Region: Telugu, 44.8 million; Tamil, 37.7; Malayalam, 21.9; Kannada, 21.7.

Eastern Region: Bengali, 44.8 million; Oriya, 19.9; Assamese, 9.0; Manipuri, 0.8; Khasi, 0.5; Garo, 0.4; Lushai (Mizo), 0.3; 14 Naga languages (Ao, etc.); North-East Frontier Agency [NEFA] languages (Dafla, etc.).

CHAPTER 1

Language in a Plural Society

THE SOUTH ASIAN LANGUAGE SCENE has provided a unique mosaic of verbal experience since historical times. In India, a land populated by over 680 million speakers, scores of small speech groups consisting of a few thousand people continue to maintain their mother tongues in everyday life.[1] During the course of history, four language families—Indo-European, Dravidian, Austro-Asiatic, and Tibeto-Chinese—represented by different ethnic groups, have acted and reacted upon one another, making for a fundamental cultural unity of the subcontinent. Several Indian languages belonging to different families show parallel trends of development during a long history and characterize a single composite region; they bear many phonological, grammatical, and lexical similarities; and they have a great susceptibility toward borrowing from languages of contact. Modern languages in the South Asian region represent a striking example of the processes of diffusion—grammatical as well as phonetic—over many contiguous areas.[2]

India is one of the most interesting laboratories of multilingual experience in the world today. The Indian census lists about two hundred classified languages,[3] out of which over forty are dominant district languages, though the Constitution puts its seal on only fifteen as major "national" languages (fourteen modern plus one classical language—Sanskrit) (Table 1). The prevalence of tiny linguistic minorities scattered in small clusters throughout the country—such as Saurashtri in Madurai, Marathi in Tanjore, Urdu in Mysore and Madras, Kachhi in Poona, Bengali in Banaras, Tamil in Mathura, Malayalam in Bombay—exemplifies a degree of tolerance of linguistic and cultural variation in India's history. Acculturation processes among migrants have, to a great extent, been voluntary and gradual.[4]

Studies in South Asian linguistics pursued during the past three decades have highlighted the diversity of linguistic systems. The multiplicity of Indian languages prevailing in a single federal polity has also received considerable attention from many social and political scientists interested in developing nations, particularly from those for whom language identity is very much a part of the identity of a nationality or a nation, as is the case in Europe.

Since the independence of India and Pakistan in 1947, the role of language in individual and social life on the subcontinent has been under constant review at different levels of the federal polity. To acquire a better understanding of the prevalent and newly emerging communication patterns in the pluralistic society that India is, it is necessary to supplement the statistical accounts enumerating the multiplicity of languages in the country with an overall ecological perspective of different regions and the dynamic patterns of diversified behavior among different speech groups.

Linguistic Regions

The federal organization of India (twenty-two states and nine union territories) comprises broadly twelve principal language areas, each dominated by a different language enjoying full or partial recognition in the sphere of public communication within that area. Much of the confusion in interpreting India's language scene comes from the tendency to deal with the subcontinent either as a whole or as a series of small, linguistically isolated units. A better understanding of trends can be achieved by grouping together these language areas into four major linguistic regions, which show many parallels in their overall communication environments in spite of a widespread linguistic heterogeneity within each region:

1. The South, dominated by four Dravidian languages, with more than 25 percent of the country's total population: Telugu in Andhra Pradesh, Tamil in Tamil Nadu, Kannada in Karnataka, and Malayalam in Kerala.
2. The East, dominated by three Indo-Aryan languages, with more than 15 percent of the population: Bengali in West Bengal, Oriya in Orissa, and Assamese in Assam. It is the most multilingual region, covering many Tibeto-Chinese and Austro-Asiatic (Munda, Mon-Khmer) languages. It also includes five multilingual states (Meghalaya, Nagaland, Manipur, Tripura, and Sikkim) and three Union territories (Arunachal Pradesh, Mizoram, and the Andaman and Nicobar Islands).
3. The West, dominated by two Indo-Aryan languages, with nearly 14

percent of the population: Marathi (South Indo-Aryan) in Maharashtra and Gujarati (Central Indo-Aryan) in Gujarat.
4. The North-Central, dominated by two Central Indo-Aryan (Hindi-Urdu amalgam and Panjabi) languages and one Dardic (Kashmiri) language, with nearly 46 percent of the population. Hindi-Urdu is spoken in six states—Uttar Pradesh, Madhya Pradesh, Bihar, Rajasthan, Haryana, and Himachal Pradesh (also in Delhi and Chandigarh Union territories); Panjabi in Panjab; and Kashmiri in the Kashmir valley (along with Dogri in Jammu, part of the Jammu and Kashmir State).

The twelve major languages listed above—eight Indo-Aryan and four Dravidian—account for 87 percent of the entire population of the country. Hindi is the official language of six states and two Union territories; Bengali of two states (West Bengal and Tripura); and the remaining ten major regional languages are recognized as state languages in ten different states. Urdu continues to enjoy the status of an official language in Jammu and Kashmir, though Kashmiri and Dogri are gradually taking its place in public communication. Manipur recognizes Manipuri, a Tibeto-Chinese language; and Goa recognizes Konkani, a South Indo-Aryan language, for official purposes. Most of the Union territories represent multilingual pockets within different linguistic regions. Some multilingual territories retain English as the administrative language.

Altogether fourteen Indian languages plus English enjoy official recognition at the administrative level in different parts of the country. At the federal level, Hindi is the declared official language, and English is being retained as the associate official language until the non-Hindi-speaking regions are equipped to accept Hindi. Apart from twelve major regional languages, the Indian Constitution recognizes three languages without any region—Urdu, Sindhi, and the classical language, Sanskrit. The 1971 populations of major national and administrative languages are given in Table 1.

Language Plurality

The plural character of Indian society is well recognized. In a plural society, there is a shared core of universe, and different partial "universes" of the groups within coexist in the region in a state of mutual accommodation. Despite several varying sociocultural characteristics, such as caste, religion, occupation, and mother tongue, cutting across over 370 districts in 31 states and Union territories, members of a group having a common identity share a core of experience. Individual identity groups crisscross in more than one manner, hardly ever coterminating within the

Table 1. Major National and Administrative Languages

Languages	Number of Speakers in 1971* (in millions)	Percentage of Total Population
Recognized by Constitution		
1. Hindi	208.5	38.0
2. Bengali	44.79	8.2
3. Telugu	44.76	8.2
4. Marathi	41.8	7.6
5. Tamil	37.7	6.9
6. Urdu	28.6	5.2
7. Gujarati	25.9	4.7
8. Malayalam	21.9	4.0
9. Kannada	21.7	4.0
10. Oriya	19.9	3.6
11. Panjabi	14.1	2.6
12. Assamese	9.0	1.6
13. Kashmiri	2.5	0.5
14. Sindhi	1.7	0.3
15. Sanskrit	(2.2 thousands)	—
Additional Administrative Languages		
16. Konkani	1.5	0.3
17. Manipuri	0.79	0.14
18. English	0.19	—

*Census of India, 1971: Social and Cultural Tables, Part II-C (i), A. Chandra Sekhar. New Delhi: Registrar General of India, 1977, 4–86.

same boundary. Each of the identities such as age, status, religion, occupation, and language may be important under some circumstances, but no single characteristic is so important that it operates to divide one group from another in all traits. Thus, individuals joined by a single trait (say, speech) are generally marked by their variety, their lack of unity, and their tendency to act as fairly discrete groups relative to the pulls and pressures of time and space. It would, therefore, be a fallacy to characterize a plural society in terms of the dominance of one unit over, or its dependence upon, another unit.[5] Insular societies such as nationality groups in Europe, in contrast, are marked by congruent identities terminating roughly at the same boundary, and thus are amenable to clear-cut categorization.

Speech behavior in a society is modulated according to the roles and the attitudes of the participants, the settings and channels of communication, situational expediency, and the communication tasks to be performed. In unilingual "standardized" societies, variation due to stratification may be limited to a narrow spectrum of speech behavior. This spectrum becomes much wider when the society is either multilingual, with its members controlling several distinct languages, or is made up of

Language in a Plural Society

fluid speech groups, with its members claiming different speech identities in response to changing contexts. Such a linguistic spectrum may even operate across "language" boundaries delineated by grammarians and other custodians of language.

Many speech groups in South and Southeast Asia associate the diversity of speech (styles, registers, dialects, and languages) around the region with differential values in social interaction. The verbal repertoire of an individual or a group in a plural society is often characterized by a creative use of speech variation in diverse combinations through linguistic stratification (such as diglossic complementation,[6] code-switching, code-mixing, bilingualism) in everyday life. In other words, diversity of speech on a societal level is not merely a convenience or an "aesthetic" choice (a luxury that can be dispensed with), but signifies subtlety of purpose in an interaction; it is highly functional. The human quality of communications in a plural society is bound to suffer when we discard such an asset in favor of standardization, as is presently being emphasized in schools.

The linguistic reorganization of Indian states enforced in 1956 was based primarily on the language identity of the dominant pressure groups. *Language-identity regions* are not necessarily homogeneous *communication regions,* as has been implied as an article of faith by many sociopolitical, administrative, and educational agencies in different states. Apart from the dominant state language, every state has from one to six outside, or minority, languages which are spoken by more than 20 persons per 1000 population (Khubchandani, 1972b).

On the basis of language-identity pressures, the country can be divided into two major zones: the *Stable Zone* and the *Fluid Zone.* The North-Central part of the country, known as the Hindustani region (also called the Hindi-Urdu-Panjabi [HUP] region) and comprising all Hindi states, belongs to the Fluid Zone, where language-identity patterns and language-usage patterns among different communities are not necessarily congruent. One notices many vacillating trends in the census declarations of mother tongues in the entire zone, representing fluidity of the language-psychological contexts and fluctuating according to the sociopolitical climate and the pressures of acculturation. Populations in the Fluid Zone have other-than-linguistic criteria for determining in-group/out-group identity (see Chapters 3 and 5). The remaining states belong to the Stable Zone, where the language identities of different populations are, by and large, in consonance with language-usage patterns. In the Stable Zone, areas of predominant languages are relatively easily identified, and the increases in regionally dominant mother tongues run parallel to the normal growth in total population (the variation in the growth rate not exceeding ±4 percent to account for territorial adjustments at the time of state reorganization in 1956) (Khubchandani, 1972a).

In the postindependence period many radical changes in the language behavior of different speech communities are being envisaged through ambitious language-promotion programs which do not give any serious attention to the sociolinguistic realities of Indian life. Some prominent characteristics of Indian communication patterns can be identified as follows:

1. *Heterogeneity.* The linguistic composition of the 330 districts, distributed in 26 states and Union territories (at the time of the 1961 census), clearly shows the prevalence of linguistically pluralistic communities in many parts of India. Nearly half of the districts (152 out of 330, i.e., 46 percent) are heterogeneous, with minority speech groups exceeding 20 percent of the district population.

Following the linguistic reorganization of states since 1956, the principles of linguistic homogeneity and of the supremacy of a region's numerically dominant language have dominated the thinking of many political and administrative agencies, making them virtually unconcerned about the heterogeneous patterns of communication in many districts. Patterns of verbal usage in the subcontinent are hardly coterminous with political and administrative boundaries. Linguistic minorities in all states, however, add up to a quarter of the total population (Khubchandani, 1972b). In such circumstances, demands for linguistic homogeneity within a state are pregnant with many complexities. Table 2 provides a general glimpse of the heterogeneity of communication environments prevailing in different states.

2. *Stratified social structure.* Indian society is characterized by interlocking hierarchies of religion, caste, mother tongue, and occupational and regional affiliations. There is differential use of caste dialects, Sanskritic, Perso-Arabic, or Anglicized varieties of the same speech; Hindi and Urdu, two sociocultural variants of Khariboli spoken in the same region, are identified as separate languages. The distribution of literacy and bilingualism in various speech varieties also shows a high correlation with sex, class, and status (see Chapter 5).

3. *Fluid language boundaries.* In a pluralistic society such as India, the interlanguage boundaries have remained fluid in many regions. Until as recently as three to four decades ago, one's language group was not generally a very important criterion for sharply distinguishing oneself from others. Hutton, in the 1931 census reports: "So deep does bilingualism go in parts of Ganjam that from very infancy many grow up speaking both Oriya and Telugu, and are so much at home in both that they can-

not tell which to return as their mother tongue" (vol. 1, p. 349). This phenomenon of plurality in mother tongues is much more widespread than has been recorded in linguistic studies of the subcontinent.

Following independence in 1947, language consciousness has grown and language loyalties have acquired political salience. In the new context, the language boundaries have acquired a new order of fluidity. The Indian census bears witness to very large fluctuations in the number of persons claiming particular mother tongues, in response to overt identity pressures; for example:

- a phenomenal increase between 1951 and 1961 of 14,611 percent in the number of persons claiming as mother tongue the Bihari group of languages—mainly Maithili, Bhojpuri, and Magahi—in Bihar;
- a move away from regional toward religious identity among bilingual Muslims throughout the country, revealed through the consolidation of claims of Urdu as mother tongue—a growth of 68.7 percent during 1951-1961;
- excitement over language identity at the time of the 1951 census in the erstwhile Punjab (details discussed in Chapter 5).

This fluidness of language identity is revealed through the speech patterns operating across language boundaries. Such communities are not very conscious of the speech characteristics which keep them in one language or the other. In such conditions, natives speak a typical "language" which defies the standard notion of "grammar." People do not associate speech labels precisely with grammatical or pronunciation stereotypes, and standardization and other propriety types of control of verbal behavior generally tend to be permissive. Consequently, it is often difficult to determine whether a particular discourse belongs to language A or language B. Such ambiguities can arise among Panjabi settlers in Delhi, urban Muslims in Gujarat and Maharashtra, and urbanized tribal communities. The fall-in-line processes of Western societies, operating through various standardization mechanisms, do not find easy acceptance in the speech behavior of even literate groups in South Asia, as revealed through "highbrow" Anglicized versions of Indian languages and through code-switching among bilinguals, that is, intermittent shifting between Indian languages and English in an interaction.

4. *Situational norms.* Most Indian languages have not gone through the so-called developmental processes of standardization and have not been explicitly described through a single writing system, spelling and grammar manuals, dictionaries, and the like. Even for the major Indian languages, these explicit imperatives—learned at school and in other for-

Table 2. Communication Environments in Indian States and Union Territories, 1961

	Total Population, 1961 (thousands)	Dominant Languages	Percentage of the State Population	Other District Languages	Prominent Contact Languages (speakers >20/1000)
States					
Kerala	16,904	Malayalam	95.0	—	English 41, Tamil 33
Gujarat	20,633	Gujarati	90.5	Sindhi, Bhili, Khandeshi	Hindi-Urdu (H-U) 66
Andhra Pradesh	35,983	Telugu	86.0	—	H-U 91, English 25
Uttar Pradesh	73,746	Hindi	85.4	Kumauni, Garhwali, Urdu	English 25
West Bengal	34,926	Bengali	84.3	Nepali, Santali	H-U 90, English 43
Tamil Nadu (Madras)	33,687	Tamil	83.2	Kannada	Telugu 112, English 37, H-U 21
Orissa	17,549	Oriya	82.3	Kui, Santali	H-U 33, Telugu 22
Madhya Pradesh	32,372	Hindi	78.1	Chhatisgarhi, Rajasthani, Marathi, Bhili, Gondi, Urdu	H-U 160, Gujarati 30, English 26, Kannada 21
Maharashtra	39,554	Marathi	76.6	Khandeshi	H-U 103, Marathi 43, Tamil 42, Konkani 21
Karnataka (Mysore)	23,587	Kannada	65.2	Telugu, Tulu, Coorgi	H-U 68, English 24
Assam (incl. Meghalaya, Mizoram)	11,900	Assamese	57.1	Bengali, Khasi, Garo, Bodo, Mizo, and other Tibeto-Chinese languages	—
Rajasthan	20,156	Rajasthani Hindi	56.5 33.3	Bhili, Panjabi, Urdu	
Panjab (incl. Haryana, Chandigarh)	20,300	Hindi Panjabi	55.6 41.1	Urdu, Pahari	English 36

Jammu and Kashmir	3561	Kashmiri Dogri (Panjabi)	54.4 27.5	Pahari, Ladakhi, Balti	H-U 93, Rajasthani 59
Bihar	46,456	Hindi Bihari languages	44.3 35.4	Bhojpuri, Maithili, Magahi, Urdu, Santali, & other tribal languages	—
Union Territories					
Goa, Daman, and Diu	627	Konkani	89.1	—	—
Pondicherry	369	Tamil	88.1	—	—
Lakshadveep Islands	24.1	Malayalam	83.3	—	—
Delhi	2659	Hindi	77.4	—	English 158, Panjabi 127
Tripura	1142	Bengali Tripuri	65.2 24.9	—	—
Manipur	780	Manipuri	64.5	—	—
Dadra and Nagar Haveli	58.0	Varli (Marathi)	58.1	—	—
Andaman and Nicobar Islands	63.5	Nicobarese Bengali	21.9 21.8	—	—
Nagaland	369	14 Naga languages	98.4	—	—
Himachal Pradesh	2812	8 Pahari languages	79.8	Hindi-Urdu, Panjabi	—
Arunachal Pradesh (North-East Frontier Agency)	337	Tibeto-Chinese languages	—	—	—
Sikkim	162	Nepali Bhotia	45.9 22.6	—	—
INDIA	439,235				

mal settings—have been too recent to have seriously challenged the dominant implicit identity pressures whose influence depends largely on situational expediency.

These speech pressures are different in character from the explicit prescriptions, with sanctions from the language elite in a community, which can be irrelevant even to the immediate demands of verbalization activity. Implicit pressures form a kind of etiquette made up of rules agreed upon ad hoc by those who participate in the situation; whereas explicit standards form a rigorously defined value system acquired through education and various other socialization processes.

Bilingualism

India has become proverbial for the diversity of the language and culture of its inhabitants. Grass-roots knowledge of more than one language has been a marked feature of Indian society from time immemorial. The complex segmentation of Indian society and the frequent migrations, conquests, and internal colonizations in the past have established conditions for an extensive "folk" multilingualism in the country, despite a high percentage of illiteracy and the absence of any strong tradition of systematic language teaching (Pandit 1972; Khubchandani, 1972b).

Many ecological and socioeconomic factors determine the incidence of bilingualism in a community. These factors include size of the mother-tongue group, contact environments (heterogeneity, urbanity, etc.), schooling opportunities, economic strata of individuals, and occupational conditions. Apart from such practicalities, a contact language often is acquired because of the privileges and status accorded by it; the prestige attached to it; or some other pressures of social identification.

Three patterns of contact languages are observable among Indian bilinguals (or multilinguals) for intergroup communication:

1. Local languages (ten major ones) are predominant in their respective regions.
2. Hindustani, identified as Hindi or Urdu (hereafter, Hindi-Urdu), is used mostly for oral and informal communication throughout the country, with varying degrees of intensity in different regions.
3. English is used, to a great extent, for formal and written communication throughout the country, with varying degrees of intensity in different regions.

The education system of the country and patterns of intergroup communication in multilingual regions facilitate the use of more than one contact language:

Language in a Plural Society

1. Hindi-Urdu native speakers residing in their home region (over 30 percent of the country's population) have a somewhat restricted pattern of intergroup communication. They are generally exposed only to one prominent contact language—English—as they tend to perceive many distinct languages in their repertoire as mere dialects of their mother tongue (for details, see Chapter 5).
2. A large majority of the non-Hindi-Urdu-speaking groups residing in their respective home regions (over 46 percent of the country's population) are exposed to two contact languages: English and Hindi-Urdu.
3. A majority belonging to various minority speech groups and those staying outside their home regions (constituting roughly 24 percent of the population) are potentially exposed to three contact languages: English, Hindi-Urdu, and a regional language (when it is different from Hindi).

Owing to a number of sociopsychological factors, the census returns give a rather conservative account of bilingualism among the Indian population. The 1961 census records only 43.5 million people (9.7 percent of the entire population) who claim to have subsidiary languages. The underrepresentation of bilingualism claims is attributed to various traditional convictions about the knowledge of a language, such as:

- ability to write the language in its prevalent script;
- identification considerations of communication overriding linguistic characteristics;
- sense of belonging to a tradition encompassing more than one language, which treats multilingualism as similar to a diglossic variation of one's "own" speech (see Chapter 5).

According to the 1961 census returns, English ranks first among the contact languages, with 26 percent of the total bilinguals in the country declaring English as their first subsidiary language; Hindi is a close second, with 22 percent bilingual speakers. The combined total percentage of Hindi, Urdu and Panjabi speakers—three mutually intelligible languages sharply divided on the issues of writing system and literary trends —comes to 28 percent. Forty-five percent of the total bilingualism is shared among eight prominent regional languages: Tamil, Kannada, Telugu, Marathi, Bengali, Assamese, Oriya, and Gujarati, in that order; 194,000 bilinguals (0.5 percent) declare the classical language Sanskrit as their subsidiary language.

Hindi is claimed as the primary contact language by 30 persons per 1000 among the non-Hindi-speaking population, and the ratio of Urdu claimants is 5 per 1000; English is claimed by 25 persons per 1000. The ratios of other regional-language claimants among those who are not native speakers of the respective languages are as follows: both Tamil and Kannada are claimed as contact languages by 9; Telugu by 8; Marathi by 7; Bengali by 5; Assamese by 4; Oriya by 3; Gujarati by 1.4; Panjabi by 1; and Sanskrit, Malayalam, and Kashmiri each by fewer than 1 per 1000 population.

There is yet another significant feature of Indian bilingualism. Very often, in urban-educated settings, the capacity to use one or more Indian languages and English to refer to the same event results in code-switching between those languages, with a speaker using more than one language interchangeably in the same discourse or even within the same utterance without being conscious of switching. An occasional switchover to classical languages (Sanskrit, Persian, or Arabic) in Indian elite discourse has been a quite common phenomenon, and it finds expression in the form of bilingual poetry as well. But the high intensity of switching between two codes (Indian languages and English) at the phrase level in daily intercourse among the urban educated is rather a recent characteristic of Indian bilingual communities.

The incidence of English and Hindi-Urdu bilingualism is more prominent in urban than in rural areas. In urban areas one notices that both languages are frequently used in communication among those who do not speak them natively. A sample study of two districts in Maharashtra provides a vivid contrast between the bilingual claims of the urban and rural populations. The Bombay district's population is 100 percent urban, whereas the Sangli district's urban population is only 18 percent. Ratios of different contact-language claimants per 1000 of the nonnative language population in the two districts (as per the 1961 census) are as follows:

Bombay Hindi-Urdu 202 (195 + 7), English 137, Marathi 61, and Gujarati 97
Sangli   Marathi 530, Kannada 32, Hindi-Urdu 27, and English 10

In the Bombay district, Hindi-Urdu and English occupy a more prominent position as contact languages than the regional Marathi, whereas in the Sangli district, Marathi is claimed by more than half of the non-Marathi population, and Kannada, a neighboring southern language, is recorded as the most prominent contact language among the Marathi population.

The extent to which Indian languages have functional value for wider communication can also be ascertained through their use in the press.

Language in a Plural Society

Newspapers and periodicals are published in about seventy Indian languages. Hindi and English claim a major share of the total number and the circulation of dailies and periodicals in the country. According to the 1978 Press Registrar's Report (for the year 1977), the Hindi press accounts for 26 percent of the total number of newspapers and 23 percent of the circulation in the country. The English press's shares of the total number and circulation of newspapers are 20 and 24 percent, respectively. The daily reading habits of a large number of literate bilinguals still seem to be English-oriented.

Almost half of the press activity in India is conducted in English and Hindi. The share of fourteen main languages in the Indian press is given in Table 3.

The English press and the Hindi and Urdu press are spread throughout the country. The four metropolitan areas with a total of more than 600 publications each (newspapers and periodicals in all languages) during 1977 published 63 percent of all the English newspapers in the country: Delhi (803), Bombay (519), Calcutta (300), and Madras (205), whereas only 24 percent of the Hindi papers were published in these cities: Delhi (745), Bombay (69), Calcutta (91), and Madras (8). A glimpse of English and Hindi readership patterns can be had from the content classification of periodicals shown in Table 4.

English information media are the most organized in the country, and they are supported by relatively affluent bilinguals. Many Indian-lan-

Table 3. Percentage Distribution of the Press in India by Language, 1977

Language	All Newspapers and Periodicals		Only Dailies	
	Percentage of Papers	Percentage of Circulation	Percentage of Papers	Percentage of Circulation
Hindi	26	23	30	20
English	20	24	9	24
Urdu	7	4	10	4
Gujarati	4	6	4	8
Bengali	7	5	3	7
Marathi	6	6	10	10
Tamil	5	9	7	7
Malayalam	4	8	10	11
Telugu	3	4	2	3
Kannada	3	4	6	3
Panjabi	2	1.6	1.6	1.1
Oriya	1	0.7	1.1	1.2
Sindhi	0.4	0.2	0.3	0.1
Assamese	0.3	0.4	0.3	0.4
Others	1.3	0.4	1.9	0.1
Bilinguals and Multilinguals	10.1	3.4	2.8	0.5

Table 4. Classification of Periodicals according to Contents, 1977

Contents	All Languages Number	All Languages Circulation (thousands)	Hindi Number	Hindi Circulation (thousands)	English Number	English Circulation (thousands)
News and Current Affairs	4830	7820	2159	2696	524	1519
Literary and Cultural	2038	6465	468	1529	225	725
Religion and Philosophy	1375	2235	242	452	246	467
Commerce and Industry	512	534	37	45	365	399
Medicine and Health	408	779	58	112	185	494
Social Welfare	358	384	97	93	66	121
Film	319	1450	79	368	55	517
Agriculture and Animal Husbandry	298	483	63	100	113	135
Law and Public Administration	289	412	13	13	219	334
Labor	284	289	59	28	88	158
Engineering and Technology	254	310	9	7	220	265
Education	246	381	25	115	71	53
Science	188	316	8	43	148	232
Children	165	1938	34	788	10	175
Finance and Economics	105	162	12	23	77	115
Insurance, Banking, and Cooperatives	103	240	16	13	34	139
Transport and Communication	96	141	10	12	60	102
Women	76	692	19	40	19	338
Sports	72	148	9	3	27	82
Radio and Music	47	70	6	2	12	11
Art	39	28	3	1	20	17
Unclassified	1422	1346	3	1	10	9
TOTAL	13,524	26,623	3429	6484	2794	6407

guage newspapers rely, to a great extent, on English information agencies for broad-based coverage and for authentic and detailed accounts. Hence the impact of the English press on the national scene is out of all proportion to its circulation.

As discussed earlier, the intragroup and intergroup communication patterns reveal that the language-usage regions do not coterminate with language-identity regions. Bilingualism is characterized by socioeconomic strata and the density of population (metropolitan cities, towns, and rural areas). In many regions one finds a rough correlation between the degree of heterogeneity in the native population and the intensity of bilingualism. Different regions show a predominance of the state language, Hindi-Urdu, and/or English in different combinations (Khubchandani, 1972b).

In general, the high incidence of English bilingualism is attributed mainly to occupational specialization and functional superiority. English, at the present time, continues to be an important part of the communication matrix of urban India. Hindi bilingualism is generally attributed to the mobility of the population and to its use in the spheres of trade, employment, the military, and mass entertainment. Both Hindi and English have acquired the position of pan-Indian languages at different strata of society, and their functional importance exceeds mere communication needs. A bilingual with a smattering of Hindi, English, or both feels quite assured about coping with the demands of ordinary communication amidst the diversity of local languages.

NOTES

1. "Mother tongue" is used here in a specific sense, that is, "as a speech variety which members of a group identify as their own." For a fuller description of the term, see Chapter 3.

2. Scholars like Chatterjee (1945), Emeneau (1956), and Katre (1961) deal at great length with the characteristics underlying affinities among Indian languages. Emeneau (1956), in a comment highlighting the common linguistic traits across genealogical boundaries in the South Asian subcontinent, points out: "The end result of the borrowings is that the languages of the two families, Indo-Aryan and Dravidian, seem in many respects more akin to one another than Indo-Aryan does to the other Indo-European languages" (p. 16).

3. The 1961 Indian census classified 1019 mother tongues reported by 439 million people into nearly 200 languages—60 belonging to the Indo-European family (322 million speakers); 21 to the Dravidian (108 million); 20 to the Austro-Asiatic (6.2 million); and 98 to the Tibeto-Chinese (3.2 million). The census, in addition, lists 530 unclassified mother tongues whose affiliation could not be determined, spoken by only 63,000 people. There are also 103 languages of foreign origin spoken by 315,000 people, the most prominent being English.

4. M. B. Emeneau (1962): "It is clear that in the West, specifically in the United States of America, the prestige of the old established English-speaking community works with such powerful pressure for conformity that the languages even of sizeable immigrant groups are generally wiped out in a very few generations. . . . In India immigrant situations often result otherwise than in America. After a period of at least fifteen centuries of migration Saurashtran still survives as the domestic language of the immigrant silk weavers in Madura [Tamil Nadu State]."

5. In the context of the interdependence of man and society, Gandhiji explains individual units in terms of "concentric circles" in an ocean that keep on widening to the outer periphery, but never ascending like "a pyramid with the apex sustained by the bottom." In such a plural pattern, the "inner" circle forms an integral unit of the "outer" oceanic circle, and will not be crushed by the overwhelming power of the outer periphery; on the other hand, each should give strength to the other (1958: 110-111).

6. Diglossic complementation refers to a functional compartmentalization by a society of its linguistic resources, such as the use of a vernacular and a classical variety of the same language or of several distantly related (in some cases, even unrelated) languages. The term "diglossia" was originally introduced by Ferguson (1959) in the sense of "a relatively stable language situation in which, in addition to the primary dialects of [a] language . . . there is a very divergent, highly codified superposed variety, the vehicle of a large and respected body of written literature."

CHAPTER 2

Language Modernization

So PERVASIVE IN OUR TIME is the distinction between developed and underdeveloped (euphemistically called developing) stages of economies, societies, and even cultures that many language experts are led to employ the same dichotomy for languages. "A high degree of arbitrary social and linguistic heterogeneity" in a region is characterized as a feature of less developed modernizing societies, whereas, "the fast growth of functional heterogeneity" within a language is associated with more developed industrialized societies (Neustupný, 1974:43-44). Several homogenization processes in the language behavior of many European societies, stimulated by trends begun during the Renaissance and Reformation, such as the creation of new standard languages and the assimilation of neighboring dialects and unwritten languages of minorities (Breton in France, Frisian in the Netherlands, etc.), are regarded by many language-elites as inevitable in the contemporary stages of modernization in Asia and Africa as well.

"Center-Periphery" Hypothesis

In the same vein, modernization in "traditional" languages is compared on the scale of "intertranslatability" with the languages of already industrialized, secularized, and differentiated societies. Here intertranslatability is regarded as an adequate rendering of lexical and grammatical features, along with conversational as well as literary styles, which are already accurately and easily expressible in one or another crucial language of reference communities considered to be modern (Ferguson, 1968; Fishman, 1974).

This approach to language development relies, to a large extent, on the "center-periphery" hypothesis of politicoeconomic development. According to this hypothesis, the so-called developed and undeveloped stages of language can be determined in accordance with a set of ecological, social, and projectional dimensions, as shown in Table 5.

Guided by such "imported" models, Westernized language elites in many developing countries, in their thrust for "modernity," either seek to have their speech recognized as a developed, "absolute" language or abandon the "handicapped" speech altogether in favor of the one touted as the "privileged" variety, as per the dicta of newly established politicoeconomic institutions. In this dichotomous process, many less favorably placed speech varieties—which may be dialects, vernaculars, minority languages, or may have nonelite styles—stand in danger of becoming extinct.[1] Disturbance of the age-old, harmonious hierarchic patterning of different speech varieties (or languages) in one's verbal repertoire (diglossic, pluralistic, etc.) creates disharmony among heterogeneous societies, centering on such issues as language privileges in education and state-boundary disputes over language identity (see Chapter 7).

In a way, the dichotomous approach in language development depicts the futile race of trying to keep up with the Joneses, as is evident from the more-than-a-century-old program of "refining the vernacular dialects" expounded in the "Macaulay Minute" of 1835:

> To that class [Indian in blood and colour, but English in tastes, in opinions, in morals, and in intellect] we may leave it to refine the vernacular dialects of the country, to enrich those dialects with terms of science borrowed from the Western nomenclature, and to render them by degrees fit vehicles for conveying knowledge to the great mass of the population. (Sharp, 1920:116)

The targets of vernacular development in response to the demand for a vernacular university in 1867 were also spelled out in the same vein. The British rulers rejected the vernacular medium for higher education on the ground that "the vernaculars of the country do not as yet afford the materials for conveying instruction of the comparatively high order" (Documents 6 and 7, Naik, 1963:21–32).

Today, many educators continue to emphasize the utility of a highly cultivated language medium as a precision instrument of thinking and communication through which students can be trained in logical thought and in the disciplined use of words. A committee of the University Grants Commission reporting on standards of university education (1965) went to the extent of saying: "A change is justified only when the university is confident of raising standards by doing so. Unless an Indian language has grown up to its full stature, with a good literature in science and other subjects, the move for its acceptance as the medium of instruc-

Table 5. Dimensions of Language Development

Dimension	"Developed" Languages	"Underdeveloped" Languages
Ecological		
Utilization	wider communication "world" languages	languages limited to a region (national, local languages)
Population strength	dominant "majority" languages	dominated "minority" languages (often treated as "dialects" in policymaking)
Social		
Legitimization	standard languages (acceptable to the elite)	nonstandard regional varieties, substandard languages (slangs, hybrids)
Domains of use	full-fledged "autonomous" languages	languages with restrictive use (vernaculars in diglossia situations)
Projectional		
Graphization	written languages	unwritten languages
Literature	literary languages	colloquial *bazaar* languages
Medium of education	advanced "cultivated" languages	preparatory "ethnic" languages
Technologization	languages suitable for typing, shorthand, and telecommunication purposes	languages not extended for technological tasks

tion immediately would be a retrograde step" (p. 71). It is interesting to note that the same argument against Indian languages has been made by some Indian elites for over a century. The objection of the Lahore Indian Association in 1876 against establishing a vernacular university at Lahore was couched in almost the same terms: that the vernacular medium would be a "retrograde and reactionary" step as there was "in the vernacular languages a sad want of text-books for the higher examinations" and "the English being dispensed with, the standard of instruction must necessarily be lower than that of other universities" (Naik, 1963:283–296). The controversy provides a classic example of the tendency to dodge the issue on the basis of such illusionary demands, which can be compared to expecting someone to acquire mastery in swimming before he enters the water.

Hence, as a result of a hard struggle the Indian languages are now proving themselves increasingly acceptable for a wider range of study in the "elitist" framework of education. Today, more than a century later, the citadels of higher learning have yielded only to the extent of providing an alternate medium of regional language use, usually associated with the "ordinary" tradition in education, for humanities and commerce courses up to the graduate level (discussed at length in Chapters 6 and 7).

According to this "evolutionary" scale of development, it is assumed that the newly independent societies are to strive for "secondary modernization," trailing behind the path taken by "advanced" societies. Consequently, many of the transformations sought through language modernization in these societies (such as targets of language learning, standardization, coining technical terminologies) are "externally" induced rather than internally generated, unlike the classical European modernization. These processes eliminate many interim stages; involve rapid transformations, sudden thrusts, and dramatic reconstructions; and also have to cope with pressures from politicized masses (Das Gupta, 1970).

By the same token, languages of newly emerged nations are considered to be "deficient" communication systems with all "the unprecedented disadvantages of the latecomers" (Fishman, 1974:84). As such, in this unending chase of the mirage, by the time the vernaculars have finished struggling to acquire the credibility of "developed" languages, the latter will have moved higher, with additional honors, such as usability with computers, space satellites, and so on.

Assumptions of Language Development

The simplistic projection of education in a mother tongue as a means of establishing equality of opportunity for individual self-advancement has

Language Modernization

led to discarding the principle of language hierarchy in education, which has given way to the demands of language autonomy, that is, "the promotion of full-fledged or autonomous status for a language as an exclusive vehicle for full expression in different fields of knowledge and in all walks of life" (Khubchandani, 1974b). It is taken for granted that the "highbrow" values of speech communication—uniformity, precision, elegance, purity of form, allegiance to literary tradition, and the elaboration of language through the coinage of technical terms—are essential means of developing a language.

This aim encourages two types of activity in a speech community guided primarily by its language elite:

1. *language codification:* prescribing "standards" (i.e., authentic versions) for a language through a writing system, spelling and grammar manuals, dictionaries, style sheets, and so on;
2. *language elaboration:* expansion of language domains, especially for formal communication (education, administration, mass media, etc.), by devising new terminologies, providing translations, encouraging original writing in the new domains, and so on, under modernization programs (see Chapter 4).

Taking their cue from the path of "development" as envisaged by the high priests of economic and technological planning in developing nations, many language experts concerned with language policies of "traditional" societies tend to equate the range and quantity of communication projections achieved through technology (cf. Table 5) to the communication quality in these languages. The societal characteristics of restrictions in role access (or mobilization) and range of experience, and of structural compartmentalization between segmental identities in the traditional order, are axiomatically correlated with the nature of communicative restrictions in the traditional verbal repertoire. In this regard, "predevelopmental" segmentation clusters intensifying intragroup compartmentalization within a polity or region—as revealed from the European experience—are assumed to be "universal" characteristics of underdevelopment, such as Polish ethnic groups linked with the landholding class, with the Catholic faith, and speaking Polish as their mother tongue; Ukranian ethnic groups identified as peasants, of the Eastern Orthodox faith, and with Ukranian as their mother tongue (Fishman, 1974:87–88).

According to Fishman (1974), "the social context of language modernization is most commonly discussed in terms of (a) the growing identification with the standard version of the national language on the part of the general public, (b) the (at least theoretically) increased accessibility of all varieties within the speech community, and (c) the more rapid diffusion of linguistic innovations and status markers, resulting in repertoire continuity rather than discontinuity across classes" (p. 91). In this framework, one notices an evident bias toward evaluating language development in terms of increasing rate of role mobility, wider range of functional domains, and clearly categorized "insular" distinctions in speech varieties—labeled as registers, dialects, and languages. Language experts suggest taxonomical classification of sociolinguistic types of languages as "tribal, early modern (developing), modern (developed), contemporary, etc." In this taxonomy "linguistic modernization" is notionally plotted as "a process the sense of which is to remove the inadequate premodern features from language" (Neustupný, 1974:35). But the features characterizing "inadequacy" or "modernity" in a language system (lexical, syntactic, etc.) are left to the subjective evaluation of other-than-language dimensions—ecological, social, projectional, and so on (cf. Table 5). In this context, intellectualization—a tendency toward increasingly definite and accurate expression—is equated with language modernization (Garvin, 1973).

According to this model, Westernization is projected as a further intensification of modernization based upon both methods and substance overtly borrowed from successful foreign models, such as intertranslatability with "currently prestigeful" languages (Fishman, 1974:91). Garvin (1973) aptly draws attention to the frequent implication in the language-planning literature that the European and Europeanized experience, duplicated in some other parts of the world, constitutes a valid basis for developing language communications on a universal level. Neustupný's (1974) four indices of modernization—homogeneity, development, equality, and alliance—seem to be based primarily upon "analytical developments" in contemporary European languages. In the absence of any firm "communicative" evidence, such generalizations should be regarded merely as "rationalization of a basically modern system" (which Neustupný himself would like to discard, p. 43). At this "developmental" stage of the language-planning theory itself, the universality of such modernization processes in mobilizing deliberate changes in the speech behavior of traditional societies is yet to be proven.

One finds such parallels in the linguistic scholarship of the eighteenth century as well, when many overt similarities between language and other-than-language traits in developing societies attracted the attention of many Indo-Europeanists (Max Müller and others), who sought to correlate language development to the realities of everyday life. The Indo-European languages of agricultural settlers were assumed to be superior by virtue of representing "perfect morphological inflection" compared with the "agglutinative" Mongolian languages of the nomadic races and the "monosyllabic" Chinese languages. Led by the dominant theory of genealogical development, many Western philologists at that time regarded the characteristics of their own speech as the epitome of language development and believed that "exotic" features like agglutination or monosyllabicity characterized "frozen" languages—somewhat primitive languages which never blossomed into Indo-European![2] Hence, in the context of formulating a theory of language development, it is all the more necessary to examine critically the assumptions of extending sociopolitical trends of modernization and Westernization as "superior" tools for enriching communicative competence.

Functional Heterogeneity

A critical appraisal of the sociolinguistic realities in traditional societies in the South Asian subcontinent reveals the noncongruence and crisscrossing of identity affiliations, segmented in overlapping or even contrasting groups, on the basis of occupation, caste, religion, mother tongue, region, and so on (cf. Chapter 1). Many of these speech communities demonstrate the magnitude of "functional heterogeneity" in their verbal repertoire, even to the extent of being characterized by a certain amount of fluidity in their language identities, depending on circumstances and setting. Such pluralistic speech communities tend to organize their repertoire through diglossic patterning, grass-roots "folk" multilingualism (distinct from "elegant" bilingualism or trilingualism learned through conscious effort), code-switching, pidginization, and other such processes of language contact.

Identity preservation and distance characteristics signifying heterogeneity of communication among many pluralistic speech communities in the subcontinent do not result from a mutual isolation that causes a communication barrier per se, as is often implied by the language-planning agencies attuned to the values of homogenized societies. *Stratificational* characteristics, emerging from intense social contact, play a significant role in explicating full meaning in a discourse. These characteristics are markedly different from those of *regional* differentiation, which result from isolation or lack of interaction among different groups. In this respect, the cultivation of "caste dialects" among traditional societies on the subcontinent signifies a system of linguistic stratification among different castes in the midst of a fuzzy diversity in everyday repertoire (Pandit, 1969b:207-228). Rigid adherence to caste dialects in certain parts of India, characterized by acute awareness of propriety and deference considerations to "higher" castes, greatly resembles the obsession with propriety evident in the pervasive use of so-called standard diction among "modern" technological societies.

Several diglossic and pluralistic communication patterns, based on the elaborate oral or written styles of "highbrow" and "lowbrow" speech, and the "ornamental" or "instrumental" uses of speech prevailing among traditional societies (as is the case of the Hindi-Urdu amalgam; cf. Chapter 5), appear to be the direct consequence of functional heterogeneity. These patterns provide a rich example of linguistic cultivation resulting from the handling of complex tasks of societal stratification. One does not find any conclusive evidence for assuming that such codes represent "deficient" communication systems, as implied by Neustupný (1974) and Fishman (1974). In making such an assumption, we may be committing an error similar to that of the eighteenth-century Indo-Europeanists who were swayed by ethnocentric bias.

In a hierarchical patterning of speech variation, no one variety can be associated with the dominant role of a "standard language" appropriate for all members of the speech community at all times and on all occasions, as is found in many homogenized societies in Europe. Indian society as a whole, particularly among Indo-Aryan and Dravidian speakers, shows variation in speech related to identity and purpose of interaction. Examples of such variation include:

sex class	In Sanskrit plays, royal male characters speak "formal standard" Sanskrit (etymologically, it means "well-cultivated" speech), royal females speak "colloquial standard" Prakrit ("natural" speech), and commoners speak "grass-roots" Apabhraṃsha ("contaminated" speech).
age	Vernaculars like Bhojpuri and Maithili are spoken with elders, and Khariboli with peers and juniors among many communities in Bihar.
caste	Brahmin and non-Brahmin varieties of speech are used in Dravidian languages.
setting	"High" Hindi and "high" Urdu are spoken in formal settings, and "Bazaar Hindustani" is identified with informal interaction.
medium	Sanskritic Hindi is used in elegant writing, and its Anglicized version in urban oral speech.
attitudes	Permutation of varied Sanskrit and Perso-Arabic characteristics in Hindi-Urdu, Panjabi, and Sindhi identifies stylistic variation on the scales of formality-intimacy, seriousness-joviality, etc.
domain	In Hindi *Bhakti* poetry during the medieval period, the Awadhi variety was cultivated for poetry on Rama, and the Braj variety for poetry on Krishna throughout the North-Central Hindi belt.
genre	In Hindi literature during the late nineteenth century, the

Language Modernization

	preferable vehicle for poetry was Braj, and for prose, Khariboli.
writing	Many regional systems of writing vary according to locality and occupational groups for the same language (cf. Chapter 6).

In this regard, the Hindi-Urdu amalgam spread throughout North-Central India and Pakistan also represents a classical case of "multimodal standardization." Ferguson (1962) refers to it as "bi-modal standardization," showing a religiocultural split between Hindi and Urdu, a literary and colloquial split between Hindi-Urdu on the one hand and Hindustani on the other, and a split among various regionally stabilized forms of Hindustani in the Hindi-Urdu-Panjabi (HUP) and non-HUP areas; that is, Panjabi-ized Hindi differs from Bombay Hindustani, and Dehlvi (Delhi's local speech) differs from Dakhini (of the South).

In this entire area, commonly known as the Hindustani region, one finds a superposed homogeneity in communication patterns based on different linguistic hierarchies. It is regarded as the Fluid Zone where areas of predominant languages are not clearly marked and declarations keep fluctuating in every census, representing constant shifts in the mother-tongue allegiance of the local population (cf. Chapter 1). It represents a typical case where identificational considerations of communication (constituting 46 percent of India's total population) override the linguistic characteristics. Many markedly different languages in the region, such as Rajasthani, Bhojpuri, Maithili, Pahari, Chhatisgarhi, and Awadhi, are functionally as well as psychologically accepted by their speakers as "dialect-like tools for informal and oral communication" (Kloss, 1967b); and many communities live under "stable diglossia" conditions (for a more elaborate discussion, see Chapter 5).

Owing to various historical accidents (religiocultural ideologies, elite pressures, etc.), there have been considerable shifts in the nucleus of speech norms in the vast Hindustani region, resulting in new models for a supradialectal communication network. It was only during the past one hundred years that the increasing rivalry between the Hindi and Urdu elites prompted Braj- and Awadhi-speaking elites to shift their patronage to Khariboli, the speech of the capital, Delhi, as a literary basis for Hindi, thus voluntarily reducing the Braj and Awadhi varieties, with a rich literary heritage, to vernacular status.

Language Standardization

Language as an institution, like religion and law, presents a distinct "profile" to a society (Hertzler, 1965). One's speech behavior reveals a profound human desire to be accepted in a group. Transmission of institutional meanings through speech obviously implies control and legitimation procedures in speech activity.

Studies of language as a social process point to the fact that different varieties of speech enjoy differential prestige in a community. Patterns of social interaction are differentially valued within a culture. Often, different roles in a setting or different identities or cultural legacies transmit from one generation to another some prominent values of interaction—ways of interpreting and sharing experiences—known collectively as the communication ethos. On the one hand, there are implicit identity pressures such as "linguistic etiquette" (*śiṣṭācār* or *tamīz* in Hindi-Urdu), adhered to by the participants in an ad hoc fashion, depending upon situational propriety. On the other hand, there is an explicitly defined value system—a prescriptive code with sanctions from the language elite in a community, an authentic "standard" version of which is mirrored in its writing system, grammatical description, lexicons, and other standardization processes. Together, the various implicit and explicit social norms provide a distinct communication ethos to a speech community.

In compact homogeneous groups, a participant shares maximum verbal experience with other members of the group and is bound by feelings of group solidarity. In such cases, language operates with subtle or implicit mechanisms of control, whereas in widely spread heterogeneous groups, pressures of identification through speech may become loosened, so that the group imposes explicit sanctions in regard to verbal behavior. In such cases, adherence to the explicitly described code—a "correct," "proper," standard variety—becomes essential for one's identity and competence.

In everyday verbal communication one notices an enormous fluidity and diversity of codes dealing with informal situations, whereas in formal situations, particularly in the written form, one demands compartmentalized "appropriate" usage according to the professed dictum. One or more socially favored styles of verbal expression (generally promoted through literature and schooling) are labelled as "standard language"; its communication networks are marked by a wider spread in the society. Speech varieties with smaller or specialized communication networks—dialects, slangs, jargons, and so forth—are considered as uncouth or quaint in the elite judgment.

Standardization of language, in this sense, can be regarded as a legitimizing activity expanding its institutional order through a "programmed course" in socialization (Berger and Luckmann, 1966). Through different standardization techniques, the self-evident "situational" affirmations of linguistic rules of etiquette and rudimentary pragmatic nuances give way to formalized explicit procedures, as prescribed by the officially accredited custodians of linguistic practice in grammar manuals, dictionaries, style sheets, and so on. In standard usage, the emphasis shifts from an "event-centered" discourse to an ideal-oriented "expression-concentrating" discourse. "What expressions are right" (as ultimately defined by the language elite) attains pride of place at the cost of "what expressions actually occur spontaneously" (in response to a situation or event). Thus, rigidly standardized societies can turn the effortless gift of social verbalization into a directed effort of learning the elite-acceptable diction of their own speech. Language "boundaries" become sacred, and spontaneity and creativity leading to hybridization are filtered through the standardization processes. In such situations the contextual and functional fluidity in speech which manages to cross the boundaries of language and diction, is deprecated by the custodians of language.

Most of the languages in the subcontinent cultivated through the plural character of the society have not been subjected to the pressures of standardization, as is implied in the West, and have not been explicitly formulated through spelling and grammar manuals, dictionaries, and so on. For many major Indian languages, standardization imperatives and literacy drives have been introduced so recently that these have not yet seriously challenged the dominance of implicit identity pressures.

Traditionally, linguistic studies have presented each language as having a uniform and invariant structure. But contemporary research suggests that the entire speech matrix in use in a community may be an amalgam or a conglomeration of different speech varieties with diverse and heterogeneous structures (Weinreich, Labov, and Herzog, 1968). These varieties have been identified under various classificatory labels—registers, styles, codes, dialects, and so on. A number of common historical associations, however, lead a speech community to cherish all such speech varieties as part of its shared "tradition" through one or more "language" labels. In genealogical terms these varieties may be closely or distantly related: Khariboli and Braj are examples of "closely related" varieties, whereas Khariboli and Maithili can be regarded as "distantly related" varieties of Hindi. Through such associations a group develops a set of social attitudes toward the entire speech matrix, attitudes which find expression in highly stratified variations in actual speech. A basis of identity can be attributed to a common set of geographical, political, sociocultural, and even legendary experiences (see Chapter 5). A community's identification through a uniform "standard" language in the midst of a diversified speech matrix could be regarded as a matter of idealization, conditioned by the "bonds" of tradition. The notion of uniformity and homogeneity, even in the speech behavior of an individual, is only a myth. In a sense, speech behavior can be regarded as a coherent cerebral activity having a wider or narrower spectrum in an individual or in a speech community.

The "literate" world seems to be circumscribed by the myth of treating language in everyday life as a "crystallized entity" characterized by a distinct "tradition" embodied in its literary heritage. Qualities of language in a literary creation are quite different from those required in actual communication. In a sense, a literary creation comes closest to being regarded as an "artifact"—utilizing speech as its raw material and crystallizing it within a language "boundary"—and is distinguished from everyday communication, which is regarded as a "fact."

This myth is shared by many "underdeveloped" speech communities in their drive for modernization, just as they accept many other institutions and values from developed societies in attempting to transform the economic and technological patterns of their own societies. Many visionaries of language, by accepting language as a "social artifact" instead of as an "ongoing activity," commit themselves to applying the authenticating apparatus to the one or more chosen speech varieties around them. This leads to crystallizing the preferred speech more or less arbitrarily, guided mainly by literary styles and pressures from the elite, and proclaiming the "autonomy" of the variety (or varieties) in all domains of communication.

For a better understanding of speech as living phenomena, it may be useful to examine the distinction between "speech process" in everyday life and the "normative entity" proclaimed by the language elite.[3] Certain prominent features distinguishing process from entity are informally presented in Table 6.

The three aspects of a speech community's verbal behavior—as a communication device, as a strategy of control, and as a total repertoire—reveal the divergent characteristics of "speech process" and "language entity." An interplay of centripetal and centrifugal factors in a community, as indicated in Table 6, provides a base for the natural growth of a living language. This distinction makes us aware of the apparent paradox in the speech behavior of plural societies, and at the same time helps us realize the complementarity of speech variation and language standardization in a speech community. Such an understanding should go a long way in formulating a sound basis for language-planning theory.

Language Cultivation

Speech behavior, in a sense, can be compared with mapping activity, the full significance of which can be explicated only by the imperatives of context and communicative tasks (illocutionary and perlocutionary forces; cf. Austin, 1962). Speech becomes understandable only in connection with social interactions, situational expediency, and the purpose of communication.

The entire variability phenomenon in language activity has been regarded in sociolinguistic studies as a conditioning process, reflecting the underlying constraints exerted by social relations in different interlocutions. With this approach, one finds that various repetitive and innovative faculties in an individual's performance leading to fluidity in his verbal repertoire do not receive adequate attention. There are variable characteristics in a repertoire, conforming, on the one hand, with the demands of interactional role (such as transitional versus stable, sociocentric versus egocentric); of setting (home, market, work situation, etc.); and of channel of communication (spoken, written, interpersonal, group media, etc.). But at the same time, a repertoire is also structured by various regulating processes of selection (relevant to a presupposed knowledge of the theme, individual disposition to the interaction, and ethos of communication in general). A speech act, that is to say, is designed to achieve the desired effect on the audience in a covert manner by applying several selection mechanisms of pragmatic use in specific communication task(s).

A speech event carries a "formal" meaning within sentence unit(s) signifying subject, predicate, and so on; a "specificational" meaning within a context (conditioned by interactional roles, setting, channel, etc.); and an "affective" meaning within the discourse emerging from the relevance of interaction. Winograd (1974:75) observed, "A sentence does not convey meaning the way a truck conveys cargo, complete and packaged. It is more like a blueprint that allows the hearer to reconstruct the meaning from his own knowledge." In short, a message can convey meaning not merely through its "intent" in isolation (as indexed in the dictionary) but also in the context of its "identity" and through its "affect" on the participants.

Among traditional speech communities, interactional settings characterizing *inherited* (or ascribed) roles are generally marked by a certain amount of flexibility in adjusting to "situational" needs, as speakers' identities are stabilized irrespective of maintaining propriety in speech; whereas in an interaction characterizing *achieved* (or mobilized) roles, one notices a marked difference in the degree of expectancy of the "standardized" norm—a sort of prerequisite for entry into the aspired-to "club." Hence, societies structured around role ascription need not necessarily be handicapped by communicative restrictions, as is assumed by many language-planning experts (Fishman, 1974). Similarly, the restrictive range of experience in the traditional repertoire is at the same time compensated by the absorbing qualities of depth in "personalized" interaction. On the other hand, a wider range of experience in modernistic

Table 6. Speech as Living Phenomena

	Speech Process	Normative Entity
I.	*Communication Device*	
1.	An organic process, potentially diverse and heterogeneous.	A formalized entity, emphasizing uniformity and homogeneity.
2.	Regarded as a nonautonomous device, communicating in symphony with other nonlinguistic devices; its full signification can be explicated only from the imperatives of context and communicative tasks.	Ideally aiming at the targets of being an autonomous and unambiguous tool of communication.
3.	Interpretation dependent on the focus of communication "field" and the degree of individual's "sensitivity" toward it.	Interpretation relying heavily on explicit formulas—grammars, dictionaries, etc.; efforts for consistency made through the standardization apparatus.
4.	An effortless integral activity; discourse centers around the "event" with the support of ad hoc "expression" strategies.	An ideal-oriented representation requiring directed effort; discourse concentrates on "expression," which measures the "event."

II. *Strategy of Control*

5. Guided by implicit identity pressures—a sort of etiquette agreed upon ad hoc by those participating in it.

   Characterized by explicitly defined value system—a prescriptive code with sanctions from the language elite in the community.

6. Regulated by "situation-bound" propriety in which ecosystems, constituting the social reality "here and now," claim a prominent share.

   Conditioned by "tradition-inspired" profiles in which "time-honored" standard practices (spelled out through the grammatical accounts, lexicons, and style sheets) dominate the scene.

7. Permissive toward inherited variations linked with region, class, etc.

   Less tolerant toward such ascribed deviations; assimilatory pressures in favor of the elitist standard variety.

III. *Total Repertoire*

8. Total verbal repertoire is malleable, responsive to contextual expediencies resulting in uninhibited convergence between speech varieties with the contact pressures of pidginization, hybridization, code-switching, etc.

   Total verbal repertoire is demarcated for the demands of different normative systems (specified by a "distant" elite) involving stress on maintaining divergent development of a different system, and insistence on exclusiveness or "purity" of tradition.

9. Greater scope for functional fluidity leading to innovations and creativity of expression in negotiating the "event."

   Restrictions over the scope for spontaneity and creativity due to the pressures of exclusive conformity to different systems.

10. Fuzzy speech boundaries; interlocking variations responding to covert stratificational and situational differences.

    Sharp language boundaries; compartmentalization through overt linguistic differentia.

societies tends to promote "transitional" characteristics in speech, with insistence on explicit norms for standardization. In the present context, language-cultivation programs for many technologically developing societies are being recommended on the assumption that the imitation of communication models of affluent societies is inevitable (Neustupný, 1974).

Linguists, in their structural pursuits, generally pay attention to explicit, unambiguous, overt manifestation through language. Such *rationalized* use of language is only one of the sociolinguistic variables in actual speech activity. A native speaker's use of speech in everyday life is an *integral* activity, relevant to the context and purpose of verbalization. His actual discourse is modulated on the scale of *rational* and *reflexive* extremes. At the rational end, thought processes are sequential through calculated (audio-monitored) speech, verbalization is overt and deliberate, and attention in the discourse is concentrated on "expression." On the other hand, at the reflexive end, communicative processes are simultaneous with extemporized speech (being integrated with somatic reactions), verbalization is spontaneous and involuntary, and attention in the discourse is concentrated on "event" (see Table 6). The reflexive use of language is characterized by implicit regulation, depending on reference- or peer-group pressures, and on suggestion and covert design.

Many language experts, concerned with language primarily as a system of informational signaling, tend to regard explicit and overt correlations of speech variation as "functional" but stratificational and pragmatic manifestations in speech as "nonfunctional" (Neustupný, 1974:39). In this sense, elaborate networks of address and reference systems in many Oriental languages, identifying generation, sex, group, and other social hierarchies, are interpreted as nonfunctional "early modern" characteristics in language (for a treatment of the address system in Japanese, see Neustupný, 1974).

In several studies of pronouns in different languages, there seems to be much concern over clear-cut categorization of the modes of address. Attempts have been made to dichotomize these modes on the universal planes of "power" and "solidarity" and to show how these universal characteristics can distinguish "feudal" and "modern" pronominal patterns to suggest the "static" and "dynamic" stages of different speech groups. Brown and Gilman (1960) interpret the nonreciprocal, asymmetrical usage of Hindi and Gujarati pronouns within the family, such as between husband and wife and between elder and younger brothers, as a "truly feudal pronominal pattern," suggesting "a more static society and a less developed equalitarian ethic."

In a plural society such as India the same language speakers are not necessarily part of the same social group. It is not unusual to find several social groups belonging to the same language but adhering to different types of conformity pressure in its usage. It is a distinct characteristic of many Indian languages that the semantic content of pronouns keeps shifting according to the setting and the communicative task of a speech act. Fluidity in the use of the Hindi-Urdu pronominal system provides strong testimony to the interplay of formal (cognitive), institutional (identifying), and pragmatic (focusing) factors which make it necessary for a speaker to operate in various speech matrices (cf. Khubchandani, 1973b).

In the static view of language, modes of address and reference are treated as having a fixed attribute associated with an individual in the interaction dyad. But looking at the speech behavior of Hindi-Urdu speakers from a dynamic point of view, the ascending or descending shifts in assigning pronouns can be better understood in terms of their having variable values within a certain scale. The pronominal field in a language can be potentially organized differently among different social groups on the basis of the space- and time-bound abstract patterns of social dyads.

One can postulate two primary axes regulating the differential assignment of a pronoun to individual(s) in a Hindi-Urdu discourse:

1. *propriety,* that is, identity related to role, setting, channel, etc.;
2. *compatibility,* that is, pragmatic function related to communicative task.

Selection mechanisms of pronouns reveal the "elasticity" of the address-and-reference system in Hindi-Urdu, malleable to diverse settings, and susceptible to manipulations in negotiating optimal payoff in everyday communication. The collapsible nature of the pronominal system in many Oriental languages provides a basis on which to critically examine the characteristics of social variability and expressive fluidity in language activity.

One can identify at least three distinct "world views" of the conceptualizing address-and-reference system in Hindi-Urdu:

1. *group propriety,* emphasizing in-group/out-group relationships on the power-solidarity scale, in the speech of rural speakers (mostly in the vicinity of the original Khariboli belt).
2. *individual propriety,* emphasizing equal-unequal relationships according to age, status, and so on, on the deference (necessary-unnecessary) scale, among urban speakers; it includes Muslims as well as Hindus who have inherited the aristocratic culture of the Muslim court.

3. *contact propriety*, emphasizing the nature of contact on the formality-informality scale, among urban progressives who cherish egalitarian values.

Though in the patterns of language elaboration (i.e., orthography, borrowing of lexicons and rhetorics), "high" Hindi and "high" Urdu go in diametrically opposite directions, both languages show remarkably similar characteristics on the propriety scale as far as the pronominal usage is concerned.

In standard Hindi-Urdu one notices a marked distinction among the patterns of address referring to male and female. Male address is mainly guided by the patterns of individual propriety among the urban nobility, whereas female address is generally conditioned by the patterns of group propriety among the rural acculturated. The male-female differentials in this regard could possibly be explained as follows: in most parts of the Hindi-Urdu region, the male population, with a greater exposure to alien "aristocratic" values through Persian during the period of Muslim rule, demands a "higher" form of address, for example, use of the pronoun *aap* after the fashion of "nobility," thus causing "higher" asymmetry when addressing the female population, whose interactions were mostly confined to the family. On the other hand, the female population, even in urban areas, tends by and large to remain aligned with the "tradition-culture" syndrome and thus uses standard Hindi-Urdu speech, retaining the rural female address system based on "group" solidarity.

In the modern, "progressive" use of pronouns, the criteria of contact propriety—formal-informal—are gaining ground, at least in the spoken idiom. Informality, which is winning out over deference, usually permits "higher" *aap* or a "lower" *tuu/tum* symmetry. Thus, in private a modern young wife may exchange mutual *tuu/tum* with her husband; but in a formal setting or when writing to her husband she may revert to the standard usage of "higher" asymmetry: *tuu/tum* → *aap* (for details, see Jain, 1973). Due to the stigma associated with the "lower" pronoun—*tuu* in urban usage—its use is now being discouraged for the sake of egalitarian propriety, at least in teaching Hindi-Urdu as a second, or foreign, language. Thus, now the "elaborate" three-tier address system *(tuu/tum/aap)* is again being reduced to the two-tier system *(tum* and *aap)*, contrasting with the original rural "fluid" symmetry between *tuu* and *tum*.

In a changing society there is an ongoing redefining of relationships. Considerations of class mobility in a rapidly changing social structure provide many instances when the same person can be involved as an addresser or addressee in different interlocution systems. A Hindi-Urdu speaker does not see anything unusual in frequent shifts of pronominal axes for different social dyads, or even for the same dyad functioning in different settings or channels. For example, a "modern" young lady focuses on the *contact* relation (informal-formal) when addressing her husband in private, using *tum;* she operates on the *individual* propriety dimension (deference-nondeference) when addressing her father, her urban teacher, as well as her husband in public settings and in writing, using *aap;* and she utilizes the *group* identity (in-group/out-group) when addressing her mother and her rural grandparents, using *tuu/tum*.

Everyday reality in many Indian languages is not organized around the consistent use of the same pronouns for the same participant by the same addressee all the time. Different focuses in conceptualizing the address-and-reference system among different social groups speaking the same language show man's ingenuity in abstracting or transcribing everyday reality through speech.

Contemporary Trends

As discussed earlier, many of the Indian languages have reacted to influences of foreign languages as a composite linguistic unit (cf. Chapter 1). Many major languages of the subcontinent appear to be very susceptible to borrowing from different classical and modern languages. English also shares this characteristic of "loan proneness." There are various other languages, such as German, Hebrew, and Chinese, which instead show preference for translating a term or a phrase from the foreign language, copying only the arrangement of the model (known as "loan translation").

Two significant trends are noticed among contemporary major Indian languages to suit their new roles in the changed conditions: classicalization and Westernization. These "modernizing" drifts have greatly affected the phonological, grammatical, and lexical patterns of the languages involved and have also contributed to the widening gulf between their spoken and written styles (Khubchandani, 1968, 1969d).

1. *Classicalization,* that is, borrowing and reborrowing from classical languages. Many Indo-Aryan and Dravidian languages depend on Sanskrit; Urdu, Kashmiri, and Sindhi on Perso-Arabic elements; and Tamil on Old Tamil stock. This trend has led to the development of "highbrow" literary, academic, and administrative writing styles. To equip Indian languages for new roles in administration, technical occupations, higher education, and research, classicalists have begun a new trend of translating technical terms and concepts from the Sanskrit stock; for example, *jalayān* for "ship," *dūrvāṇī yantra* for "telephone." The chances of success in this direction appear to be rather dubious, since Indian

speakers are prone to borrowing terms from living situations rather than coining artificial terms from the classical stock.

2. *Westernization.* The impact of urbanization and technological advancement has accelerated the trend of borrowing from European languages, especially from English. This tendency has given birth to a "highbrow" spoken style which is gaining popularity among educated people in various Indian languages. Compound bilingualism of Indian languages and English (two or more languages being used in fused contexts for referring to the same environmental event) has led to code-switching, which has further escalated this process. It bears some connotations of sophistication and intimacy in the spoken register, and many contemporary writers have started using this style in avant-garde literature.

In recent years, there have been sharp reactions against these two diametrically opposite trends:

1. As literacy is increasing, the common man is reacting sharply against the "highbrow" styles, which are rather unintelligible to him.
2. As prose styles in various major languages acquire stability, writers realize the potentialities in indigenous patterns of their language instead of looking to outside sources for refining and polishing their diction.
3. Due to chauvinistic pride in their native language, writers are making a conscious effort to give prestige to the elements indigenous in the language and even to revive the obsolete forms with modernistic connotations.

The handicap in language transition, particularly in the domains of science and technology, is not due to inadequate cultivation of Indian languages to the extent that is generally presumed but to the lack of linguistically reoriented personnel to take up the task, and also to the purists' reluctance to accept borrowed expressions for new concepts from living situations. Development of a "highbrow" *tatsamized* style,[4] based on artificial coinage from nonnative classical stock, has been a great deterrent to adopting Indian languages for this purpose (see Language Elaboration, Chapter 4).

Under the influence of the purists' tradition in philology, many language-planning agencies seem to regard concepts like language hybridization, grass-roots "folk" multilingualism, and other such processes arising from contact situations as serious problems of human adjustment. Guided by such assumptions, agencies concerned with social planning analyze linguistic heterogeneity as a serious challenge to them.

NOTES

1. In this context, Spolsky (1971), discussing the language problems of blacks and Hispanic Americans, also points out cases where "language is used as an excuse, like race or skin color or sex, for not hiring someone. No amount of language training will change this for the discrimination exists in the hearer and not the speaker" (pp. 1-5).

2. R. Austerlitz, in his presentation on internal reconstruction of Altaic and Uralic languages at the Linguistic Society of Hawaii, University of Hawaii, Honolulu, March 1975.

3. In this regard, Saussure's dichotomy of parole and langue (1959), Pike's etic and emic approach to language (1967), and Chomsky's model of language distinguishing performance from competence of the ideal speaker (1965) provide useful insights concerning the plurilateral facets of speech activity. Braga (1972), discussing the dialectical premise for developing a comprehensive model in sociolinguistic studies, introduces a distinction between expectations concerning linguistic behavior and actual performance.

4. Loan words from Sanskrit retained in a language without any phonological adaptation are termed *tatsama* (unassimilated) words, in contrast to those adapted to the phonological system of the borrowing language, which are called *tadbhava* (assimilated) words.

CHAPTER 3

Language Manipulation

THE MAGNITUDE of various linguistic and education problems in newly independent nations appears to be quite outside the experience of most European countries either in the past or in the present. In most of the Western homogenized nation-states, identification of the "standard" core and demarcation of boundaries of a mother tongue are no longer sources of tension. Textbook standards of different languages, drawn from respective literary traditions, were stabilized along with the continuing processes of urbanization. One does not find any apparent conflict between the stabilized standard and actual speech variations in a language area. By and large, a speech community's *image* of language, its *identity postures* through language, and its *actual use* of language have acquired some congruence within a language *territory*. But the intricacies of language behavior in the Indian context reveal apparent ambiguities in defining the concept of mother tongue itself. The posture toward and image of a mother tongue do not necessarily claim congruity with actual usage, and these, again, are not rigidly identified with specific language territories.

Contours of Speech Behavior

Language is a complex multilateral phenomenon, manifested in physiological, psychological, institutional, and other forms. Various overt and covert characteristics in verbal communication point to at least three distinct contours of speech behavior: (1) what people do with speech, that is, language usage; (2) what people think they do with speech, that is, language image; and (3) what people claim they do with speech, that is, language posture.

In many plural societies one often finds inherent contradictions in the language scene concerning different aspects of speech behavior, namely, patterns of language use, levels of competence, unconscious attitudes (images), and conscious assertions (postures) about speech activity. Elicitation techniques for ascertaining speech behavior developed through language surveys and a decennial census in various countries tend to provide stigmatized responses from people about their claims, which are conditioned by the propriety of domains or tasks associated with different languages. In reacting to the questions concerning language, a respondent unconsciously or deliberately reveals certain patterns of "acculturation" or "manipulation." So far, language postures of many "exotic" societies have often been badly misunderstood and their language images ridiculed, with the result that no serious thought seems to have been given to the patterns of actual linguistic usage in many sociolinguistic and demographic investigations.

Numerous apparent contradictions in the language policy decisions and the actual speech behavior of many plural societies in Asia and Africa should make one realize that behavioral decisions are not necessarily made explicit in minute detail. In the case of Kenya, the assertions made for replacing English with Swahili are not actually against the use of English as such but are in fact used as a posture against the dominance of major ethnic languages in the political structure (Gorman, 1973:75–79). One also finds ambivalent attitudes toward language image and language usage on the Marquesas Islands in French Polynesia, where the knowledge of French is regarded as an ideal but the knowledge of Tahitian is an easily accessible goal: "a gallicization desired by the administration, accepted by the missionaries, and dreamed of by the people is opposed by a de facto tahitianization" (Lavondès, 1974:262). The same can be said about the Indian situation: "Champions of regional languages and Hindi, under the spell of a hyper-sensitive nationalism complex, are mostly guided by the presumption that Indian languages cannot be developed for full expression in different fields of knowledge unless English is dislodged from its present privileged position. This demand for the creation of a 'vacuum' in favour of Indian languages, apart from having the overtones of national pride, is to a great extent motivated by the issues of employment and economic opportunities" (Khubchandani, 1973c:204). The struggle for leadership between the Westernized and the regional elites (both relying heavily on English in everyday life) has been at the root of various conflicts over language privileges.

Language Claims

The language claims of many societies can be characterized as tips of icebergs: much more is hidden under the surface than is revealed through an individual's declarations. A language census accounts for information on one or more aspects of speech behavior:

1. Population aggregates portraying a picture of language *usage* in a region or society. The data highlight the significant characters of performance (intensity, domains, etc.) in different languages.
2. Head counts according to the levels of proficiency in different languages. The data highlight information graded on the basis of language *competence* in a variety of skills in a particular language.
3. Populations signifying unconscious attitudes or values regarding the languages with which they feel concerned in one way or another. The data provide a picture of language *image,* characterizing the pressures of identity within a particular group.
4. Populations asserting conscious alignments toward different languages in a particular context. The data characterize the signals of language *posture* in a region or society, implicitly revealing the scope of manipulation through language returns.

A general tendency seems to prevail among those interpreting language census data to assess the quality of a census on the basis of authenticity concerning the first two types of information: (1) the actual usage of a particular language in general or specifying domains—home, school, public, and so forth; and (2) the degree of competence in general or according to specific skills—speaking, writing, and so on. The latter two types of information—(3) identity pressures and (4) implicit assertions made through language returns—do not receive adequate attention from language investigators. Very often, the insistence on "face-value" interpretations of the implicit assertions give a distorted picture of a population.[1] In order to evaluate the language scene of a community, it is essential to process language statistics in a sociolinguistic framework that accounts for all relevant aspects of speech behavior.

Since language is primarily a time-and-space-bound institutional reality, it would be rather idealistic to subject language claims to a universal "standard" interpretation in all regions and for all times, as is being argued by many social and political scientists (Kloss and McConnell, 1974). There is no uniform procedure for interpreting language statistics into patterns of speech behavior, just as there is no single procedure for interpreting phonemic systems of languages from their writing systems. Nor for that matter, can one even find a one-to-one correlation between the perceived (auditory) speech sounds and the spectographic evidence which provides visual signals for the acoustic sounds. Each language has its own intrinsic patterns of correlating the two. In a simple monolingual situation or in a well-formalized speech group, census returns pertaining to mother tongue may run parallel to the prevailing communication patterns of the mother tongue, whereas in a complex multilingual society or where speech conventions are relatively less stabilized, seeking an exact parallel between the two may be quite misleading.

One notices many instances in the pluralistic societies of Asia and Africa where the boundaries distinguishing two languages, two castes, or two religions are not sharply delineated. Linguists and social scientists have made many attempts to distinguish "language" from "dialect," "register," and other speech labels by applying various parameters, such as percentage of cognates, mutual intelligibility, autonomy of morphological systems, functional dominance, literary achievements, writing systems, lexical and stylistic elaboration, standardization, and even juridical considerations.[2] But we are still far from having any objective criterion for quantifying linguistic differences and for determining the boundaries between "language" and "dialect."

In this regard, Sledd (1972) cites the contradictory conclusions reached by Loflin (1967) and Labov et al. (1969) in treating nonstandard black English as a dialect of standard English or as a separate language. Loflin finds the nonstandard speech of blacks so unlike the standard speech of whites "that a fuller description . . . will show a grammatical system which must be treated as a foreign language" (pp. 1312-1314). On the other hand, Labov is equally emphatic in rejecting such claims:

> In dealing with the structure of NNE (Nonstandard Negro English), we do not find a foreign language with syntax and semantics radically different from SE (Standard English): instead, we find a dialect of English, with certain extensions and modifications of rules to be found in other dialects. (p. 339)

As such, one cannot claim to possess a standard measuring index of identifying one's mother tongue or the knowledge of other languages.

Often, different political and educational agencies interpret the concept of mother tongue in narrow or broad terms according to the exigencies of the situation—juridical, functional, linguistic, and so on.

1. According to the juridical approach, an officially accredited "national" speech variety is considered as a language, and unrecognized varieties are treated as dialects. Provençal and Breton in France are regarded as patois. Between the two Celtic varieties, Welsh and Breton, in the United Kingdom Welsh is recognized as a language, while in France Breton is treated as a dialect.

2. The functional approach regards as languages only those tongues that are carriers of a literary tradition; all other preliterary vernaculars are regarded as dialects (supposedly at the lower level of development). Intrinsic distance from the dominant literary language is of no consequence.
3. The linguistic approach, based on intrinsic distance (such as percentage of cognates between two speech varieties; differences in morphological structure; degree of mutual intelligibility, i.e., the amount of information transferred), has been utilized so far only for classifying preliterary speech varieties.

The seemingly innocent question asked in the census, "What is your mother tongue?" could be projected as: (1) language first learned or used (which favors the reporting of minority-language maintenance); (2) language usually used in everyday life (which favors reporting assimilation trends toward the dominant language); or (3) all languages which the individual knows (which maximizes the number of speakers of the dominant language) (Kirk, 1946). Knowledge of the criteria employed is a great help in making a critical evaluation of language statistics.

Similarly, we do not have any clear-cut operational definition with which to quantify the knowledge of a particular language. Such knowledge largely depends on an individual's degree of awareness, subjectively interpreted on the basis of: (1) fluency, that is, spontaneity in expression; (2) intensity of use, that is, varieties of communicative tasks being performed; (3) proficiency, that is, grasp of the standard variety, (4) knowledge of the script associated with that language; and so on. A perfectionist may hesitate to claim knowledge of a language in spite of having a fairly advanced grasp of that language but about which he is not satisfied, whereas a trader may claim to know a number of languages merely on the basis of knowing a few phrases in those languages.

Because of the bias in favor of clear-cut categorization, language information in many demographic accounts is often mistakenly handled like physical data (birth, death, sex) without evaluation of subjective factors. The anomaly of analyzing the abstract attributes of institutional reality on the same basis as physical reality becomes evident when treating the statistical information concerning speech communities which are not explicitly defined.[3] Language claims in such communities remain quite unpredictable, varying with prestige and other politicoeconomic fluctuations.

Since language enumeration is primarily a statement based upon an individual's assertion, an exact (i.e., objective) statement about the actual speech behavior of a speaker is not possible. Census figures attain only the appearance of precision. Numbers by themselves do not tell the whole story. A critical appraisal of Indian census returns reveals the extent to which "absolute" numbers could present a blurred picture of the language scene (cf. Chapter 5).

Mother-Tongue Identity

The notion of "language" to a speaker is not the same thing it is to a linguist. Languages are generally classified according to their grammars. To a linguist, the formal characteristics of a particular speech have a priority in determining whether it can be grouped with language A or language B. But to a speaker, language is more significant symbolically in terms of identifying himself with a group than in terms of its purely formal criteria, which are a priori considerations for a linguist in defining language. Consequently, in a pluralistic society a speaker's declaration about his or her mother tongue is purely individual, based mostly on considerations of social identification and group loyalty rather than on the speech he or she uses for primary communication.[4]

In linguistic and educational jargon, the terms "mother tongue" and "native speech" are often used indistinguishably, which leads to some indeterminacy when applied in different contexts. In terms of language proficiency and language loyalty, a distinction has been suggested between the two (Khubchandani, 1974a):

- *native speech* as "the first speech acquired in infancy, through which a child gets socialized. It claims some bearing on 'intuitive' competence, and potentially it can be individually identifiable."
- *mother tongue* as "[speech] categorized by one's allegiance to a particular *tradition,* and it is societally identifiable." In the in-group/out-group dichotomy, a speech variety which members of a group (or, in extreme cases, even an individual) regard as their "own" is accepted as their mother tongue.

In this respect, "language" can be regarded as being closer to "mother tongue." It represents an institutional reality, being space- and time-bound to a specific society or culture.

Though the actual speech of an individual is marked by various diverse and heterogeneous characteristics revealing stratificational demands of the context, people perceive their own and others' speech in categorical terms as discrete language A or discrete language B, as if it were uniform and homogeneous. This paradox of "heterogeneous" performance and "homogenized" perception (i.e., categorization) is one of the characteristic features of speech behavior. As already discussed, an amalgam or conglomeration of many speech varieties is identified through one or more "language" labels, depending upon a number of historical associations which are cherished by its members as a part of their shared "tradition." A speech can be distinguished on the basis of:

1. physical or political environments providing opportunities or imposing restrictions on the mobility and contact among different groups. Many language boundaries are stabilized with geographical or political borders; for example, between Dutch and Low German; and between Danish, Swedish, and Norwegian.
2. emphasis on sociocultural affinities (ethnic, religious, nationality, and/or occupational affiliations), such as the distinction asserted by the language elites between Hindi and Urdu and between Serbian and Croatian.
3. convictions or beliefs based in legend, such as Bihari or Panjabi rural speakers claiming "Hindi" as their mother tongue, and individuals belonging to different speech groups similarly claiming Sanskrit.

In the Indian situation one finds evidence of multiple criteria by which language labels become identified. Very often, identificational correlations override such linguistic criteria as structural distinctions or mutual intelligibility in determining one's mother tongue.

1. *Physical or political environments.* Structurally, Kachhi is regarded as a dialect of Sindhi (a Northwest Indo-Aryan language) . But the political and social separation of the Sind and Kutch regions for over three centuries has given a distinct identity to Kachhi speakers. Now Sind forms a part of Pakistan and Kutch is part of India. Although the standard Sindhi (i.e., the Vicholi dialect) is quite intelligible to a Kachhi speaker, he is not motivated to acquire the prestige variety of Sindhi and thus regards himself closer to being a Gujarati (a Central Indo-Aryan language) speaker (Khubchandani, 1969a).

2. *Sociocultural affinities.* In many urban and border regions in South Asia, one often notices a citizen identifying his language with caste or class or original (ancestral) regional affiliations, and not so much with the actual speech he uses as a native speaker. According to the 1961 Indian census, Bihari was identified as mother tongue by fifteen thousand individuals from twenty states and Union territories, but not a single individual from Bihar claimed Bihari as his mother tongue. Similarly, six thousand South Indians settled outside South India claimed languages

like "Madrasi" and "Dravidam" as their mother tongue in the 1961 census.

In multilingual societies, a community often asserts its group identity by claiming a language of its own for reasons of caste loyalty, religious affiliation, and so on. The language returns recording such languages as Reddi Bhasha, Muslim Pahari, Ahiri Hindi, Kshatri, Rajputi, Mughaliya (of Mughul descent), Ad Dharmi (of the foremost religion; cobblers' speech), Islami, Musalmani, Christian, Kerala, and Andhra in the Indian census illustrate this fact.

3. *Legendary convictions.* In societies where speech habits are not rigidly identified with a particular language label, esteem for a particular ideal of speech, or any set of fanciful beliefs, may lead individuals to identify with a prestigious major language group which need not necessarily be one's native speech; for example, many monolingual speakers (mostly rural) of diverse languages of the North-Central region, such as speakers of Garhwali, Marwari, and Bhojpuri, claim Hindi as their mother tongue (though they need not know Khariboli, which forms the basis for standard Hindi), since they regard themselves as part of the great Hindi "tradition." Their speech, in the strict formal sense, will be classified as a distinct language different from the so-called Hindi (i.e., Khariboli) as understood by structuralists, academicians, and other custodians of language standardization.

In this connection, it is interesting to note that among 1019 classified mother tongues in the 1961 Indian census, 247 are claimed by fewer than 10 speakers each. In this list there are as many as 81 language labels which can be counted as simply "whimsical" inventions claimed by only one speaker each, depending upon his or her fancy, place of origin, caste, and so on. Examples of such language labels are: Vedic, Riyasati (of princely state), Mulki (of native place), Swadeshi (of homeland), Tibia (of the tradition of medicine), Nepali Hindi, Patiali Pahari, Nagpuri, Travankorian, and Mysore. Further, other declarations of languages like Indian, Bharati, Roman, Nagari, Pakistani, Bolti Zaban (spoken language), Deshi (local speech), Sarnarthi (refugee speech), Pahlwani (wrestlers' speech) given as mother tongues in the 1961 census also stand as testimony to the trend toward "exclusiveness."

Two major characteristics in speech behavior lead to homogeneity in communications in the midst of considerable variation in speech activity: (1) speech as an expression of cohesion; and (2) speech as an abstract categorization of heterogeneous performance.

A variety of the affiliations discussed above bind members of a community together. The affiliations are expressed through:

1. sharing a common set of normative patterns in their speech behavior (Labov, 1970); for example, adherence to a common variety of speech—Ferguson (1968) calls it a "supradialectal norm"; a general consensus concerning language "elaboration" processes, that is, equipping it for new functions (Haugen, 1966; Khubchandani, 1969d; also discussed at length in Chapter 4); or
2. in certain cases, sharing the mere conviction of common ideal of speech functions, even when it is not exemplified in actual speech; for example, allegiance to a particular literary tradition or to a writing system, or having common attitudes toward the patterning of verbal repertoire (diglossia structure, etc.).

Since language is one of the fundamental elements of social life, it is a prominent mark of differentiation and collective cohesion. It forms a strong tie among the members of a community and strikes a note of unity to the ear. Hence, a common language label, like other subjective traits (such as customs, tradition, faith, nationality, race), gives people a sense of common feeling. One notices an instinctive adherence to one's own native speech. In many newly independent countries, with the overt language-loyalty pressures found in the political and educational structures, language is emerging as the most important element in identifying with a "group." It is displayed as an emblem of national or group solidarity.

During periods of political or social unrest, however, one may find that sharp awareness of language traits is often confused with physical traits, and many claimants erroneously regard them as an index of physical descent. Many campaigns based on linguistic and religious claims for resolving disputed "nationality" boundaries in post-Renaissance Europe and also in South Asia during recent decades provide ample evidence of this vital "folk" reality.

An individual's identification through a particular language label is a categorically determined institutional attribute and does not necessarily have an exact parallel with the structural characteristics in his speech matrix. Mother-tongue identity is a discrete alignment by an individual or a group with certain cultural or formal attributes, whereas speech behavior is not necessarily so. A variety of consequential associations may result from such discrete operations, such as different elite-group pressures or different pulls of tradition on a community's speech norms that affect speech attributes. Language returns in a census, therefore, should be regarded as "indexing devices" through which one obtains the results of this categorization process.

The degree of stability of such a categorization process in a speech community can be assessed on a scale indicating:

Language Manipulation

1. the level of social awareness of certain structural features marked "linguistic stereotypes" (Weinreich, Labov, and Herzog, 1968);
2. the degree of consensus among its members in their subjective reactions to the norms in actual speech or in cherishing them as an ultimate goal or out of conviction; and
3. the degree of diglossic complementation among speech varieties regarding their propriety in the total verbal repertoire: "the sharpness with which constituent varieties are set off from one another" (Gumperz, 1968).

In well-formalized speech groups, it is basically as the result of an explicit standardization process (through prestige-group pressures and/or education) that allegiance to a particular mother-tongue label and to a particular set of "stereotypes" (inflection system, etc.) in speech is taken for granted by its members; for example, "English," with the general acceptance of the RP (Received Pronunciation) model by the British.

On the other hand, in a heterogeneous situation, communication is organized on the basis of different linguistic hierarchies (with many speech varieties enjoying different status privileges), and social and political changes bring the conformative values of a speech community into sharp conflict. Also, there are regions where populations remain in perpetual flux (in urban and industrial areas, along migration routes, in transient border territories, and in other watershed regions) which can be characterized by the lack of uniformity among speakers concerning their subjective reactions to speech variations, resulting in the loosening of propriety controls in verbal behavior in the group as a whole. In such circumstances, a community's claims that a particular language is the mother tongue keep fluctuating, sometimes even "shuttlecocking" according to overt identity pressures (see Chapter 5).

A society may have certain overt linguistic traits, the identities of which do not cause much ambiguity in a particular group, region, or country, as the result of implicit social awareness or explicit standardization efforts (e.g., the identity of the standard languages in Europe). But the lack of standardization or of overtness of a particular trait is characterized by fluidity in identifying abstract attributes. Such traits are selected on the basis of various prestige factors, reference-group pressures, and the sociopolitical climate. Response to such attributes may be a product of subjective evaluation conditioned by the degree of awareness in a group with which the claimant desires to be affiliated (e.g., mother tongue in plural societies in the Indian context).

Most of the time an individual's claim to a mother tongue and the normative attributes of his native speech behavior go hand in hand; but this is not always so. In multilingual societies, we do find that the ideal claim and the real function of a language might be at variance. As an example, in the 1961 Indian census, 2544 individuals scattered throughout the country testified that Sanskrit, a classical language, was their mother tongue, though one could easily detect that most of them natively spoke different modern languages in their respective regions and did not form a single speech community.

Communication patterns in South Asia, characterized by a plurilingual hierarchy, pose a serious challenge to the monistic norms of underlying univariability in interpreting diverse speech behavior. On the basis of such norms, communicative competence is evaluated by razor-edged boundaries between languages, by the dominating extension of standard usage, and by notions of language purity and language elaboration (through meticulous coinage of technical terms and translations). In this regard, Steiner (1975) also, in rejecting a theory of *language* in favor of a theory of *languages,* makes a decisive break with both traditional and fashionable linguistics. In his view, a metamathematical "universalist" view of language is bound to fail to account for the nature of relations between languages (or speech varieties) as they actually exist and differ (Cranston, 1975). "A genuine philosophy of language must grapple with the phenomenon and rationale of the human 'invention' and retention of anywhere between five and ten thousand distinct tongues" (Steiner, 1975).

One speech variety can be distinguished from another in a number of ways. In a preliminary comparison of social borders, Jennie Ross (1975) suggests the identification of four degrees of definition: category, collectivity, intensive contact, and formal assocation focused on the border. "Just as geographical borders vary from discreet signs announcing the existence of a boundary to the intricacies of customs inspections and military checkpoints, social borders vary in degree of definition from minimal acknowledgement of social similarity to its public and formal proclamation" (p. 54). Similarly, varying degrees of boundedness between languages, dialects, or speech varieties can be explained only through a "pluralistic" view of language.

In the course of history, language boundaries become stabilized, not primarily because of the barriers of intelligibility between two speech varieties, but because of the considerations of identity and value systems among the speakers of those varieties. The "highbrow" registers of Hindi and Urdu are sharply marked by the polarization in the patterns of borrowing, whereas at the "lowbrow" level the distinction between the two is not regarded as so significant. Identification through a particular language label is very much a matter of social awareness on the part of an individual.

Bilingual Identity

In a multilingual interaction no single language caters to all needs of the participant. Since language is a form of dyadic behavior, the choice of using a particular language is determined by: (1) the pragmatic demands of the situation, depending on the listener's capacity and the speaker's ability as well as their cultivation of the language; and (2) the institutional factors of identification, language here serving as a label for status, prestige, and fashion. The second factor adds sentimental affiliations with one or the other language.

People have feelings about different languages varying in intensity from positive to neutral to negative—love, sympathy, indifference, aversion, antipathy, or hate (Fodor, 1966). People in general tend to have possessive feelings about their mother tongue and the languages (dialects, styles) of their region, partly owing to cultural inheritance and partly to which languages lead to various cultural and economic gains such as employment, political power, and cultural dominance.

A critical study of the 1961 census returns on mother tongues and bilingualism brings into the limelight several convictions founded in tradition and other sociopsychological characteristics of different speech groups which have a great bearing on the individual's claims to his "own" and his "contact" languages. Patterns of intragroup and intergroup communication and the education system that encourages the "three-language formula" show that many parts of the country find utilization of more than one contact language to be congenial.

Bilingualism claims in India, by and large, reveal the extent of pressures developed among different speech groups for intragroup and intergroup communication. In a situation of multiple choice, different factors —such as heterogeneity, demands made by the dominant speech group, contiguity of language borders, levels of education, occupational specialization, urbanity, and prestige—contribute to the claims of regional languages, Hindi-Urdu, and/or English as contact languages in a state. In many cases, the degree of proficiency or the intensity of use of the declared contact language does not correlate exactly with an individual's claims, which are made under social-identification pressures on him to associate with a particular group equivalent to his educational and economic standing, or are made because of his affiliations in the language controversy in the transient postcolonial period of shift in language functions and privileges. In order to arrive at a rough correlation of the bilingual experience in the country, Khubchandani (1972b) has suggested the compilation of "pressure indices" of prominent languages in a region.

1. *State Language Pressure Index.* State language claims depend largely on the demands made by the dominant speech group on the rest of the

population in the state. A "State Language Pressure Index" is obtained on the basis of the proportion of minority speech groups claiming the dominant state language as their contact language:

$$\frac{\text{state contact-language claims}}{\substack{\text{linguistic minorities population} \\ \text{(in the state)}}} \times 100$$

For example, in Tamil Nadu, 6 out of 10 non-Tamilians claim Tamil as their contact language, but in Rajasthan only 1 out of 100 non-Hindis claim Hindi as their contact language (Khubchandani, 1972b, Table D).

2. *Hindi-Urdu Pressure Index.* The spread of Hindi-Urdu as a contact language throughout the country can be attributed to two major factors: (1) Speakers of Hindi-Urdu as mother tongue proliferate in almost all neighboring and nonneighboring states outside the six Hindi states. Six out of 10 non-Hindi states (at the time of the 1961 census) had contiguous borders with the Hindi region, and 9.5 million Urdu natives (42 percent) and 4.5 million Hindi natives (3 percent) were reported from outside their home region. (2) The Hindi-Urdu amalgam, by the virtue of being the dominant language of the largest region, exercises a good deal of influence in intergroup communication throughout the country (of course, with varying degrees of intensity in different regions). It had virtually acquired the position of a lingua franca for trade, entertainment, and informal communication in heterogeneous situations (mainly in urban, industrial, and military settlements) throughout the country, well before the hectic involvement of official and semiofficial agencies in the promotion of Hindi.

The "Hindi-Urdu Pressure Index" outside Hindi states is worked out on the basis of the first major feature, that is, the proportion of speakers claiming Hindi-Urdu as a contact language to the number identifying Hindi-Urdu as mother tongue settled in these states:

$$\frac{\text{claimants of Hindi-Urdu as contact language}}{\text{speakers of Hindi-Urdu as mother tongue}} \times 100$$

For example, in Gujarat we find 75 persons speaking Hindi-Urdu as a contact language per 100 speaking Hindi-Urdu as mother tongue, whereas in Tamil Nadu there are only 10 Hindi-Urdu contact speakers per 100 persons citing Hindi-Urdu as their mother tongue (Khubchandani, 1972b, Table E).

3. *English Pressure Index.* Even after independence English has con-

Language Manipulation 53

tinued to be an important part of the communication matrix of urban India. Throughout the country, English contact speakers are approximately 50 times more numerous than those speaking English as their mother tongue. The spread of English in different states is due primarily to schooling opportunities and to the degree of occupational specialization, which demands a certain minimum proficiency in English. In situations of multiple choice, the prestige attached to an international language also seems to be one of the vital factors in causing people to claim English as their primary contact language. One finds a remarkable correlation between the ratio of the literate population and English claimants in different states, which is here taken as the basis for obtaining the "English Pressure Index":

$$\frac{\text{English claimants}}{\text{literate population}} \times 100$$

For example, in Panjab 16 percent of the literates know English, whereas in Jammu and Kashmir only 4.5 percent of the literates claim to know English (Khubchandani, 1972b, Table F).

By and large, these pressure indices signify the degree of disposition of the bilingual population of a state toward a particular contact language.

Under these circumstances, claims of a subsidiary language depend very much on the psychological distinction one consciously makes between one's native speech and the formal "standard" speech. For many speakers in the North-Central region, Hindi-Urdu is like an "associate" native speech, and for them the switching of linguistic codes from native speech to Hindi or Urdu is similar to the switching of styles in a monolingual situation. As was pointed out earlier, most of the people in the region are quite unaware of their plurilingual behavior and consider themselves "monolinguals" belonging to the Hindi or Urdu tradition. This phenomenon appears to be one of the primary reasons for the HUP region which, though relatively heterogeneous, shows very low claims of bilingualism in the census returns. Bilingual claims in the 1961 census for all of India are 9.7 percent of the entire population; the South claims 13.5 percent bilinguals; the West, 12.4 percent; the East, 10.9 percent; and the North-Central region, 5.9 percent (for details, see Khubchandani, 1972b).

The population of nearly half the total number of districts (46 percent) is exposed to heterogeneous surroundings, where minority speech groups exceed 20 percent of the total population (cf. Chapter 1). Such widespread heterogeneity can be considered as a potentially significant factor in promoting bilingual interaction among different speech groups. But the low returns of bilingualism do not testify to the intensity of such interaction.

A major factor contributing to the low claims to bilingualism in many linguistically pluralistic societies in India seems to be the conviction among many speech groups that knowledge of a contact language is associated with the ability to write that language in its prevalent script. Overlapping claims of Urdu (identified by Arabic script) and Hindi (identified by Devanagari script) made by nearly two million Hindi and Urdu natives is sound evidence in support of this tendency, as shown in Table 7.

To what extent this conviction can blur the bilingualism picture is evident from the claims of Sindhi immigrants as reported in the 1951 census: "Gurumukhi" is reported as a subsidiary language by Sindhi immigrants from Bombay Province in this census; Sindhi is primarily written in Arabic script. But some Sindhi Hindus, especially women, read and write Sindhi in Gurumukhi script. Some people equate having this knowledge of Gurumukhi script with acquiring another language. There is a widespread traditional conviction among many speech communities in India that associates the mastery of any additional script with the knowledge of another language. The Panjabi language is predominantly written in Gurumukhi script. Hence, Sindhi speakers' claims to know "Gurumukhi" were interpreted in the census as knowing the "Panjabi" language, and over two thousand Sindhi native speakers (mostly women) were shown claiming Panjabi as their primary contact language in the 1951 census, which is far from true (Khubchandani, 1963).

Many such traditional convictions distort the objective account of bilingualism among the Indian population. The extent to which many contact languages are spoken or merely understood cannot be fully discerned through census returns. Hence, one has to accept these returns as presenting a rather conservative account of bilingualism. At the same time, these returns present a valuable picture of the attitudes of speakers and trends of social identification at a particular moment in time. In spite of their limitations, one cannot underestimate the importance of the data made available through these returns.

Politicization of Language Data

Because of its subjective definition, language identity is particularly susceptible to manipulation by individuals, groups, and the state. Until the recent mobilization of pressure groups over language, one noticed that among many Indian communities the urge to belong to a particular language group was often relegated to somewhat less significant status in one's subjective evaluation of strata (cf. Chapter 1). Since independence

Table 7. Claims of Hindi-Urdu in the 1961 Census

State	Claimants of Hindi or Urdu as Mother Tongue (thousands)	Contact Speakers			Native plus Contact Speakers† (thousands)
		Claimants (thousands)	Overlapping Claims* (thousands)	Net (thousands)	
Andhra Pradesh	2693	634	39	595	3288
Tamil Nadu	656	66	1	65	721
Karnataka	2117	318	12	306	2423
Kerala	16	37	—	37	53
West Bengal	2731	511	118	393	3124
Orissa	433	139	7	132	565
Assam	535	275	3	272	807
Maharashtra	3956	2526	161	2365	6321
Gujarat	787	585	12	573	1360
Jammu and Kashmir	35	306	2	304	339
Hindi States					
Uttar Pradesh	70,867	1014	618	396	71,263
Bihar	24,730	1784	300	1484	26,214
Madhya Pradesh	26,012	1658	187	1471	27,483
Panjab	11,557	916	269	647	12,204
Rajasthan	7225	215	64	151	7376
Delhi (Union territory)	2210	183	52	131	2341

*Speakers of Hindi as a mother tongue claiming Urdu, and speakers of Urdu as a mother tongue claiming Hindi.
†The sum of speakers of mother tongues plus net contact speakers.

in 1947, language consciousness has been growing rapidly, and language loyalties have acquired a new order of fluidity in responding to overt identity pressures. Individuals in such communities select a particular language label according to the unconscious language image, that is, what they think of their speech; or according to the deliberate language posture, that is, the language they prefer to be aligned with under the circumstances (discussed earlier in this chapter).

In recent decades language privileges have become the rallying ground of most demands in many newly independent nations. "Unlike socioeconomic interests, the cultural and linguistic interests admit of greater subjective definition and, therefore, a greater possibility of political manipulation and negotiation, especially in a situation of plural groups where the very nature of segmentation imposes a limit on the possible dimensions of a group" (Das Gupta, 1970). At the time the census is taken in India, one often comes across such reactions in the vernacular press; for example: "Unless certain needs of a particular village were not immediately attended to, all people in that village would return a different language as their mother tongue in the census."

Often political considerations, such as the adjustment of district, state, or national boundaries on the basis of language, tend to politicize pressure groups around language and influence the language returns of a region. It is rather amazing to note that when agitations on the demarcation of boundaries of linguistic states reach a high pitch in Indian politics, even state officials resort to appealing to people to return a particular language label in the census. Thus, it is not altogether surprising that census data on the linguistic composition of a region are inevitably weighted in favor of the dominant language label in such a way that:

1. questions are often phrased to favor the dominant group in interpreting borderline cases;
2. political and economic advantages result in an exaggeration of responses in favor of the majority or elite group (a characteristic similar to the "heaping" of age declarations); and
3. manipulations by statistical authorities in the projection and selection of the information highlight certain results at the cost of others.

1. *The way the questions are posed.* One comes across various restrictions on the choices made available to the respondent, such as drawing the line between language and dialect (in tune with manipulations to achieve certain objectives); deliberately not providing for certain labels in the census (e.g., literary varieties of the Serbo-Croatian language—Serbian and Croatian—are not identified in the Yugoslav census); bilingualism in a foreign language was not recorded in the 1951 Indian census

Language Manipulation 57

(not accounting for English bilingualism in the country), which was rectified from the 1961 census onward.

2. *The way the questions are answered.* In an intensely charged environment, answers are often influenced by emotional and other considerations; for example, claims of Irish or of Sanskrit as the mother tongue are revived in Irish and Indian censuses; prestige and other politicocultural assertions lead to vacillation between religious and regional identities among Muslims in India through language claims of being bilingual in the dominant language regardless of its correlation with proficiency (cf. Chapter 5). Often, negative reasons also affect answers: individuals are afraid to admit knowledge of certain languages due to prevailing hostilities among the groups (e.g., many South Indians not recording the knowledge of Hindi). Such biases can scarcely be measured.

3. *Tabulation biases.* Often arbitrary systems of classification are introduced in presenting the results, by applying varying criteria: (1) The inclusive criterion. In order to boost the majority claims, many spoken languages of the region are included as dialects of the dominant language (e.g., the Austrian census classified Yiddish as a German language; the Indian census classifies Awadhi and Chhatisgarhi as Hindi). (2) The exclusive criterion. In order to minimize the importance of a minority group, dialects and local varieties of a language are enumerated in detail under different language labels in order to draw one's attention away from the whole entity (e.g., in Austria, Caranthian is distinguished from the Slovenian language of Yugoslavia; Hungary treats Serbian and Croatian as separate languages, whereas the Yugoslav census treats them as one language, namely Serbo-Croatian; Russians treat Moldavian, spoken on the Rumanian border, as distinct from the Rumanian language).

The European censuses demonstrate the inaccuracy of their linguistic and ethnic interpretations. Utilizing the inherent ambiguity in the terms "language" and "dialect," various governments make intentional distortions in taking the censuses of their populations. A normal pattern in these censuses emerges as: (1) maximization of the apparent proportion attributed to the dominant national language; and (2) corresponding minimization of the size of linguistic minorities. The British census tabulates language data in the framework of English and non-English speakers, and thus the 1931 England and Wales census reported only 98,000 non-English speakers (i.e., monolingual Welsh speakers), though at the same time there were 909,000 Welsh-speaking people in the region. The 1931 Scottish census in Scotland listed only 7000 non-English speakers, though the population included 136,000 Gaelic speakers.

The Indian census also presents an interesting picture of the manipulative game of language classification, beginning as early as 1881, particularly in the Hindi-Urdu-Panjabi region. It is somewhat amusing to find the Indian language census being absorbed, for over half a century, in preparing genealogical classifications of languages, and especially to note its obsession with modifying and remodifying Grierson's grouping of languages, which could be of direct interest only to historical linguists (cf. *Linguistic Survey of India,* 1903-1928). It is of particular interest to note the varying criteria (inclusive as well as exclusive) applied in successive censuses (or even different provinces applying different criteria during the British period) of grouping over 330 mother tongues under a few generic "umbrella" labels, such as Hindustani, Hindi, Western Hindi, Eastern Hindi, Urdu, Bihari, Rajasthani, Panjabi, Pahari (Western, Central, and Eastern), with very little regard for their characteristics as "institutional" realities.[5]

Census figures thus do not warrant assertions of accurate distinctions per se. With a critical evaluation one can detect many possible sources of bias.

In the controversy over language privileges, particularly in the sphere of education, two differing interpretations of what constitutes a mother tongue have been emphasized by conflicting pressure groups. According to the narrow interpretation, the home language of each child—"the language spoken from the cradle" (the 1951 census of India, 1954, p. 1)—is accepted as the mother tongue. However, the broad interpretation regards all minority languages not having any written tradition as "dialects" of the dominant language in the region, by which one implicitly denies equal rights to linguistic minorities on the grounds of practicability. In the early stages of educational development, the British rulers and the Indian elite gave greater weight to the broad interpretation. This view had prevailed in the post-Renaissance period in Europe as well, when language was claimed as a major criterion for stabilizing nationalistic states; for example, the French viewed minority languages—Provençal (another Romance language), Breton (a Celtic language) and Basque (a non-Indo-European language)—as dialects of the dominant French (a Romance language).

Attitudes of language loyalty tend to unite diverse local groups and social classes whose members may, at the same time, have distinct heterogeneous norms of speech for specific limited purposes. Haugen (1966), analyzing the correlation between language and nation, points out that the ideal of a nation is based on internal cohesion and external distinction. It stimulates loyalty beyond the primary group by minimizing internal differences and maximizing external ones. Congruence among language, culture, and territory tends to foster an intense in-group feeling. "The greater the intensity of in-group loyalty the greater the possibility, not to say danger, of alienation from the out-group which may even culminate into hostility towards the out-group" (Damle, 1968:28).

In modern times, with the growing sentiment of minority groups for equal language privileges, many authorities seem to be becoming more sensitive to the narrow interpretation of the mother-tongue concept, though a good deal of ambivalence still prevails over the issue. Such ambivalence is also evident from a UNESCO committee's (1953) definition of *vernacular:* "a language which is the mother tongue of a group which is socially or politically dominated by another group speaking a different language. We do not consider the language of a minority in one country as a vernacular if it is an official language in another country."

Colonial rulers often exploited the issue of language privileges as an effective means of transmitting their cultural heritage in the colonies. One finds that the language question in every Indian decennial census since 1881 has been handled either arbitrarily or with some preconceived notions, giving rise to various doubts and misinterpretations in the minds of people of different regions, as well as intriguing the British administrators who were "alien" to the relatively fluid segmentation patterns in the language behavior of Indian society.

Fluctuations in language returns of the North-Central region in India provide good evidence that census declarations of mother tongue do not necessarily correspond to the actual speech used in everyday life, but are guided mainly by the shifts in social identification under changed circumstances. In the 1911 census, Gait (1913) reports threefold difficulties in language enumeration:

1. The Aryan languages of India have no hard and fast boundaries between them.
2. The want of the precision of the people themselves in describing the dialects spoken by them.

    Over a large part of Upper India the only general term in use is Hindi—the language of Hind—a comprehensive word which includes at least three distinct languages, Western Hindi, Eastern Hindi and Bihari. . . . Lahnda in NWFP (North Western Frontier Province) is commonly regarded as a form of Panjabi, but it is quite distinct from that language.
3. Political considerations:

    [These] have given more trouble than heretofore. . . . Amongst many educated Hindus, there is a tendency *to belittle the great differences* which actually exist between the different parts of the Empire: and it is sometimes alleged that there is practically only one language spoken throughout northern India. . . . On the other hand, Muhammadans often declare that Urdu, the Persianized form of Hindostani is the language, not only of their co-religionists, but also of a large number of Hindus in the north of India. [emphasis added]

In the 1931 census, Hutton also expresses the difficulty of distinguishing various dialects of Hindustani classified by Grierson as different languages. He comments: "Generally speaking one dialect fades into another by indistinct and gradual changes so that it is very difficult to draw a hard and fast line" (pp. 355–356).

A sense of annoyance on the part of the British administration concerning language fluidity finds further expression in the 1913 Gait Report:

[In the United Provinces], as in 1901, there were undoubtedly steps taken to cause the returns of language to be falsified. . . . Simply because they *refused to define their terms* before they argued, or rather because they *would not take the trouble to understand the terms* as used by the census authorities, the controversialists, who were really quarrelling about the respective *merits of certain styles* as vehicles of instruction, succeeded in utterly falsifying a set of important statistics relating to something entirely different. (p. 320) [emphasis added]

In the 1931 census, Hutton also cites the same handicap:

The distinction between Eastern and Western Hindi in the Central Provinces and Central India, and between Lahnda and Panjabi in the Punjab was more than the census enumerators could grasp. As for the enumerated, each of course very properly considers his Hindi to be the true Hindi and is not prepared to qualify it by an adjective of locality implying that it is merely a dialect. Too much precision must not therefore be expected of figures representing the use of Eastern and Western Hindi and of Lahnda and Panjabi. . . . In the case of the spoken language admittedly the use of the terms Urdu and Hindi does give rise to embittered controversy between two schools which are generally speaking coterminous with Hinduism and Islam in religion. In point of practice it is *impossible to define any boundaries between Urdu and Hindi as spoken,* since the difference consists merely in a preference for a Persian or for a Sanskrit vocabulary, and as an illiterate man uses only the languages of common speech it is generally the bias of the enumerator which would determine the category of his return. As far as spoken lan-

Language Manipulation 61

guage goes therefore it was decided, as in 1921, to use the term Hindustani *only in the return for the United Provinces* and with the omission of the script of literacy the use of *the term Urdu disappeared.* This disappearance caused some searching of heart among Muslims who did not realise that the reason for omitting the term Urdu was that no general record of the script was being made at the Census. (pp. 355-356) [emphasis added]

As such, the semantic acrobatics over the issue of defining Hindi-Urdu-Hindustani to suit different audiences, treating all claims under one language (Hindustani), two languages (Hindi and Urdu), or three languages (Hindi, Urdu, and Hindustani), have been going on throughout the last eighty years.

Many political observers usually dismiss language as a question involving primordial loyalties (Geertz, 1963; Harrison, 1960; Shils, 1961). Language groups, according to them, cannot possibly contribute to the institutional development of political life; such groups, because of selectivism and particularism, retard political modernization. But recent developments on the subcontinent indicate that particularist loyalties of several language organizations are not necessarily inconsistent with national loyalties. Where social cleavages are crosscutting and mutually offsetting in a pluralistic decision system, "these concrete political conflicts may prove to be a factor of positive sociation lending to a possibility of integration" (Das Gupta, 1970:13). The very nature of language politics permits a special degree of flexibility.

In considering language in the Indian context as a role symbol for political mobilization rather than as a symbol of primordial loyalty, the Hindi particularist elite have not only formulated the cause but have also created a new form of Hindi, and "in this respect they have not behaved as traditional actors defending a given primordial cause" (Das Gupta, 1970:65). In this manipulative game, apart from Hindi-Urdu elites, the British administrators have at times also played contradictory roles, as is evident from the census data. However, it ought to be pointed out that throughout the struggle for power among competing language elites, the common man has shown very little awareness of distinguishing Hindi from Urdu in his actual speech behavior. The masses' involvement in the language agitation, to a large extent, has been manipulated by the power elite.

Language Manipulation as a Tool for Social Planning

Statistics are put to both proper and improper use, over which statisticians have hardly any control. Statistical data are often interpreted differently by the authorities and by the pressure groups in many countries. There has been a general concern regarding the use of language data from decennial censuses conducted at different times in different countries. Many political agencies interpret the language census rigidly, that is, evaluating language information arithmetically (such as numerical majority versus minority) and incorporating compulsory changes in the administrative or educational structure based on the given information. Issues such as the demarcation of state boundaries, or the recognition of administrative and educational languages in the Indian and Belgian contexts, are often resolved by "face-value" interpretations of the language census.

One finds many deliberate attempts at influencing the results obtained from the census for the political or cultural advantage of one or another section of the population. Examples of such manipulation are classifications of the populations of Alsace-Lorraine in France and of Upper Silesia in Poland, as reported by Kirk (1946): French authorities count the Alsace population as belonging to "French nationality" on the basis of historical association and tradition, while Germans regard them as belonging to the "German nationality" on the basis of linguistic affinity. In the Upper Silesia region in Poland, German authorities claimed historical affinity and economic unity with the people of the region, whereas Polish authorities were claiming them as "Polish nationals" on the basis of the patterns of language use of the population.

A census would lead only to the politicization of an institutional trait like language if it were aimed at introducing compulsory shifts in the patterns of speech behavior of a population, and if the language "identity" data (providing accounts of language image and/or language posture) were utilized for bringing about mandatory changes in language usage. That this is so is evident from the situation in Belgium, particularly in the Enghien region where the ethnic image concerning language is in sharp contrast with actual usage (Levy, 1960).

Many linguists often question the reliability of language statistics in various censuses and attribute the unreliability to the "ignorance" of the population or to the lack of "trained" enumerators, without themselves realizing the inherent limitations in quantifying abstract traits like language in objective terms. Looking at the matter purely from the point of view of the consumers of language censuses in different countries, it is not an exaggeration to say that political pressure groups in general show a rather more realistic approach in utilizing census material pertaining to language than do social scientists and linguists.

Language declarations, at best, can be regarded as effective indicators of the attitudes of speakers at the macro-level and of the trends of social identification at a particular point in time, and not necessarily of actual interaction patterns in a population. Census data on language can provide an overall understanding of the complexities of different institutional parameters which supplement the ecological perspective of a group, region, or nation. The census can be used as an important tool in interpreting, at the macro-level, the trends of population concerning speech behavior and in correlating them with other trends, and *not* as a depository of "absolute" numbers accounting for the speech behavior at the micro-level, concerning the proficiency or domains of one or another language.

There have been two basically different approaches among social scientists with regard to utilizing the language census as a tool for social planning:

1. Universalists show concern for soliciting information on language in standardized categories: (1) framing of language questions for eliciting precise and unambiguous responses; (2) orienting the population to provide "objective" responses; and (3) interpreting responses. The basic aim of inquiry as claimed by universalists is to enhance human understanding through statistical information in standardized categories. This could, in my view, lead to pseudo-questioning and pseudo-responses, which may or may not represent the facts in a population.
2. Pluralists lay emphasis on the relevance of questions specific to a context. Responses and interpretations are regarded as conditioned by ecological and historical perspectives. This view implies that investigators should be equipped with the tools to dig out covert implications of the statistical information by meaningful projections. According to this approach, a broad aim of a language census is to understand the significance of a particular trait, the trends of its change in a particular time and space, and its significance in problem-solving and policymaking for a society, region, or nation. A census can profitably be used for promotional or preferential purposes in social planning. One can avoid absurd results in social planning by spelling out the dangers of the misuse of language statistics in the absence of a relevant context.

The language census as a tool for scientific inquiry can provide useful insights into such concerns as language-and-dialect relationships, the conceptual fluidity regarding the mother tongue in plural societies; attitudes regarding one's "own" and "contact" languages in multilingual populations; difficulties in standardizing the units for counting speech variations in language behavior; language as an instrument as well as a product of "cohesion" and "distance"; the reflection of language shift and language modernization in a community; and diagnosis of communication environments of different regions.

Correlational studies should be able to distinguish language image from language posture, and both as distinct from language usage or language competence. A comparison of the language factor with other relevant variables—such as age, education, religion, density, mobility, and urbanity—can help in understanding the speech phenomenon of human behavior in more transparent terms so that the information can be more meaningfully utilized in the sphere of social planning.

NOTES

1. A social scientist unacquainted with the variable factors of the region and of that particular period could not but possibly interpret language data in purely statistical terms. This is especially true if the goal is to predict the language trends of a given population. Erroneous projections regarding the assumed English and Hindi literate populations in India by A.D. 2000 attempted by Deutsch (1953) are a glaring example of drawing inferences about the language trends of a population in purely statistical terms.

2. For an elaborate treatment of the possible criteria for delimiting languages, see Kloss (1972).

3. Kirk (1946) has rightly pointed out: "All these elements do not have any consistent *weights,* nor does the *chemistry,* in which they are mixed, always yield predictable answers."

4. The branching of the Makedonian standard language from the Bulgarian standard is an example of where political identities, in this case of Makedonia (in Yugoslavia) and Bulgaria, respectively, overshadow the linguistic similarities between the two speech varieties.

5. In the light of such ambiguous criteria for classifying languages, the district and state tallies of mother tongues and bilingualism from the 1971 census were not released for over five years so as to avoid certain political objections raised in the Parliament concerning language classification.

CHAPTER 4

Language-Promotion Activities

LANGUAGE PLAYS AN IMPORTANT ROLE in the social, economic, and educational development of a nation. With a clear perspective and proper planning, developing nations with pluralistic societies, most of them possessing a rich multiplicity of languages, can think in terms of utilizing this potential as an accelerating factor of rapid social change and other modernization programs. For many newly emerged nations, it has become a matter of primary concern to frame an appropriate language policy which can materially assist in social and national integration and in providing an economic uplift of their people, while maintaining a balance between internal needs and external necessities in the modern world.

Many Asian and African nations were submerged under one or another dominant European language at a time when tremendous scientific and technological progress was achieved. In the postwar phase of decolonization, many of these countries have been passing through a linguistic and literary upheaval, a consequence of the shift in emphasis from colonial languages (English, French, Dutch, Portuguese) to their native languages in education, administration, and other spheres of formal communication.

Language Politics

In the debates on language policy for the vast Indian subcontinent, many politicians and language experts invariably think of the roles and the privileges of different languages—Hindi, English, regional languages, minority languages, classical languages—in the life of a nation. For the past three decades various governmental agencies have been quite active in this area. At times, one finds these agencies acting willy-nilly on ad hoc solutions for quick results, hoping to contain rival language claims of various pressure groups competing on behalf of their divergent regional, economic, and educational interests.

Though at times governmental agencies may be blamed for misplaced enthusiasm in favor of one or another language, on the whole, far from being authoritarian or doctrinaire, language policy at the national level appears to be susceptible to the sensitivities of different pressure groups within the federal democratic order. In contrast, language policies of individual states have been rather slow in responding to the sensitivities of linguistic minorities, possibly because the representation of these minorities in state politics tends to be relatively low, and also because many of them have not kept the same pace as the dominant groups in socioeconomic development. However, the language scene of South Asia during the past quarter century has undoubtedly been fraught with discord and tension resulting from the new political situation following colonial withdrawal.

Contrary to the traditional Indian accommodation to linguistic heterogeneity based on grass-roots multilingualism, which readily responds to situational needs, recent decades have seen strong drives for language autonomy in the name of "language development." In recent years, the tendency to struggle for language privileges in all walks of life has been a main factor in promoting political discord among competing language groups. In light of this fact, many political experts believe the diversity of languages is an unmanageable phenomenon for this poverty-stricken subcontinent. Many of them somewhat pessimistically cast doubts on India's viability as a nation and its capacity to meet this gigantic challenge (Harrison, 1960).

Conservative accounts of Indian bilingualism obtained through the census returns (cf. Chapter 1) give the impression that the people of India are mostly monolingual and that the degree of interaction among two hundred-odd speech groups must be quite low. Such assumptions lead to the erroneous conclusion that the diversity of languages must be causing strong communication barriers, hampering the growth of a nation (Davidson, 1969). But if one takes into account the stratified caste structure of Indian society and the frequent migrations, conquests, and internal colonization during the course of India's history, the condition of extensive folk bilingualism (or multilingualism) at the grass-roots level in most parts of the country raises serious questions about the prevalent belief that linguistic heterogeneity is a freshly acquired "handicap" in Indian life, resulting from recent modernization processes such as technological and urban growth, accelerated mobility, and mass communication.

Hence, viewing the multiplicity of languages in pluralistic societies as a "handicap" may turn out to be an illusion. The ad hoc solutions of

Language-Promotion Activities

the three-language or two-language formulas, however well intentioned, may be quite inadequate for tackling Indian realities.

Following the departure of the imperial powers, Asia and Africa have undergone a linguistic and literary upheaval. Battles for linguistic succession have come to life in India as they have elsewhere in Afro-Asia. One notices an evident contrast between the effects of the external direction of language matters under the colonial rule until 1947, directly or indirectly prescribing "elegant" solutions in the name of rationalistic modernization of underdeveloped (primitive) societies, and the effect of "haphazard," flexible behavior of language interest groups after independence in the newly emerging pluralistic decision system. Within such a framework, language groups in India have been seeking viable solutions, leading to a convergence of conflicting interests, though at times these efforts have led to considerable tension, agitation, and sporadic violence. Since independence in 1947, one has seen an intricate battle of wits among competing language interest groups over the issues of deadlines, modes of changeover, privileges, guarantees, communicability, stylistic content, and so on, concerning "national," "official," and "link" languages.[1]

This language consciousness among hitherto unpoliticized groups on the Indian social and political scene is characterized by the lack of harmony and goodwill among different language pressure groups. In the polemics over the language issue, no effective demarcation of the roles of different languages is acceptable to the country's social architects, who represent different segments of the society. One major confrontation is between the camps supporting English and those supporting indigenous languages. At issue here are not only matters concerning modernization and cultural regeneration but also the struggle for leadership between the English-knowing Westernized "established elite" and the regional "rising elite" (cf. Chapter 3). Language has become a very distinct weapon in the power struggle: during the past thirty years numerous religious, cultural, and caste battles have been fought in the linguistic arena. Clearly, however, the competing regional and pan-Indian pressure groups—and the claims they advance—totally disregard elementary sociolinguistic realities in individual and social life (cf. Chapter 1).

In the present situation one notices a great gap between the language postures of the policymakers and the language images of large numbers of the neoliterate. In spite of the policymakers' revolutionary pronouncements regarding a change in language functions to accord with national aspirations, the powerful elite in India does not seem to be very enthusiastic about the switchover from English to indigenous languages.

An individual's skill in the use of English continues to be prerequisite to social advancement. Mastery of English is associated with modernization, which puts a high premium on achievement orientation, merit consideration, specialization, mobility, and interdependence within the system. No substantial efforts seem to be put forth to induce the Hindi and other major-language-speaking elites to spearhead the modernization process through these languages. Even today in a bilingual situation, incomplete knowledge of English detracts from one's prestige, whereas one does not lose any prestige by showing incomplete acculturation with Hindi or any other Indian-language group. Change in language functions is easily transmitted through the behavioral patterns of the social elite. In this respect, leadership has to act as a model of what is expected from the masses in the period of language transition.

With the elitist approach to language development, efforts to cultivate Hindi and other Indian languages during the past three decades have been mixed up with the zealous promotion of creative literature in the major Indian languages, languages which were denied them during a long spell of Muslim and British rule. Among them, Hindi, the national link language, has been allocated preferential treatment by various governmental agencies. This situation has touched off serious psychological problems. Custodians of several regional languages with a respectable history were not prepared to forfeit their literary status. Due to cultural and literary pride, many language groups, particularly Tamil- and Bengali-speaking enthusiasts, resented the preferential treatment given to Hindi by virtue of its numerical superiority; and these groups claimed privileges for their languages on the basis of literary merit. Many speakers of other languages having a written tradition (for example, Sindhi, Konkani, Rajasthani, Maithili), and various tribal language speakers (Santali and others) have, on the basis of their numerical strength, also shown concern about the privileges accorded to major languages and have been asserting equality by advancing the claims of their mother tongues.

The principle of reorganizing states on a linguistic basis was accepted in 1956 under the assumption that linguistic homogeneity would provide a common bond among citizens and a convenient measure for better administration. But this approach resulted in the aggravation of language conflicts during the 1960s and gave birth to several issues related to language identity, such as state-boundary disputes and language chauvinism, sometimes leading to street skirmishes. The tendency to exploit the languages accorded with official recognition for various economic and political purposes, such as discrimination against linguistic minorities in job opportunities, electioneering, and preferential treatment in literary development, creates an atmosphere of mistrust resulting in clashes of narrow vested interests among the different language groups. Such clashes involve the baser instincts, producing histrionics and demagoguery. Feelings by nature have scant respect for reason.

Many Asian leaders and planning experts in the postcolonial period have been advocating "sharply defined" and "instant" solutions concerning languages and scripts. Such insistence seems to be largely responsible for promoting the mobilization of different language pressure groups in the Indo-Pakistan subcontinent.[2] Language-development programs of this sort have very little relation to the country's diversified speech patterns and values. This pluralism, which could aid in accelerating social change, has led newly emerged nations into serious difficulties in social planning.

Language and Education

For a nation such as India, with a multilingual population and a federal polity, education is made the responsibility of the states. The Constitution of India provides full freedom for the states to choose a language or languages in a region as "official" language(s) (Article 345). It also allows linguistic minority groups to receive education in their mother tongues and to set up institutions of their choice for this purpose (Article 30). Hence, one finds wide variations in different states as far as the medium, content, duration, and nomenclature of educational stages are concerned. There is inevitable flexibility in the weight assigned to different languages in the total educational programs, in the framing of language curricula, in selecting textbooks, and so on. A national policy of education emerges out of a consensus arrived at among the states constituting the federal polity. The role of the Union government is, therefore, largely confined to promoting national policies through seeking mutual accommodation among individual states, coordinating institutions of higher education and research and of vocational and technical training, dealing with language elites, and offering the incentives of the resources at its command for specific programs.

At present in the field of education all states have the capacity to teach the students of major Indian languages through their mother tongue or through their language of formal communication (e.g., Maithili and Rajasthani students are educated through Hindi, and Kashmiri students through Urdu) up to the school-leaving stage. Many universities now provide instruction in the medium of regional languages at the undergraduate and graduate levels in the arts and commerce faculties, but English continues to be the principal medium for higher education, particularly in law, science, and technology.

About eighty languages are being used as media of instruction at different stages of education (see Appendix). Many of them are used only as preparatory media at the primary education stage (for classes I and II, often extended to class IV; a few are extended to class VII as well), before a student switches over to any major language as the medium at the secondary education stage. Some tribal languages, spoken by smaller populations, are also promoted as elementary media by private institutions (missionary schools, monasteries, etc.). There are fourteen principal media languages, comprising eleven regional languages (including the pan-Indian Hindi, excluding Kashmiri); two languages without any region, Urdu and Sindhi; and one foreign language, English. Some prominent Indian languages—Hindi, Bengali, Telugu, Marathi, and Urdu—are now being extended as alternate media to English to undergraduate and graduate levels in the universities of particular regions, depending upon their developmental stages. Foreign languages such as Persian, Portuguese, and French are also retained as media in a few urban schools (Chaturvedi, 1976).

Many distinct scripts are in vogue for writing these languages. Sanskrit, Hindi, Marathi, and Nepali are written in Devanagari script; Urdu, Kashmiri, and Sindhi in Perso-Arabic script. Other major Indo-Aryan and Dravidian languages (and Tibetan) have distinct scripts derived from the early Nagari system. Some vernaculars and tribal languages have adopted Devanagari, Roman, or regional scripts. Khampti in Arunachal Pradesh uses a variation of Thai script. With the emphasis on literary programs conducted through the mother tongue, many languages of small speech groups are now being written in Devanagari or Roman script, depending upon sectarian or regional pressures.

The Education Commission (1966) envisaged setting up some institutions, at both school and university levels, with pan-Indian languages—Hindi and English—and some of the world languages as media of instruction. What this amounts to is that at every stage there will be institutions available with specialization in a particular medium, and students can select a school or college with a medium of their choice. The Union government has introduced a Central Schools system in major towns throughout the country for the children of those employed in all-India services and for those belonging to mobile occupations in business and industry, where education is imparted through Hindi, English, or through both languages.

For a nation such as India, where no single language caters to all the needs of an ordinary literate citizen, pan-Indian languages like Hindi—and, for some time to come, English—will occupy a significant functional position in national life. Considering these factors, the Union government endorses the three-language formula, which requires a student, on completing his or her secondary education, to acquire an adequate grasp of three languages, the mother tongue and two nonnative languages: Hindi and English (discussed at length in Chapter 7).

In various regions in South Asia, different socialization processes identify the characteristics of a speech stratum—local speech, subregional varieties, supraregional varieties, lingua franca, "highbrow" dictions—associating them with a variety of interactions on the cline:

close in-group → wider in-group → intergroup → mobility→ mass communication → urban contact → formal (model for prestige).

In heterogeneous plural environments, a child acquires language from everyday life situations where speech behavior is guided by various implicit pressures based on close-group, regional, supraregional, and outgroup identities. A child learns his language not from grammar books but from the behavior of adults and peers through his innate capacities. This is evident from a large gap observed between the speech patterns of typical illiterate communities and the language values promoted through school education in two regions in India, given in Table 8 (Khubchandani, 1974b).

In this study it is significant to note the literate cultures regarding hybrid varieties (patois, pidgins, creoles, etc.) as a sign of inferior socialization, and discouraging them in formal situations (such as schools). In this "filter-down" approach of the educational elite, grass-roots "folk" multilingualism is devalued, and language teaching gets focused on "remedial" programs so that the "backward" pupils speaking hybrid varieties become eligible for entry into the "advanced" world through the mastery of standard language(s).

Literacy programs in several plurilingual situations are organized through a contact language. For example, literacy in the Kashmir valley is imparted through Urdu, in Arunachal Pradesh through Hindi, and among tribal communities through the respective regional language—Telugu, Oriya, Bengali, Marathi, Hindi, and so forth. In such diversified speech areas, education programs need to be geared to facilitate the scope of communication with the prevailing socialization values in a community extending from one's native speech to "associate" native speech, a second language, and when necessary to a totally unfamiliar (foreign) language.

During the first years after the departure of the British from India, different expert bodies on education, such as the Central Advisory Board of Education (1948), the University Education Commission (1949) and the Official Language Commission (1956), gave greater weight to the broad interpretation of mother tongue, that is, regarding all minority languages

Table 8. Speech Behavior and Language Education

Typical Verbal Repertoire		Language Values Promoted in Schools	
Speech Varieties	Communication Situations	Languages Taught	Values

Rural Marathi Community Around Nagpur

Speech Varieties	Communication Situations	Languages Taught	Values
Nagpuri Marathi	close in-group	—	denied prestige, and used minimally as substandard varieties
Supradialectal Marathi	wider in-group	—	
Standard Marathi	in-group mass communication	Marathi	promoted through "autonomy" values in all situations
Neighboring varieties of Marathi	optional familiarity through mobility	—	regarded as nonprestigious and their use not promoted through mobility
Nagpuri Hindustani	inter-group	—	its use signified a nonprestigious upbringing
Standard Hindi/Urdu	inter-group mass communication	Hindi	
Regional English usage (a few phrases)	optional modernistic acquaintance	English	learned as an "exercise" for eventual use after the school career (not related to immediate use)
Sanskrit or Arabic (a few phrases)	optional ritualistic acquaintance	Sanskrit, Arabic/ Persian	learned as optional classical languages for religious and literary scholarship

Rural Santali Community in Bihar

Language/Variety	Function	Status/Notes
Local Santali	close in-group	—
Supradialectal Santali	wider in-group	—
		Santali (standard: set by language elite)
		denied prestige, and used minimally as substandard varieties
		medium for primary education
Other tribal languages (Munda, Ho, etc.)	optional familiarity through mobility	—
Sadri (Sadan)— a hybrid Bihari language	tribal inter-group	—
		regarded as nonprestigious, and their use not promoted
		its use signified a nonprestigious upbringing
Bihari languages (Maithili, Magahi, etc.), regional Bengali or Oriya	nontribal inter-group	—
Regional Hindustani	urban contact	—
		regarded as non-prestigious, and their use not promoted
		its use signified a nonprestigious upbringing
Standard Hindi/Urdu; standard Bengali or Oriya	mass communication	Hindi
		medium for further education
Regional English usage (a few phrases)	optional modernistic acquaintance	English
		learned as an "exercise" for eventual use after the school career (not related to immediate use)
—	—	Sanskrit
		learned as an optional classical language for religious and literary scholarship

not having any written tradition as "dialects" of the dominant language in the region. Many protagonists of major languages pointed out the illogic of literacy in languages that have no literature. The University Education Commission (1949) and the Official Language Commission (1956) believed that "the languages of the large advanced groups with a current literature, practice and tradition" were the only fit media of instruction (OLC: 27).

In a critical appraisal of the role of mother tongue in education, a study conducted at the National Council of Education Research and Training (NCERT) highlights wide disparities in sociocultural traditions of states and notes that consequently languages differ in their stages of development. The study points out that education through the minority languages, which hold a subordinate position in society and are relatively less cultivated, is likely to produce uneven levels of achievement. Such a situation is bound to create unequal opportunities for higher education and employment for minority communities (Goel and Saini, 1972).

However, during the past three decades the linguistic minorities have shown greater vigilance in safeguarding their rights for education in the mother tongue and have virtually succeeded in persuading the authorities to accept the narrow interpretation of mother tongue (cf. Chapter 3). Most of the state governments now show a sense of tolerance for the heterogeneity of education media in their multilingual areas. The safeguards of education in the mother tongue at the primary school stage for linguistic minorities were spelled out in the Three-Language Formula in 1956. Some concessions were even made for the continuance of secondary education through tribal language media wherever possible. But the pace of implementation has remained slow. No doubt the initial reluctance to accept the narrow definition of mother tongue has now been overcome, but several objections are still raised against its full implementation, and many states are simply waiting for minority languages to become extinct.

Theoretically, the arguments for the supremacy of the mother tongue based on "elegant" urban standards have very little substance as far as facility of expression is concerned. The sudden imposition of a standard variety through language-planning "recipes" creates serious communication gaps (Pandit, 1972). The elite-acceptable "instant standard" promoted through educational programs has remained unintelligible to the hinterland communities for a long period, as seen in Table 8, and its tyranny hampers mass literacy programs.

Many language experts have now started questioning the value of the supremacy of the mother tongue as language medium stretching over the entire education career. Under various political pressures, it is now being conceded that the mother tongue cannot be the only language of education. The scope of education in the mother tongue and of the imposition

Language-Promotion Activities 75

of urban elite standards in "school" language, therefore, needs to be critically assessed in the light of recent insights gained from studies of plural societies (discussed in detail in Chapter 6).

The demands of active bilingualism in a plural society expose an individual to doing language activity by accomplishing diverse communicative tasks through a variety of speech styles, registers, dialects, and even languages. A policy requiring every literate person to master two, three, or four distinct normative systems—nurtured in historically or geographically unrelated "traditions"—is likely to result in stifling the flexible and creative role of contact languages in a community. With such an approach, these contact languages may survive merely as "world," "national," or "classical" library languages for purposes of reference.

Language Elaboration

In the campaign for "autonomy" in the Indian context, language elites try to push forward elaborate instruction and orientation programs in order to introduce new values and bring forth what they consider to be desirable changes in the speech habits of the masses. These include:

- prescribing "urban-based elite" standards for literacy drives even in remote rural areas;
- promoting "highbrow" diction for regional languages (sprinkled with Sanskrit, Perso-Arabic, Old [Tamil], or Medieval [Telugu] flavors for formal and public meetings);
- prescribing compulsory teaching of two, three, and even four languages in the schools, and other mandatory language requirements for various careers.

The "elitist" education system does not seem to take account of the complexity of speech variation across dialects in flux (and in plurilingual societies, often across languages) at the folk level. Under such a system the development of language is erroneously linked with the clear-cut demarcation of language use. Thus, a continuum of language hierarchy becomes compartmentalized, and the diglossic complementation of different languages signifying different communicative tasks does not receive enthusiastic support from language experts.

Developing the resources of a language to fulfill its role in new situations, such as administration, law, journalism, broadcasting, higher education, and research, cannot be done in isolation. It is due mainly to the active bilingualism of Indian languages and the use of English among the educated classes during the past few decades that various styles and expressions have been added to the stock of Indian languages to qualify them for their new roles in society. Also, important reference works such as grammars, dictionaries, encyclopedias, translations, and other teaching aids have been published in these languages. It is evident that such active bilingualism is playing a very significant role in the process of standardization of the major Indian languages. Therefore, it becomes necessary to shake off the notion that the elimination of English from the Indian scene would create a vacuum, stimulating the growth of Indian languages.

From the viewpoint of "language cultivation," educational subjects can be classified in three broad categories, requiring a different type of preparation for a change in the medium, particularly at the higher education level:

1. Demonstration-oriented subjects largely dealing with concrete visual or with other-than-language symbols: subjects of "hard core" sciences and technology, such as medicine, engineering, physics, zoology, also subjects dependent on nonlinguistic symbols, such as mathematics and astronomy.

    In these subjects language expression tends to be somewhat simplified, since it is usually supplemented by visual demonstration. These subjects generally exploit only the rudiments of language structure. Information in these subjects tends to be autonomous, well formulated, and unambiguous.

    Some of the prominent Indian languages with a written tradition, drawing upon the heritage of classical Sanskrit, have acquired an adequate range of expression for such subjects as mathematics, astronomy, the natural sciences (agriculture, horticulture, forestry), chemistry, *āyurved* (Indian medicine), archery, and cottage and small-scale industries. Of course, for the expression of high-technology-oriented subjects Indian languages do not possess a well-sustained tradition, and most of the conceptualization concerning these subjects is continuously borrowed from the Western experience, mainly through English.

2. Abstract subjects dealing with human phenomena; most of the arts, religion (theology), and social sciences, such as history, philosophy, politics, economics, sociology, and psychology. Creative literature and aesthetics also fall into this category; these are further supplemented with expressions of emotions and personal feelings.

    In these subjects, language needs mature expression to be able to portray the complexities of human nature, but information tends to be less rigorously formulated, the likelihood of ambiguity is greater, and interpretations are relatively less precise than in "hard core" scientific subjects.

Most of the Indian languages with literary standing possess a long tradition in many of the arts subjects through classical literatures. With the development of prose styles in various major languages, these languages are gradually catching up in the process of so-called modernization through borrowings and loan translations from classical literatures.

3. Subjects in which the object of interpretation is "language" itself, such as law, logic, semiotics, and linguistics. These subjects develop a kind of metalanguage by exploiting subtleties of the language structure for sophisticated and well-formulated communication. Some major Indian languages, through sustained contacts with the classical heritage of Sanskrit, Arabic, and Persian, have been equipping themselves with the nuances necessary for such meta-inquiries. But so far these languages have been scantily utilized for modern scholarship.

Almost all of India's official efforts in the sphere of language planning proceed on a very simplistic basis, treating language as if it were a kind of industry or technology. This observation applies equally to its literacy drives, teaching second and third languages, and its gigantic programs for "language codification" and "language elaboration," and is typified in the setting of time limits for the switchover from one language to another, the coinage of terminologies while sitting in ivory towers, the translation of textbooks and reference books, and so on. These targets are set in a manner utterly unmindful of the natural sensitivities of plural speech communities, as discussed at length in Chapter 8. One cannot ignore the ecological imperatives of stratificational and situational multiplicity, so much more pervasive in the developing nations' pluralistic communication patterns than the new values being injected through the official programs. So far, very little experimentation has been encouraged to test the validity of these assumptions for a complex plural society such as India.

The Role of English

During the past two centuries, English has been internalized by a powerful segment of the people on the subcontinent as a linguistic projection of regional environments, as a language of cerebration revealed through frequent code-switching, and as a literary vehicle for creative expression.

Owing to the rigorous academic base and to selective education, English, in spite of such intense use by nonnative speakers, has not been so greatly pidginized in the Indian context, but it has definitely acquired a certain regional flavor which distinguishes South Asian English from native standard varieties (British English, American English, etc.). The most prominent characteristic of South Asian English is the cheerful acceptance of regional deviations in pronunciation (e.g., lack of phonemic stress, readjustment in the English consonant system with the features of retroflexion and aspiration) (Pandit, 1964; Khubchandani, 1966). Many scholars who would be very particular about the mastery of grammar and style of British English show very little concern for a wide variety of regional pronunciation.[3]

The social image in India is still in favor of English. The premium on grammatically good English is still very high. The masses do not show as much disenchantment with English, or hostility toward it, as is evident among a segment of the leadership. English-medium schools are still very much sought after by the social elite or by those who want entry into the social elite through their children.

English educationists have been rather slow in adjusting to the needs of the society, which is experiencing many changes in the phase of decolonization. This factor has, to a great extent, led many educators to worry about a general fall of standards of English in education and inadequate control of the language by students. The most significant changes which need to be recognized in formulating a new approach to the teaching of English are:

1. With the rapid spread of literacy among the masses, the scope of bilingual contact between Indian languages and English has been widening at a fast pace. The demand for learning English has been steadily growing among the masses under urban and modernized conditions. Today there is a larger population which knows English; and there are more English teachers, more English students, and more Indo-English writers than when the British left. This situation is bound to change the role of the white-collar English elite as the go-between of colonial times.
2. So far as learning conditions are concerned, the situation has changed radically to the detriment of English. During colonial rule, English was learned by a select group of people under very favorable, even luxurious, sociopsychological conditions, namely:
    a. The learning of English was greatly facilitated by strong motivation to acquire Westernized culture. In terms of language proficiency, there was more emphasis on full language in a "package," with the maximum possible grasp of style, close to that of a native speaker. Since then the emphasis has been shifting toward "fragmented" utilitarian usage.
    b. Since English was the principal medium of instruction, mastery of the language was promoted by natural contextualization of all

Language-Promotion Activities

subjects taught in school. Students acquired a greater degree of fluency and lucidity of expression in English through this medium than from what they were taught in their English lessons (Widdowson, 1968:166–167).

c. English as a subject enjoyed greater priority in the school curriculum. It was allotted about one-third of the total teaching time: twelve to eighteen hours a week for a minimum of eight years in school. Admission to specialized courses required a high degree of proficiency in English. Under these conditions, students devoted much attention to the mastery of English.

d. English teachers enjoyed a privileged position in the education system, which attracted the best talent to this profession. Supported by the students' strong motivation and by the contextualization of English in other subjects, the English teacher's role was very similar to that of a native-language teacher, monitoring the correctness and stylistic usage of the language and imparting knowledge about English literature and culture. "The Professors of English are not reporters about a foreign language, but rather transmitters of English life and letters; they belong to the early years of British education in India when they were the carriers of liberal education and the sole professors of literature *par excellence*" (Pandit, 1969a:115).

In learning English these days such luxuries can no longer be counted upon, though they still exist in certain privileged cases. In general, learners and teachers now have to operate under much less favorable conditions. They even have to cope with hostile conditions in certain states under the spell of Indian-language chauvinism.

Under these changed circumstances, English in South Asia is becoming more detached from native English speakers on the one hand, and on the other, with the growth of literacy, urbanity, and technological advancement, its scope and intensity of communication for intragroup contact is increasing. Pan-South Asian English across the boundaries of regional language sensitivities has already taken deep roots on the subcontinent. The vitality of English in the subcontinent largely depends upon the facility with which bilinguals, who have practically no living contact with native English speakers, can acquire enough proficiency in it for mutual intelligibility. For the most part, their oral as well as written reinforcement is in regional English through formal education, the press, radio, television, and so on (for a glimpse of the English press in India, see Chapter 1).

No doubt the upper English elite, who remain in constant touch with the native English speakers, are less sensitive to local conditions. Conscious of the prestige of the international standards of English, they often show a dislike for regional flavor in English. Under these conditions, attempts to retain British or American English models for South Asian bilinguals can affect the position of English in either of two ways:

1. They may reduce English to a function similar to that of a "classical" language, separated by a distance of thousands of miles, if not of years. As a result, English is likely to lose the flexibility and creativity of an effective contact language in the region and to survive merely as a "world" library language for referential purposes at the higher education level, and for a limited international elite.
2. With the persistent intensity of communication among regional bilinguals and in the absence of any effective regional model, English may become pidginized in an unrestricted manner and lose its usefulness as an international communication system.

It is necessary, therefore, to recognize the distinctiveness of South Asian contact English and to promote gradual stabilization of a panregional standard based on influential channels of communication, such as regional literature, the press, and broadcasting, in order to balance the growing "freelance" regional influences on it and to ensure its continued usefulness as an instrument of international communication (Lutze, 1968).

The English elite, instead of trying to maintain a privileged status quo at the cost of relative underdevelopment of Indian languages, can play a positive role by participating actively in developing Indian languages and making them more viable in different spheres of life (Pandit, 1969a). They will have to remove the barriers of segregation by intensifying communication with the masses in the fields of education, administration, and other spheres of public life, which is bound to escalate the process of acquiring full expression for Indian languages.

Original discourses and learned expositions in Indian languages by the intelligentsia who know foreign languages (primarily those who know English, in the Indian context), based on their mature experience, can certainly equip these languages for new roles much more soundly and cheaply than the present trend of artificially coining technical terms and translating concepts from Sanskrit, Perso-Arabic, or Old Tamil classical stocks, and then producing "highbrow" translations based on such armchair coinage. One of the serious handicaps in developing scientific prose in Indian languages is not so much the inadequate cultivation of these languages, as is generally presumed, but the reluctance of the English intelligentsia to take the lead in writing nonnarrative prose in these languages, as discussed in Chapters 2 and 8.

The future of English as an effective contact language in the region will largely depend upon the extent to which it can play a positive role as an efficient tool for intragroup and intergroup contact in a multilingual nation.

Language-planning Agencies

Today in South Asia a host of language-development agencies, isolated language institutes, and individual language advisory boards, insulated from each other by sharply defined jurisdictions and committed to diverse traditions, seem to be pulling in different, at times contradictory, directions in the name of modernization. By and large, language-planning agencies do not seem to be sensitive to the fact that the speech behavior of a heterogeneous community is guided not so much by the dicta of insulated traditions as by the demands of ecosystems. An individual or a speech community responds to the verbal needs of heterogeneous situations spontaneously by means of several "echo" processes, such as convergence, assimilation, maintenance, creativity—known in linguistic parlance as analogy, interference, pidginization, code-switching, and so on. Skillful mastery over several sharply "insulated" standard languages is a remarkable feat which only a few motivated professionals can be expected to achieve.

The moves for language autonomy in education programs have worked rather as disincentives to the active bilingualism prevailing in many regions in South Asia. Many official agencies, with a view to containing demands of language privileges, lay emphasis on mechanical duplication of information through the "ornamental" devices of parallel or simultaneous translation in public communication, based on the models of a few European multilingual countries (e.g., Switzerland, Belgium) and on such international settings as the United Nations and the international airlines. These efforts defeat the professed goals of active bilingualism as a communication style at the national level.

In the language-development programs of many Asian and African countries, modernizing imperatives of education, mass communication, industry, sciences, and arts influence, in a significant manner, the position of languages and the patterns of speech behavior through the processes of creolization, standardization, drives for language shift and language maintenance, diglossia, multilingualism, and so on.

Many of these programs seek to advance sweeping changes in the speech behavior of the Indian masses without recognizing its innate characteristics, highlighted in the discussion on language standardization (cf. Chapter 2). For example:

1. Literacy programs, through strict controls, emphasize monistic commitment to a single writing system, a single standard grammar, and a single style for each domain of use in the name of nonambiguity and efficiency in communication.[4]
2. Language-development programs, by prescribing the elite-acceptable diction of speech, make the effortless gift of social verbalization a strenuous, time-consuming task. (The drawbacks of imposing "instant" standards on a speech community have been discussed earlier in this chapter.)
3. The easygoing grass-roots multilingualism of the illiterate masses is being replaced by the elegant bilingualism (or trilingualism) with standardization pressures from different directions: for example, neo-Sanskritic Hindi, Perso-Arabicized Urdu, BBC or AIR (All-India Radio) English, medieval literary Telugu, and classicalized modern Tamil. Even though considerable time is spent on second and third languages in school (in some places these programs are allotted a disproportionate share in the total teaching priorities in order to suit the climate of language privileges), these languages often find little or no application in meaningful communicative tasks during the entire school career.
4. In predominantly illiterate societies the written word acquires an aura of authority, permanence, and judiciousness in communication —sort of a magic wand for the privileged elite. An oral transaction tends to be debased as a less authentic version of a written communication and may easily be dismissed or contradicted.

The bureaucratic machinery in these societies, which wallows in a colossal "paper jungle," symbolizes this malady. It becomes very circumscribed by the written word, which allegedly has to be meticulously consistent with precedents—a given tradition, a set of rules and norms, procedures, routing through proper channels, and so on. Behind this facade, those in power can safely make cynical interpretations, disregarding immediate situational and human needs. Such excessive allegiance to the written word gives pride of place to "what should *appear* to be right" at the cost of "what *should* be right." The consequences of this polarization between oral and written transactions in the expanding bureaucracies of modernizing societies are clear for all to see.

Language-planning agencies in many countries, under the influences of the purists' tradition in philology and pedagogy, regard concepts like language hybridization, grass-roots "folk" multilingualism, and other such processes arising from contact situations as serious problems of human adjustment. Linguistic heterogeneity is thus inadvertently projected as a serious constraint in developing strong national identity. Many of the language-planning programs in these societies—such as targets of language learning, language autonomy, language standardization, language requirements of formal communication (technical terminology, etc.)—are regarded as necessary characteristics of "universal" modernization and as such have roots in the external "developed" world.

Concern for elitist standardization and monistic commitments to "modernize" a language, in the name of bringing order from "chaotic" diversity, generally dominate the interests of language-planning investigators. The functional relevance of these changes for the "oral-tilted" mass communication needs (radio, television, and other sound-transmitting and sound-reproducing devices) of the twentieth century has not been seriously attended to. Garvin (1973) has hinted at this handicap of looking at language-planning problems from a "European" perspective and the possibility of the developing nations rejecting this approach and "passing directly into a 'MacLuhanesque' period where oral mass communication in the local traditional style would be made possible by the electronic media" (p. 32).

The requirements of "elegance" in education, apart from slowing down the pace of the switchover from developed media to emerging media, also inhibit the introduction of literacy in an economical manner.[5] The common man has to be educated to use the language in a way that is quite unrelated to the academic's facility in communication.

During the past three decades, the Union and state governments have established language units within several ministries to cater to the needs of transition from English to Hindi and/or regional languages for administration. The Central Directorate of Hindi at the Union Ministry of Education commissions the work of preparing glossaries of technical terms and of translating administrative reports in Hindi, and also conducts examinations for administrative personnel and provides incentives for the development of Hindi through official and voluntary organizations. The Hindi adviser to the Ministry of Home Affairs oversees and coordinates the programs of implementing language policies of the Union government. The Hindi unit of the Law Ministry has undertaken the task of translating significant legal documents into Hindi. The Sahitya Akademi and the National Book Trust, through various publication endeavors, contribute to the overall development of major Indian languages. Several state governments have also established language-promotion boards to advise them in matters of language policy in the respective states and also commission the work of language elaboration and cultivation.

From time to time, the Parliament and state legislative assemblies appoint several commissions of experts and public leaders to advise the

Union and state governments in formulating and implementing language policies for education, administration, and overall development of the country; among these are the Official Language Commission (1956) and the Education Commission (1966). With a view to intensifying the activities promoting language transition in state administration, the Maharashtra Government observed 1979 as the "Official Language Year."

Through annual reports the commissioner of linguistic minorities advises the Union and state governments on issues concerning linguistic minorities scattered throughout the country, constituting roughly 24 percent of the total population. Recently a high-powered Minorities Commission has been constituted by the Parliament to look into the problems of religious and linguistic minorities. The Office of the Registrar General of India, apart from conducting the regular decennial census, compiles language material for describing specific areas and for revising the Grierson *Linguistic Survey of India* conducted from 1903 to 1928. The Anthropological Survey of India and the Tribal Research Institutes in several states undertake studies of different tribal languages, devising orthographies, preparing dictionaries and teaching materials, and so on.

Apart from various efforts made by the Union and state governments, several voluntary organizations for promoting the cause of English, Sanskrit, Hindi, Urdu, Sindhi, and major regional languages have been active in influencing the directions of development of the respective languages, and also in shaping the language policy of the country (for details, see Nayar, 1969; Das Gupta, 1970; and for a comprehensive bibliography on the subject, see Khubchandani, 1973f).

In the sphere of training and research, the state institutes of education, the National Council for Educational Research and Training, the Central Institute of English and Foreign Languages at Hyderabad, the Central Hindi Institute at Agra, and the Central Institute of Indian Languages at Mysore are engaged in research to suggest methods of simplifying language-teaching processes at various levels by introducing modern techniques. These institutes also help the state governments prepare language curricula by producing instructional materials for teaching languages at different levels. Many states have established textbook research bureaus to publish books in different languages according to the prescribed curricula.

At the postgraduate level, two national centers of advanced study in linguistics (Deccan College Postgraduate Research Institute and Annamalai University) and about a dozen linguistic departments in different universities have been engaged in theoretical and applied research concerning language-teaching methods and other aspects of language development. Various regional and occupational dialect surveys have been undertaken. In this regard, the programs of compiling dictionaries (Sanskrit, Marathi, and Sindhi at Deccan College, Telugu at Osmania University, and Tamil at Annamalai University) and of conducting dialect surveys of different regions (Malayalam dialects at Kerala University, Telugu dialects at Osmania University, Marathi and Kannada dialects at Deccan College, and Panjabi dialects at Panjabi University) are noteworthy. The Indian Council for Social Science Research also supports research bearing on language problems. Moreover, professional bodies such as the Linguistic Society of India and the International School of Dravidian Linguistics have rendered significant service in highlighting the concerns of language development.

It is only in recent years that linguistics and social sciences have showed concern with the tasks of introducing deliberate change in the functions and the content of language to serve the contemporary needs of plural societies. In 1967, against a backdrop of intense language controversy in the country, the Deccan College Postgraduate Research Institute at Poona organized a seminar on Linguistics and Language Planning in India (Khubchandani, 1968), and the Indian Institute of Advanced Study at Simla conducted a seminar on "Language and Society" (Poddar, 1969). During 1970-1972, the Center for the Study of Developing Societies at Delhi collaborated with the Stanford Project of International Language Planning Processes to conduct a sample survey of the impact of language developmental activities in the country (Ford Foundation, 1973). The Indian Institute of Advanced Study at Simla conducted another interdisciplinary workshop in 1973 to identify the critical areas of research in sociolinguistics in the country. During the past decade, the three language institutes, sponsored by the Union Government at Hyderabad, Agra, and Mysore, have also been involved in conducting a series of workshops and seminars to discuss several aspects of language planning in India.

Language is a great asset of human society. With proper planning, clear perspective, and imaginative action, a developing nation like India, having a rich variety of languages, can exploit the situation toward developing insight into human behavior, utilizing the multilingual communication network for technological advancement and other benefits rather than being sentimental regarding one or another language and thus directing peoples' energies toward discord and rivalry.

NOTES

1. Recent studies on language politics in India (Das Gupta, 1970) reject the view prevailing among many political observers (including Gunnar Myrdal and Selig Harrison) as to the high incidence of group conflict generated by segmental

social divisions in some transitional political systems such as India, which concludes with a logic of despair as to the futility of democratic operations in the development of such a nation.

2. In this connection, an intense controversy raging among the Sindhi-speaking elite for over a century concerning the recognition of Perso-Arabic *or* Devanagari script for the Sindhi language can be cited as a good example of the consequences of such monistic assertions (Khubchandani, 1969a).

3. Due to the socially stratified speech structure (as represented by caste dialects among many speech groups) and regional speech distinctions, even in formal communication, one notices a greater degree of "permissiveness" for a wider variety of pronunciation among Indian speakers when speaking their native language. (This point is further elaborated in discussion of the Hindi-Urdu amalgam, Chapter 5.)

4. Before the invention of the printing press, scholarship in India was restricted to the privileged few who needed to be acquainted with a variety of writing systems in one language, distinguished according to region and domain of use.

5. The state of affairs can be visualized from a report of the Directorate of Education in Nagaland (1971) stating that textbooks (even for primary education) are being "originally written in English and then translated in local languages," since "authors in the local languages are not available" (Sharma, 1971).

Part Two

CHALLENGES OF CHANGE

CHAPTER 3

Plural Speech Communities

IN MULTILINGUAL AND MULTIDIALECTAL SOCIETIES we often come across speech groups which have virtual native control over more than one language or dialect. One notices an inevitable measure of fluidity in certain regions in India, Pakistan, and Bangla Desh and also among smaller groups throughout the subcontinent. In such situations one's total repertoire is influenced by more than one normative system, and language labels are not rigidly identified with fixed "stereotypes." Native adults of such plurilingual communities are hardly conscious of operating across language boundaries. Dialect or language boundaries in these societies remain fluid, and the masses at large do not show overt consciousness of the speech characteristics which bind them in one language or another (cf. Chapter 1).

In this regard, decennial language returns of the Indian census could be taken as a useful indicator of some of the attitudes to language underlying the speakers' assertions, and reveal evasion as well as instability, which are not always apparent on the surface. Records of the 1961 and 1971 Indian census show two opposing streams suggesting that:

1. There is anxiety to attain prestige by identifying oneself with a major language and not necessarily with one's native speech. An amazing example of this characteristic is the claim of 154 million speakers in the 1971 census (123 million speakers in the 1961 census) that "Hindi" (proper[1]) is their mother tongue, though many of them speak markedly different varieties of altogether different languages for primary communication.
2. There is inverted pride in "exclusiveness," that is, the tendency to assert one's own social identity as being distinct from that of others. Many tribal groups show this tendency because of their feelings of superiority to, or hostility against, neighboring groups.

Mitra (1964), commenting on this phenomenon, states poignantly: "[These statements] leave no doubt in one's mind that the big fish make bids to gobble up the small fish, that for some time some small fish feel content to stay inside the belly of a big fish, but at other moments they kick back and get out of the bellies again; their strength diminished or increased *for no apparent reason whatever*" (p. 6) [emphasis added]. A deeper look into the situation, however, reveals certain sociolinguistic realities which affect the strength of various mother tongues.

Identity Pressures

The Indian census enumeration shows signs of the excitement experienced in multilingual societies over the language issue. In many instances, displacement or disappearance of a mother tongue from a region is merely a signal of a change in the group loyalty rather than of the migration of the speech group to another region or its members' abandonment of their original native speech in favor of another.[2] Very often, oscillations in census declarations of a mother tongue in the Indian context reveal shifts in social identification under changed circumstances.

Changes in language labels do not necessarily signify changes in speech habits. This displacement of language labels is interpreted by demographers as "linguistic displacement" (Bose, 1969), a term which gives the impression that the use of one language is being abandoned in favor of another. The term "Hindustani/Hindostani," quite prevalent in pre-independence India, represented colloquial Urdu or Hindi. In most of the states, the 1951 and 1961 declarations reveal a rapid rate of decline in the number of speakers claiming Hindustani as their mother tongue.

A comparison of the figures of Hindustani, Urdu, and Hindi from the 1931, 1951, and 1961 censuses, given in Table 9, reveals the oscillatory trends. (No language census was conducted in 1941 due to World War II.)

The figures shown in Table 9 reveal the virtual extinction of Hindustani, mostly in favor of Urdu. In the 1961 returns, the total population of Hindustani speakers in India was reduced to a bare 122,000—a decline of virtually 99 percent in a decade. Presumably, the partition of the country in 1947 was taken by the masses as a decision against the concept of "composite" Hindustani as a bridge between Sanskritic Hindi and Persianized Urdu. In this respect, the census figures indirectly reveal the ideal standard of one's mother tongue cherished by a group or an individual, but do indicate one's choices of grammatical and lexical patterns and pronunciation habits. Shifts in declarations of mother tongue from one language to another in successive censuses, depending on the social and political climate, seem to be a frequent feature among such speech groups in India.

Table 9. Speakers Claiming Hindustani, Urdu, and Hindi as Mother Tongue, 1931-1961

State	Mother Tongue	1931 (thousands)	1951 (thousands)	Variation 1931-51 (%)	1961 (thousands)	Variation, 1951-61 (%)
Uttar Pradesh	Hindustani	46,456	6743	−86.4	101	−98.5
	Urdu	grouped with Hindustani	4300	—	7892	+83.5
	Hindi		50,454	—	62,443	+23.8
Madhya Pradesh	Hindustani	4990	59	−98.8	1.1	−98.2
	Urdu	752	368	−51.0	740	+100.1
	Hindi	2869	19,876	+592.9	21,686	+9.1
Andhra Pradesh	Hindustani	754	529	−29.8	0.03	−99.99
	Urdu	742	1600	+115.7	2554	+59.6
	Hindi	31	107	+246.7	136	+27.3
Tamil Nadu	Hindustani	393	69	−82.4	0.6	−99.1
	Urdu	—	427	—	616	+44.2
	Hindi	11	65	+505.8	39	−40.1
Karnataka	Hindustani	404	740	+83.2	12	−98.3
	Urdu	—	878	—	2035	+131.9
	Hindi	32	72	+125.0	82	+13.3
Jammu and Kashmir	Hindustani	1.1	92	+8243.4	0.006	−99.99

In fluid situations, one is under pressure to evaluate subjectively the speech varieties with which one is involved. When a person is asked to specify his mother tongue, he makes a choice according to the relevance of the prevailing context as perceived by him. One gets different answers by putting the same question differently.

In Bihar State, the 1961 returns of the Bihari group of languages—chiefly Bhojpuri, Maithili, and Magahi—show a phenomenal change, from 112,000 (in 1951) to 16.4 million (in 1961). This is an increase of 14,611 percent in one decade. In 1951, the Hindi and Bihari populations in Bihar State were 81.0 and 0.3 percent, respectively; in the 1961 census reports these populations were characterized as 44.3 percent Hindi and 35.4 percent Bihari, with the Hindi population recording a decrease of 34.6 percent during the decade. This change is due primarily to the re-emergence of various Bihari languages as distinct from the previously affiliated Hindi group and also to speakers of these languages asserting their distinct identity from one another within the state. The returns of the 1951 and 1961 censuses from Bihar State, given in Table 10, reveal the extraordinary increase in three main Bihari languages.

Saharsa district in Bihar counted only 5418 Maithili speakers in 1951, whereas the 1961 returns show 1.1 million persons speaking Maithili in the same district. Similar though less dramatic trends are also noticed among Chhatisgarhi speakers in Madhya Pradesh. The 1951 Census counted only 369,295 Chhatisgarhi speakers in Durg district, Madhya Pradesh; in 1961 the number had increased to 1,515,536, a growth of 310 percent.

Most of the sporadic minorities in different states also reveal the trend of assertion during the period 1951–1961, which is distinguished by a sharp awareness of language. Speech groups whose census claims (net gains) more than doubled during this period are:

Banjari in Karnataka	+305.4%
Chhatisgarhi in Madhya Pradesh	+204.9
Kurukh in Madhya Pradesh	+172.3
Nepali in West Bengal	+167.6
Kui in Orissa	+127.6

Table 10. Census Claims of Main Bihari Languages in Bihar, 1951–1961

Languages	1951 Claims (thousands)	1961 Claims (thousands)	Variation, 1951–61 (%)
Bhojpuri	1.9	7842.7	+412,674
Maithili	87.7	4982.6	+ 5578
Magadhi/Magahi	3.7	2818.5	+ 76,076

Plural Speech Communities

Other cases of relatively less spectacular consolidations among smaller groups are:

Rajasthani in Rajasthan	+67.8%
Kumauni in Uttar Pradesh	+63.2
Garhwali in Uttar Pradesh	+48.4
Nepali in Assam	+40.7
Bodo in Assam	+35.1
Dogri in Jammu and Kashmir	+32.1
Konkani in Maharashtra	+22.1
Saurashtri in Tamil Nadu	+13.1

The increase in Dogri is probably at the expense of Panjabi.

Santali shows signs of slight growth in West Bengal (net gain, 2.2 percent) but loss of strength in Assam (net loss, 61.9 percent) and in Bihar (−18.0 percent). Similarly, Rajasthani claimants nearly doubled their strength in Rajasthan (net gain, 67.8 percent), but practically halved their claims in Gujarat (net loss, 115.5 percent). Other notable cases of declining speech groups during this period can be cited:

Maria Gondi in Madhya Pradesh	−104.5%
Lamani in Maharashtra	−72.5
Parji in Orissa	−62.7
Panjabi in Jammu and Kashmir	−50.7
Savara in Andhra Pradesh	−30.4
Bhumij in Orissa	−28.2
Malayalam in Tamil Nadu	−13.4
Telugu in Tamil Nadu	−13.0

The decrease in Panjabi, as noted above, is probably due to the increase of the Dogri group. Changes in numbers of Malayam and Telegu speakers in Tamil Nadu result from the territorial adjustments to form linguistic states in 1956.

The 1971 language census reveals the continuation of opposing trends particularly with regard to claims of mother tongue in the North-Central (HUP) region, namely, the consolidation of "exclusive" identity on the one hand, and the assimilation of traditional identities in favor of prestigious language labels (Hindi, Rajasthani) on the other. Several mother tongues grouped under Bihari in the Grierson *Survey* are marked by this "assertive" trend (Table 11).

Maithili, a prominent language of the Bihari group, after its spurt during the 1951-1961 decade (growth of 5578 percent in Bihar) records an

Table 11. Census Claims of Bihari Languages throughout India, 1961-1971

Languages	1961 Claims (thousands)	1971 Claims (thousands)	Variation, 1961-71 (%)
Surgujia	3.1	536.3	+17,238
Surajpuri	28.1	159.7	+ 468
Panchpargania	57.9	160.1	+ 176
Magahi	2818.6	6638.5	+ 135
Bhojpuri	7964.8	14,340.6	+ 80
Khortha	283.7	503.8	+ 78
Sadan	532.7	807.2	+ 52

increase of only 23 percent during 1961-1971, which approximates the general trend of population growth in the country (i.e., 24.8 percent).

Mother tongues grouped under Rajasthani and many other vernaculars of the HUP Region, given in Table 12, oscillate between "assertive" or "assimilative" trends.

Figures of some tribal languages also reveal instability. Significantly, in 1961, Kui, a Dravidian language of Orissa, shows a 147 percent increase from the 1951 population, but again reverts to a 31 percent decrease in the 1971 census: 207,000 in 1951, 511,000 in 1961, and 350,000 in 1971.

Another classic example is of bilingual Muslims oscillating between regional and religious identities. Muslims in India have much closer ties with Urdu than do other religious groups. As the Muslim population is scattered throughout the country, so is Urdu. A large proportion of Muslims in many regions tends to have bilingual control over the various languages of the region (Telugu, Kannada, Marathi, etc.) as well as Urdu. During the period 1951-1961, the Muslim population in the country increased by 25.6 percent, whereas the Urdu-speaking population showed an increase of 68.7 percent. This trend is reversed during the decade 1961-1971: the Muslim population in the country records a growth of 30.8 percent, whereas the claims of Urdu as mother tongue show an increase of only 22.7 percent.

The consolidation of Urdu in almost all states during 1951-1961 (see Tables 9, 13, and 14) is primarily due to the preference of bilingual Muslims for religious identity at the expense of regional identity. In Table 13, the tabulation reveals variations in the percentages of Muslims and of Urdu speakers to the total population in some of the prominent states during 1951-1971.

During 1951-1961 the proportions of those speaking Urdu as mother tongue to the total population in all states register a considerable rise, ranging between 4.1 and 0.4 percent. The most spectacular shift toward Urdu is noticed in Karnataka, a Dravidian state, where despite a slight decrease (−0.2 percent) in the proportion of Muslims in comparison with the 1951 composition of the population, the proportion of Urdu speakers records the maximum rise (4.1 percent). Also, in Uttar Pradesh, the linguistic composition of the population shifted in favor of Urdu during the decade; with a net rise of 3.9 percent in the total composition of the state, the proportion of those speaking Urdu as mother tongue increased from 6.8 percent (in 1951) to 10.7 percent (in 1961).

The 1971 census shows signs that among bilingual Muslims, the preference for Urdu as mother tongue is becoming detached from religious identity. In Uttar Pradesh and Delhi, the proportions of Muslims register increases of 0.9 and 0.6 percent, whereas the proportions of Urdu claimants are decreased by 0.2 and 0.1 percent respectively. Gujarat, with a nominal decrease of 0.04 percent in the proportion of Muslim composition in the state, shows a decrease of 0.7 percent in the proportion of Urdu claimants. In Bihar, though the proportion of Muslim population registers an increase of 1.0 percent, the proportion of Urdu claimants remains unchanged. The proportions of Muslim population in Karnataka and Maharashtra record increases of 0.7 percent each, whereas the proportions of Urdu claimants are increased by only 0.4 percent in both states. It is only in Andhra Pradesh that an increase (of 0.5 percent) in the proportion of Muslims is matched by an equal increase in the proportion of Urdu speakers.

A comparison of growth rates of individual mother tongues with overall population growth in a state during a specified period indicates the consolidation of or decrease in the strength of these mother tongues in the total linguistic composition of a particular state. Tables 14, 15, and 16 reveal the extent of oscillation in the census returns on Hindi and Urdu as mother tongues in most of the states in the country.

Urdu growth rates during the decade 1951–1961 reveal dramatically the process of consolidation throughout India: Rajasthan, 200.2 percent; Karnataka, 110.3 percent; Madhya Pradesh, 76.8 percent; Uttar Pradesh, 66.8 percent; Andhra Pradesh, 43.9 percent; Bihar, 37.0 percent; and Tamil Nadu, 32.3 percent. Considering the sociocultural situation of the Muslim pockets throughout the country, one does not find any evidence of genuine language displacement in daily life, such as abandoning a regional or minority language in favor of Urdu. Hence, these astounding increases in the claims of Urdu as mother tongue can be regarded as the assertion of cultural solidarity of bilingual Muslims through Urdu and their relegating the respective regional languages to subsidiary language status in their subjective evaluation of competence (Weinreich, Labov, and Herzog, 1968), in reaction to the postindependence language politics in the country.

Table 12. Census Claims of Rajasthani Languages and Other Vernaculars of the HUP Region, 1961–1971

	"Assertive" Trends				"Assimilative" Trends		
	1961 Claims (thousands)	1971 Claims (thousands)	Variation, 1961–71 (%)		1961 Claims (thousands)	1971 Claims (thousands)	Variation, 1961–71 (%)
Rajasthani Group							
Bagri	309.9	1055.6	+241	Dhundhari	1591.8	155.0	−90
Rajasthani	804.3	2093.6	+160	Mewari	1853.5	818.0	−56
Mewati	48.4	94.7	+96	Malvi	1142.5	644.0	−44
Lamani	679.4	1203.3	+77	Marwari	6242.4	4714.1	−24
Gojri	209.3	330.5	+58	Banjari	592.7	471.9	−20
Nimadi	528.2	794.2	+50				
Other Vernaculars							
Bundelkhandi	22.1	376.0	+1604	Awadhi	528.3	136.3	−74
Chhatisgarhi	2962.0	6693.4	+126	Baghelkhandi	557.0	231.0	−58
Garhwali	809.7	1277.2	+58				
Dogri	879.8	1298.9	+48				
Panjabi	9868.3	13,900.2	+41				

Table 13. *Percentages of Muslims and Urdu Speakers to Total Population in Various States, 1951–1971*

State	Regional Language	1951		1961		Variation during 1951–61		1971		Variation during 1961–71	
		Muslims (%)	Urdu Speakers (%)	Muslims (%)	Urdu Speakers (%)	Muslims (%)	Urdu Speakers (%)	Muslims (%)	Urdu Speakers (%)	Muslims (%)	Urdu Speakers (%)
Uttar Pradesh	Hindi	14.3	6.8	14.6	10.7	+0.3	+3.9	15.5	10.5	+0.9	−0.2
Bihar	Hindi	11.3	6.8	12.5	8.9	+1.2	+2.1	13.5	8.9	+1.0	0.0
Karnataka (Mysore)	Kannada	10.1	4.5	9.9	8.6	−0.2	+4.1	10.6	9.0	+0.7	+0.4
Gujarat	Gujarati	8.9	2.4	8.46	2.9	−0.4	+0.5	8.42	2.2	−0.04	−0.7
Andhra Pradesh	Telugu	7.8	5.2	7.6	7.1	−0.2	+1.9	8.1	7.6	+0.5	+0.5
Maharashtra	Marathi	7.6	6.5	7.7	6.9	+0.1	+0.4	8.4	7.3	+0.7	+0.4
Delhi	Hindi	5.7	not available	5.9	5.8	+0.2	—	6.5	5.7	+0.6	−0.1
Panjab	Hindi-Panjabi	1.8	not available	1.9	1.3	+0.1	—	0.8*	0.2*	—	—
Haryana								8.5	2.0	—	—

*Figures for 1961 and 1971 are not comparable, as the state was divided in 1966 into Panjab, Haryana, and Chandigarh.

Table 14. Increase (or Decrease) of Percentages in Hindi and Urdu Populations, 1951–1961

State	Total Population Growth (%)	Increase (or Decrease) of Claimants, Hindi as Mother Tongue (%)	Hindi Variation from State Growth (%)	Increase (or Decrease) of Claimants, Urdu as Mother Tongue (%)	Urdu Variation from State Growth (%)	Remarks
Fluid Zone						
Uttar Pradesh	16.7	+23.8	+7.1	+83.5	+66.8	Switch from Hindustani to Urdu or Hindi
Madhya Pradesh	24.2	+9.1	−15.1	+101.0	+76.8	Assertion by smaller speech groups: Chhatisgarhi, Kurukh, Maria Gondi, etc.
Bihar	19.8	−34.6	−54.4	+56.8	+37.0	Hindi yields ground to Bihari languages
Rajasthan	26.2	−79.2	−105.4	+226.4	+200.2	Labels like Khariboli, Rajasthani, etc., have displaced Hindi; consolidation of Urdu
Panjab	25.9	+27.0				Increase of Hindi claimants represents the total of Hindi, Urdu, Panjabi, and Pahari

Jammu and Kashmir	9.4	not available			—
Stable Zone					
Andhra Pradesh	15.7	+27.3	+11.6	+59.6	+43.9	Switch from Hindustani to Urdu or Hindi
Tamil Nadu (Madras)	11.9	−40.1	−52.0	+44.2	+32.3	Setback to Hindi
Karnataka (Mysore)	21.6	+13.3	−8.3	+131.9	+110.3	Consolidation of Urdu, with some losses to Hindi
Kerala	24.8	not available				
West Bengal	32.8	−10.6	−43.4	+52.0	+19.2	Setback to Hindi
Orissa	19.8	+40.4	+20.6	+33.9	+14.1	Gains to Hindi and Urdu
Assam	34.5	+52.8	+18.3	not available		Gains to Hindi
Maharashtra	23.6	+19.7	−3.9	+31.0	+7.4	Minor fluctuations in favor of Urdu and against Hindi
Gujarat	26.9	+83.7	+56.8	+50.1	+23.2	Consolidation of Hindi and Urdu at expense of Rajasthani
INDIA	21.5					

Table 15. Profile of Urdu as Mother Tongue, 1961-1971

State	Total Population Growth (%)	Urdu Mother Tongue Speakers, 1971 (thousands)	(%)	Increase (or Decrease) of Claimants (%)	Variation from the State Growth (%)
Uttar Pradesh	19.8	9273	10.5	+ 17.5	− 2.3
Bihar	21.3	4993	8.9	+ 20.3	− 1.0
Maharashtra	27.5	3662	7.3	+ 34.4	+ 6.9
Andhra Pradesh	20.9	3300	7.6	+ 29.2	+ 8.3
Karnataka	24.2	2637	9.0	+ 29.6	+ 5.4
Madhya Pradesh	28.7	1001	2.4	+ 35.2	+ 6.5
West Bengal	26.9	950	2.1	+ 14.1	−12.8
Tamil Nadu	22.3	760	1.8	+ 23.4	+ 1.1
Rajasthan	27.8	651	2.5	+ 27.7	− 0.1
Gujarat	29.4	582	2.2	− 2.2	−31.6
Orissa	25.1	287	1.3	+ 34.6	+ 9.5
Delhi (UT)	52.9	231	5.7	+ 50.8	− 2.1
Haryana	—	196	2.0	—	—
Panjab	—	29.0	0.2	− 11.4	—
Goa, Daman, and Diu (UT)	36.9	19.2	2.2	+101.8	+64.9
Jammu and Kashmir	29.7	12.7	0.3	− 0.95	−30.6
Kerala	26.3	11.4	0.05	+ 24.1	− 2.2
Himachal Pradesh	23.0	10.1	0.3	+ 61.4	+38.4
Assam	35.0	6.3	0.04	− 43.8	−78.8
INDIA	24.8	28,621	5.2	+ 22.7	− 2.1

Table 16. Profile of Hindi as Mother Tongue, 1961-1971

State	Speakers Classified under Hindi as Mother Tongue		Percentage of Total Population		Variation, 1961-71 (%)
	1961 (thousands)	1971 (thousands)	1961 (%)	1971 (%)	
Uttar Pradesh	62,975	78,215	85.4	88.5	+ 3.1
Bihar	20,581	44,954	44.3	79.8	+35.5
Madhya Pradesh	25,272	34,698	78.1	88.3	+10.2
Rajasthan	6715	23,481	33.3	91.1	+57.8
Haryana	—	8975	—	89.4	—
Delhi (UT)	2057	3089	77.4	76.0	− 1.4
Himachal Pradesh	144	3006	10.1	86.9	+76.8
Panjab	11,299*	2712	55.6*	20.0	—
Chandigarh (UT)	—	144	—	56.0	—
West Bengal	1898	2715	5.4	6.1	+ 0.7
Maharashtra	1230	2528	3.1	5.0	+ 1.9
Andhra Pradesh	139	994	0.4	2.3	+ 1.9
Assam	524	798	4.4	5.3	+ 0.9
Jammu and Kashmir	22	695	0.6	15.1	+14.5
Karnataka	82	527	0.4	1.8	+ 1.4
Gujarat	192	430	0.9	1.6	+ 0.7
Orissa	220	342	1.3	1.6	+ 0.3
Tamil Nadu	39	77	0.1	0.2	+ 0.1
Tripura	18.6	23	1.6	1.5	− 0.1
Andaman and Nicobar Islands (UT)	3.6	18.5	0.6	1.6	+ 1.0
Nagaland	4.5	17.4	1.2	3.4	+ 2.2
Meghalaya	—	17.2	—	1.7	—
Arunachal Pradesh (UT)	7.0	15.4	—	3.3	—
Goa, Daman, Diu (UT)†	1.7	11.8	0.3	1.4	+ 1.1
Manipur	2.4	11.6	0.3	1.1	+ 0.8
Kerala	7.3	11.6	0.05	0.05	0.0
Sikkim	2.2	6.2	—	2.9	—
INDIA	133,435	208,514	30.4	38.0	+ 7.6

*1961 figures include Haryana and Chandigarh, which were a part of the erstwhile Punjab state before its bifurcation in 1966.
†The rest of the Union territories—Dadra and Nagar Haveli, Pondicherry, and the Lakshadveep Islands—together record less than 2500 Hindi speakers.

In the 1971 census many states show signs of an overall stabilization of Urdu claims (with modest changes ranging from an 8.3 percent increase in Andhra Pradesh to a 2.1 percent decrease in Delhi, Table 15), after the postpartition spurt of expressing "religious" identity through Urdu at the time of the 1961 census. On the other hand, Assam, Gujarat, Jammu and Kashmir, and West Bengal are marked by a spectacular decline in the claims of Urdu (ranging from a 12.8 percent decrease in West Bengal to a 78.7 percent decrease in Assam), probably reverting back to the "regional" identity. Orissa and Maharashtra represent cases of steady consolidation in favor of Urdu during the two decades 1951–1971 (cf. Tables 14 and 15):

	1961 Variation	1971 Variation
Andhra Pradesh	+ 43.9	+ 8.3
Madhya Pradesh	+ 76.8	+ 6.5
Karnataka	+110.3	+ 5.4
Tamil Nadu	+ 32.3	+ 1.1
Rajasthan	+200.2	− 0.1
Bihar	+ 37.0	− 1.0
Delhi	—	− 2.1
Kerala	—	− 2.2
Uttar Pradesh	+ 66.8	− 2.3
West Bengal	+ 19.2	−12.8
Jammu and Kashmir	—	−30.6
Gujarat	+ 23.2	−31.6
Assam	—	−78.8
Maharashtra	+ 7.4	+ 6.9
Orissa	+ 14.1	+ 9.6

The most radical case of fluidity in claims of mother tongue is found in Bihar, where the predominant language population (Hindi speakers) registered a decrease of 34.6 percent during the decade 1951–1961. When compared with the overall population growth rate in the state (19.8 percent), this amounts to a dramatic decline of more than half of the Hindi-speaking population (a net loss of 54.4 percent), without any mass exodus of Hindi speakers or any influx of non-Hindi-speaking population into the state during the decade. A clue to the mystery is provided by the phenomenal increases in the returns of the Bihari group of languages (chiefly Bhojpuri, Maithili, and Magahi) (cf. Table 10). These increases

Plural Speech Communities 103

signify the change of language (not necessarily speech habits) by speakers of these vernaculars (which had enjoyed the status of literary languages in the past) in order to assert their identities as distinct from Hindi and from one another within the state.

Less spectacular is the case of the slower growth of the Hindi-speaking population in Madhya Pradesh (only 9.1 percent when compared with the total population growth, 24.2 percent), registering a net loss of 15.1 percent during 1951-1961, again due to the assertion of smaller vernacular and tribal groups (Chhatisgarhi, Kurukh, etc.). Hindi, as the dominant language in Uttar Pradesh, consolidated its strength by registering a net gain of 7.1 percent during this decade.

Another case of spectacular fluidity is provided by Rajasthan, where the claims of Hindi as mother tongue were slashed by over 79 percent during 1951-1961, registering a net loss of over 105 percent. This extreme change is accounted for by the phenomenal increases in the returns of the Rajasthani group of languages and Khariboli, which again signifies the assertion of their identities as distinct from Hindi, and does not necessarily represent any change in their speech habits.

Claims of Hindi as mother tongue representing a prominent minority group suffered heavily in Tamil Nadu and West Bengal during this period. Maharashtra and Karnataka also recorded a slower growth in returns of Hindi as mother tongue. Variations in the state's overall growth and in growth rates of Hindi as mother tongue, signifying the losses of Hindi in various states, are: Tamil Nadu (−52.0 percent), West Bengal (−43.4 percent), Karnataka (−8.3 percent), Maharashtra (−3.9 percent).

In other non-Hindi states, Hindi claims record some gains, though these are not as extreme as the losses in other states. Variations in the two growth rates, signifying the consolidation of Hindi in a few states, are: Gujarat (+56.8 percent), Orissa (+20.6 percent), Assam (+18.3 percent), Andhra Pradesh (+11.6 percent).

Such glaring instances of oscillation in the census returns regarding mother tongue have often been a source of tension affecting policymaking processes in many states. The composite characteristics of communication patterns in the entire Hindi-Urdu-Panjabi region (comprising eight Hindi states and Union territories, one Panjabi state, and one Kashmiri state; cf. Chapter 1) are at variance with the concerns for identity expressed through the claims of mother tongues, which have a marked tendency to shift in every decennial census depending on the prevailing sociocultural climate. The region, therefore, has earned the identity of "Fluid Zone." Assertions of "exclusive" identity noticed in the census claims of mother tongue of the Bihari, Rajasthani, and Pahari groups of languages have a particular bearing on Hindi as the state language of Bihar, Rajasthan, and Himachal Pradesh.

In this light, the 1971 census makes a major departure by tabulating the data on mother tongues in accordance with the "institutional" imperatives of different regions, and shelving altogether the language classification scheme introduced by Grierson in the 1901 census, which is based on comparative methodology and genealogical considerations. The Grierson classification has been subjected to ad hoc modifications from time to time; the 1951 census modified it by amalgamating "Eastern" Hindi (including Awadhi and Chhatisgarhi) and "Western" Hindi (with major dialects: Khariboli, Bangru [Haryanvi], Braj, Bundelkhandi, Kanauji) under a common label—Hindi. Under the 1971 reclassification scheme, the canvass of Hindi has been further widened by incorporating vernaculars grouped under Bihari, Rajasthani, and Pahari (excluding Nepali). Prominent vernaculars added to Hindi under the new scheme are:

	Most returns from
Bhojpuri, Maithili, Magahi, Sadan, Khortha	Bihar
Rajasthani, Marwari, Dhundhari, Mewari, Malvi	Rajasthan
Hindustani, Kumauni, Garhwali, Jaunsari	Uttar Pradesh
Nimadi	Madhya Pradesh
Pahari, Mandeali, Sirmauri, Kului, Chameali	Himachal Pradesh
Gojri	Jammu and Kashmir
Lamani	Andhra Pradesh, Maharashtra
Banjari	Karnataka, Maharashtra

As a result, Hindi growth rates during the decade present a radically different picture (Table 16). The claims of Hindi record substantial gains in all the states (except the Union Territory Delhi). Himachal Pradesh, Rajasthan, and Bihar benefit the most from the revised classification, showing a spectacular 35.5–76.8 percent rise in the proportion of Hindi speakers in these states. The ratios of Hindi speakers also show significant improvement in Jammu and Kashmir (+14.5 percent), Madhya Pradesh (+10.2 percent), Uttar Pradesh (+3.1 percent), Nagaland (+2.2 percent), Maharashtra (+1.9 percent), and Karnataka (+1.4 percent).

Stable and Fluid Zones

On the basis of the overall stability of language returns, the four macroregions have been grouped together into two zones: (1) the Stable Zone, comprising the first three regions—the South, the East, and the West; and (2) the Fluid Zone, covering the remaining vast North-Central region (cf. Chapter 1). In the Stable Zone, areas of the predominant languages, which formed the basis of the reorganization of states in 1956, are clearly marked. In Table 17 it is significant to note the relative stability of census returns on mother tongues in the Stable Zone in contrast to the fluctuations in the returns in the Fluid Zone.

During the period 1951–1961, maximum consolidation of regionally dominant mother tongues in the Stable Zone is shown in West Bengal and Assam. Bengali in West Bengal registered a net gain of 3.0 percent and Assamese in Assam of 2.0 percent, which were very likely due to the continuous inflow of Bengali and Assamese-speaking refugees from erstwhile East Pakistan (now Bangla Desh) during the decade. In this respect, predominant mother tongues in the southern states improved their positions slightly. Tamil in Tamil Nadu gained by 1.4 percent, Kannada in Karnataka by 1.0 percent, and Telugu in Andhra Pradesh by 0.5 percent, due mainly to territorial adjustments made to form linguistic states in 1956. In Maharashtra, Kerala, Gujarat, and Orissa, growth in the populations of the predominant mother tongues was somewhat slower than the overall growth in the state during this period. The strength of Marathi in Maharashtra diminished by 1.8 percent, of Malayalam in Kerala by 1.7 percent, of Gujarati in Gujarat by 0.9 percent, and of Oriya in Orissa by 0.2 percent.

The 1971 census also registers a steady consolidation of predominant regional languages in most of the states in the Stable Zone except in Assam, Jammu and Kashmir, Gujarat, and Andhra Pradesh. Orissa records a maximum gain of 2.8 percent, reversing the adverse trend of the previous decade. Predominant mother tongues in three Southern states maintain upward consolidation: Tamil in Tamil Nadu registers a net gain of 2.0 percent, Kannada in Karnataka of 1.5 percent, and Malayalam in Kerala of 1.3 percent reversing the pattern of 1951–1961, when its strength was diminished by 1.7 percent. Bengali in West Bengal also improved its position by a net gain of 1.5 percent. The increase of Marathi in Maharashtra almost matches the population growth of the state: it records an edge of 0.1 percent over the population growth and thus arrests the downward trend of the previous decade (showing a net loss of 1.8 percent).

The slower growth of the predominant mother tongues in Assam, Jammu and Kashmir, Gujarat, and Andhra Pradesh can be attributed

Table 17. Growth Percentages of Dominant Languages Other than Hindi-Urdu, 1951-1971

State	Total Population Growth		State Language	1951-61		1961-71	
	1951-61 (%)	1961-71 (%)		Increase of Claimants, Predominant Mother Tongue (%)	Variation with Population Growth (%)	Increase of Claimants, Predominant Mother Tongue (%)	Variation with Population Growth (%)
Stable Zone							
Andhra Pradesh	15.7	20.9	Telugu	16.2	+0.5	20.0	−0.9
Tamil Nadu	11.9	22.3	Tamil	13.3	+1.4	24.3	+2.0
Karnataka	21.6	24.2	Kannada	22.6	+1.0	25.7	+1.5
Kerala	24.8	26.3	Malayalam	23.1	−1.7	27.6	+1.3
West Bengal	32.8	26.9	Bengali	35.8	+3.0	28.4	+1.5
Orissa	19.8	25.1	Oriya	19.6	−0.2	27.9	+2.8
Assam	34.5	35.0	Assamese	36.5	+2.0	31.3	−3.7
Maharashtra	23.6	27.5	Marathi	21.8	−1.8	27.6	+0.1
Gujarat	26.9	29.4	Gujarati	26.0	−0.9	27.8	−1.6
*Fluid Zone**							
Rajasthan	26.2	27.8	Marwari	36.6	+10.4	(included in Hindi)	
Jammu and Kashmir	9.4	29.7	Kashmiri	28.4	+19.0	26.6	−3.1
INDIA	21.5	24.8					

*Only states with other than Hindi as dominant language.

Plural Speech Communities

mainly to the increasing movement of native populations away from their home states. The strength of Assamese in Assam is diminished by 3.7 percent (reversing its consolidation in the previous decade), probably as a result of a heavy influx of non-Assamese population in the state. Gujarat is the only state which registers a slower growth of its predominant mother tongue, Gujarati, in two successive censuses: there is a loss of 1.6 percent during 1961–1971, following upon the loss of 0.9 percent during the previous decade. This can be accounted for by the trend of outmigration among the state's Gujarati-speaking population. Telugu in Andhra Pradesh has maintained relative stability during both decades; it shows marginal variations with the population growth of state (a net gain of 0.5 percent during the earlier decade is matched by a reversal of 0.9 percent during 1961–1971).

The stability of dominant mother tongues in this zone is attested by the fact that in no case does variation between the rates of overall state growth and of dominant "home" language growth exceed ±4.0 percent.

The North-Central region, on the other hand, is characterized by fluctuations in the declarations of regionally dominant mother tongues and is hence labeled the Fluid Zone. Areas of predominant languages in this zone are not clearly marked, and the growth rate of regionally dominant groups of mother tongues does not parallel the overall growth in the total population of the region (cf. Table 14). Language attitudes of speakers in the Fluid Zone are represented by frequent shifts in language allegiance, a pattern revealed by the oscillating returns claiming Hindi, Urdu, Panjabi, Kashmiri, and the various vernaculars as mother tongues in this vast area. This characteristic seems to have weighed heavily with the authorities in their decision to reclassify languages in the 1971 census.

In this "shuttlecock" phase of mother-tongue claims, the predominant mother tongues in Jammu and Kashmir, Rajasthan, and Uttar Pradesh consolidated their strength during 1951–1961. Kashmiri in Jammu and Kashmir gained by 19.0 percent (although during 1961–1971 the earlier growth has been reversed by a net loss of 3.1 percent), Marwari in Rajasthan by 10.4 percent (classified under Hindi in the 1971 census), and Hindi in Uttar Pradesh by 7.1 percent during 1951–1961. Tabulation of the data on mother tongues according to the new scheme has significantly contributed in consolidating the position of Hindi throughout the country, particularly in resolving the indeterminacies of language returns in the states of Bihar, Rajasthan, and Himachal Pradesh.

Homogeneity in Communication

The issue of language privileges during the postindependence period has served to heighten consciousness and strengthen loyalties among different speech communities. Three major languages—Hindi, Urdu, and Panjabi—representing the polarization of literary trends and writing systems (Devanagari, Perso-Arabic, and Gurumukhi scripts, respectively) and recognized by official policies, dominate the entire Fluid Zone in India as well as the Panjabi-, Lahnda-, and Pashto-speaking areas in Pakistan. Hindi, apart from being the state language of six states and two Union territories (Delhi and Chandigarh) in the North-Central region, is also the declared official language of India. Urdu is the state language of Jammu and Kashmir and of Delhi and is also the declared official language of Pakistan. Panjabi is the state language of Panjab in the North-Central region.

On the basis of the communication patterns that prevail among different speech groups and the identificational characteristics attached to their languages, this entire region, divided between two nations—India and Pakistan—is treated as a composite communication region and is often referred to as the "Hindustani" region. Until recently, Kashmiri (a Dardic language) and Pashto (an Iranian language) enjoyed only vernacular status in their own regions, namely Jammu and Kashmir and the North-West Frontier Province (NWFP), respectively. They remained subordinate to Urdu, which was used for the purpose of wider group communication. In recent years they have shown signs, in the fields of education and literature, of asserting their separate linguistic identities. Also, Pashto in Afghanistan long remained under the domination of the Persian language (known as Darri), but now it claims an independent identity as one of the official languages of that country.

In the Panjabi region, on the Indian as well as on the Pakistani side, census returns on mother tongues seem to be influenced by religious affiliations. At the expense of slight statistical inaccuracy, one can say that the three religiocultural groups (the Sikhs, Hindus, and Muslims) show preferences for aligning themselves with three different "language traditions," Panjabi, Hindi, and Urdu, respectively, although one would not find any sharp distinction in the speech the three groups actually use for primary communication. In the past three decades, one notices a great degree of fluctuation in proclaiming loyalty to one or another "tradition" due to the rapidly changing sociopolitical situation in this region—so much so that in the 1951 Indian census language tabulation in the northern states (now comprising Delhi, Haryana, Panjab, Chandigarh, and Himachal Pradesh) was abandoned because of the emotionally charged atmosphere surrounding the language issue at the time.

Language returns on the Indian side of Panjab and its neighboring states can be broadly interpreted as follows:

1. Among those natively speaking Panjabi, Lahnda, Dogri, Rajasthani, Hariani, Khariboli, and neighboring vernaculars (in some cases,

Plural Speech Communities

even Pashto), people who regard *Panjabi in Gurumukhi script* as a fit vehicle for formal communication (particularly for education and administration) declare *Panjabi* as their mother tongue, regardless of the language or dialect they actually speak at home;
2. Similarly, those native speakers (as characterized above) who regard *Hindi in Devanagari script* as suitable for such purposes declare *Hindi* as their mother tongue; and
3. Those native speakers who regard *Urdu in Perso-Arabic script* as suitable for such purposes declare *Urdu* as their mother tongue (mostly in the urban centers of the Panjabi, Lahnda, and Pashto regions in Pakistan).

The actual number of Lahnda (mainly Multani) speakers is much greater than the 1961 census reveals (only 9000), and their speech enjoys high prestige in society at the spoken level. But generally speaking three religiocultural groups align themselves with three different "traditions," namely Panjabi, Hindi, and Urdu.

One notices a superposed homogeneity in communication patterns in the entire HUP region, with varying degrees of diglossic complementation among many speech varieties. Verbal repertoire in a community is hierarchically structured, with many speech varieties enjoying different status privileges according to overt identity pressures.

A typical example of sociocultural affinity in India's North-Central region is revealed in the fact that 123 million speakers identified "Hindi" proper as their mother tongue in the 1961 census, though a large population among them consists of many heterogeneous speech groups who natively speak markedly different varieties (Braj Bhakha, Bangru, Bundelkhandi, etc.) or altogether different languages (such as Panjabi, Dogri, Pahari, Rajasthani, Marwari, Awadhi, Chhatisgarhi, Bhojpuri, Maithili, Magahi) for primary communication. The heterogeneous speech groups claiming Hindi as their mother tongue can be placed in five broad categories:

1. Those bilingual speakers belonging to the North-Central region (characterized as the Fluid Zone) who retain their regional or caste dialects either of Western Hindi or of altogether different languages of the region (such as Pahari, Lahnda, Panjabi, Rajasthani, Awadhi, Chhatisgarhi, Bihari) for informal communication within their speech group but prefer to use Khariboli (standard Hindi) for formalized communication. In this diglossia situation, these speakers think of Khariboli as having a more prestigious role than their native speech, which has a casual use. They regard their native speech

habits as mere substandard variations of the all-powerful standard Hindi.
2. Those bilinguals who reserve their native speech varieties (as stated above) merely for communication with elders in deferent-intimate speech events but use more and more Khariboli in other situations within their speech group. These speakers associate Khariboli with urbanity and modernity and their actual native speech with rurality and orthodoxy.
3. Those bilinguals who use their native speech varieties (as stated above) for oral communication (informal as well as formal) but who regard Khariboli in Devanagari script as the fit vehicle for written purposes (education, literature, administration, etc.) within their speech group. The expression of solidarity among Hindus of the Fluid Zone through *Khariboli in Devanagari script* (Hindi) in response to the similar feeling among Muslims (primarily among urban and aristocratic classes) expressed through *Khariboli in Perso-Arabic script* (Urdu) has been a major factor in this trend.
4. Those monolinguals (mostly rural) speaking regional vernaculars or languages other than Khariboli but giving "Hindi" as their mother tongue, since they regard themselves as part of the great "Hindi tradition."
5. Those belonging to the narrow Khariboli region around Delhi who do not natively speak any other dialect or language, and those belonging to various urban and semiurban centers in the Fluid Zone who have not acquired sufficient control over the language of their region because of the genuine displacement of the local or subregional dialect or language in the thrust for urbanity, modernity, and/or solidarity realized through Khariboli.

For a majority of the urban speakers in the region, Hindi provides a nucleus for "a single inter-urban speech community, connected by a super-regional network of communication (newspapers, books, radio, etc.) which extends from one urban center to another without directly touching the intervening rural areas" (Gumperz and Naim, 1960:100). As is the case with Muslims and Urdu throughout the subcontinent, Hindi serves as a model for prestige imitation among Hindus throughout the Fluid Zone. "[It] acts as a unifying force linguistically as well as culturally, a common mould which counteracts diversity at the local level" (Gumperz and Naim, 1960:99). The number of such urban speakers of Khariboli is rather small, though in the course of time, with progressive discarding of the diglossic function of local dialects and subregional vernaculars, the number of speakers of this sort has gradually been increasing among the younger generation. One notices a gradual decline of "lowbrow" Hindi (i.e., colloquial Hindustani) and of regional vernaculars of the Fluid

Zone in favor of "highbrow" Hindi (Sanskritic or Anglicized Hindi) among urban-educated youth. But, relatively speaking, the proportion of native Khariboli speakers grouped under Urdu is still much higher than that grouped under Hindi.

The concept of mother tongue is closely linked with the awareness of one's identity affiliations in one's society. As discussed earlier, a declaration of a mother tongue by an individual can be regarded primarily as a conscious or subconscious identification of one's speech habits with others by viewing the general label as a sign of cohesion, or as distinguishing them from others as a mark of distinction. The mother tongue is usually identified by a conventional name, such as English, Arabic, Chinese, or Hindi; or, in the absence of strong standardization pressures, it could still be in flux; for example, a variety of Hindi spoken in Haryana State is known by different names—Hariani (Haryanvi), Deswali, Bangru, Jatki, etc.

Many speakers of the North-Central region of India who are not native speakers of Hindi or Urdu in the strict linguistic sense but who claim Hindi or Urdu as their mother tongue in the census returns command, by and large, nativelike control over Hindi-Urdu, and either of the languages is virtually an "associate" native speech to them. For such people Hindi or Urdu represents a particular tradition. Most of the speakers in the region, particularly those in Uttar Pradesh, Madhya Pradesh, and Bihar, remain unaware of their bilingual or multilingual behavior. These people are mostly declared as monolinguals in the census. For them, the switching of linguistic codes from native speech to Hindi-Urdu is similar to the switching of styles (such as formal, informal, intimate) in a monolingual situation. Kloss (1967a) calls such vernaculars "near dialectized" languages: "Functionally as well as psychologically they are accepted by their speakers as dialect-like tools of oral communication (plus, at best, of unassuming poetry)."

In the realm of literature, a Hindi speaker regards works of creative writing of the entire HUP region as belonging to Hindi, even though, on the basis of their structural characteristics, these writings may be classified as Braj, Awadhi, Maithili, Rajasthani (Dingal), and so on. Only a few decades ago, even writings in Panjabi and Lahnda (including the holy scriptures of the Sikhs) were included in the Hindi literary tradition. In fact, the chief centers of Hindi literature fall outside the Khariboli region—in Agra, Allahabad, Benaras, Patna, and in prepartition times, Lahore (now in Pakistan). The origin of the Urdu literary tradition may be traced to the writings of Khariboli in Perso-Arabic script, the chief centers being at Delhi, Aligarh, Lucknow, Hyderabad (Deccan), Lahore, and, after the creation of Pakistan, Karachi.

On the other hand, with the emergence of language chauvinism in the postindependence period, there are now signs of a reversal of this trend.

There is a growing tendency of various native speech groups of the HUP region to assert their "exclusive" identity. In contrast, Hindi figures show a decline or a low rate of growth in many states in the 1961 census. Some of the vernaculars, such as Awadhi, Maithili, and Rajasthani, have enjoyed the status of literary languages in the past. Ironically, most of the claimants to "exclusive" identity are persons from urban and semiurban centers who have already acquired nativelike control over Khariboli and use it more and more for their primary communication needs as their associate native speech. But they are now consciously reverting to their original native speech in order to "restore their dethroned dialects to their former status" (Kloss, 1967a).

The Hindi-Urdu Amalgam

The vast Hindi-Urdu-Panjabi (HUP) region is characterized by loyalties to the Hindi, Urdu, and Panjabi languages that extend beyond their linguistic characteristics in the thrust to assert rival claims of solidarity. These three languages incorporate many vernaculars of the region—Pahari, Lahnda, Rajasthani, Maithili, Bhojpuri, Awadhi, and Chhatisgarhi—in their overall speech matrices.

Cohesive tendencies in communication patterns coupled with divergent speech attitudes of those claiming Hindi or Urdu as their mother tongue illustrate a unique case, where the cake is cut both ways, vertically as well as horizontally. On the one hand, many different languages of this Fluid Zone, stretching from Pashto (an Iranian language) to Maithili (an East Indo-Aryan language, structurally closer to Bengali), are identified by their speakers as mere dialects or style variants of one language amalgam, Hindi-Urdu; Kelkar (1968) calls it "Hirdu." On the other hand, two sociocultural styles of the same speech—Khariboli—belonging to the same region are identified as distinct language "institutions"—Hindi and Urdu. Kloss (1967b) discusses the twin concept by which a society recognizes a language: "Abstand," that is, by intrinsic distance, and "Ausbau," that is, by independent development; it can also be regarded as the "malleability" of language. Hindi and Urdu represent an interesting case of two "Ausbau" languages developed in the same region from a common base, Khariboli—loosely known as Hindustani.

The distinction between standard Hindi and standard Urdu is marked by emphasis on allegiance to two different literary traditions and writing systems (Devanagari and Perso-Arabic). Linguistically, the difference between the two hinges mainly on the patterns of borrowing, Hindi drawing on Sanskrit and Urdu on Perso-Arabic sources for their respective "high" vocabularies. These borrowings have to a certain extent subsequently affected the phonological and derivational features of the two standards, but both still retain the common inflectional system, syntax, and general vocabulary. Patterns of borrowing in both these standard languages are not as compartmentalized as are those of two distinctly prescribed literary standards of a Yugoslav language, Serbo-Croatian (Serbian in the Cyrillic and Croatian in the Latin script).[3] Hindi and Urdu speakers, on the basis of diverse family and regional backgrounds and with different social attitudes and types of education, can admix varied Sanskrit and Perso-Arabic characteristics with enormous possibilities as mere stylistic variations in speech as well as in writing. These can be regarded as two styles of the same linguistic code: "Hindi and Urdu therefore might best be characterized not in terms of actual speech, but as norms of ideal behavior in the sociologist's sense" (Gumperz and Naim, 1960:100).

The North-Central region of India is a characteristic example of the "melting-pot" situation, where native speech distinctions are undermined because of a preference for wider group affiliations. The speech behavior of these people represents a pattern of the "divided joint family," where different languages—Pahari, Rajasthani, Maithili, and others—enjoy hierarchical positions under a single umbrella, but once again are split in diametrically opposing camps, namely Hindi and Urdu. In some regions the split between Hindi and Panjabi is also claimed more on ideological than on linguistic grounds.

Divergent trends of classicalization and Westernization have led to a great diversity of styles in Hindi-Urdu. Both Hindi and Urdu are identified with two major styles: formalistic speech and casual speech. These two styles operate at three sociocultural levels of elegance: (1) highbrow; (2) middlebrow; and (3) lowbrow.

1. *Highbrow.* Most elegant formalistic Hindi speech depends on heavy borrowings from the Sanskritic stock or on new coinages based on Sanskrit derivations; elegant Urdu relies to the same extent on the Perso-Arabic stock, in preference to indigenous usage. Both "high" Hindi and "high" Urdu are used in the urban contexts of power and religion, particularly in pedantic and ornate discourse, oratory, and religious sermons.
2. *Middlebrow.* (1) Formalized but less elegant Hindi and Urdu depend on Sanskrit or Perso-Arabic stocks to a lesser extent, and at the same time cultivate some of the indigenous usages as well. The "middlebrow" nuances of Hindi and Urdu are predominantly found in popular literature, songs, films, theater, mass communication, and so on. (2) Elegant casual Hindi-Urdu leans heavily on Western languages, particularly English, in preference to the indigenous languages. With the increasing impact of urbanization and

technologization on Indian society, Anglicized Hindi or Urdu has been gaining popularity among the educated upper middle classes along with frequent code-switching between Hindi-Urdu and English.
3. *Lowbrow.* Casual Hindi-Urdu has no specific bias in favor of Sanskrit, Perso-Arabic, or English. It is evaluated as the substandard speech of uneducated urban speakers and is labeled "Bazaar Hindustani." Its written usage is rather infrequent, except in detective fiction and cheap publications.

During the Independence movement, through the initiative of Mahatma Gandhi, the use of Hindustani was promoted in the areas of education and literature both to bridge the gulf between the divergent attitudes among Hindu and Muslim language elites and to bring these language activities closer to the masses.

Apart from the sociocultural manipulations leading to stratificational heterogeneity in speech, regional variations in the Hindi-Urdu amalgam are also very conspicuous. One can easily detect a greater degree of permissiveness for a wider variety of pronunciation among Indian speakers. Language custodians with puristic leanings, who tend to be very concerned about the correct usage of grammar and vocabulary, do not seem to mind regional distinctions in pronunciation, even in formal communication. Under such sociolinguistic conditions, strict observance of all-pervasive standards like the Received Pronunciation (RP) in British English would be unthinkable in the HUP region (cf. Chapter 4). However, one often notices an acute awareness of Perso-Arabic sounds in borrowed words in Urdu, namely in the letters *f, x, z, q, G*. Urdu pronunciation generally tends to the westward Panjabi, and Hindi pronunciation to the eastward Awadhi.

One can classify two types of regional variation within the HUP region: (1) those found in the speech of Hindi-Urdu native speakers being affected by dominant vernaculars in the area, such as Awadhi, Maithili, Panjabi, Pahari, etc.; and (2) those found in the speech of "associate" native speakers of Hindi-Urdu, retaining the diglossic function of their native vernaculars but accepting the use of Hindi-Urdu for wider communication.

Domain of a Language

A cursory look at the histories of different languages of South Asia provides numerous instances of shifts in the communication environments of a speech community or of sharp value conflicts among its subsections. Diverse historical accidents could lead to an expansion, split, shift, or

Plural Speech Communities

compromise among the domains of different languages (or speech varieties) available to a speech community. Such identity characteristics are quite noticeable in societies where speech conventions are not crystallized or are not explicitly defined through writing systems, grammatical descriptions, dictionaries, and other tools of standardization.

The processes resulting in the reshaping of the domain of a language (or speech variety) are elaborated below:

1. Expansion of the domain of a particular normative system by incorporating hitherto exterior speech varieties in its overall speech matrix.

In the thrust for solidarity and urbanity, the domain of Hindi has been progressively expanding by incorporating many vernaculars of the HUP region. The growing number of "associate" native speakers of Khariboli provides good evidence of this expansion (discussed in the previous section).

2. Overt split between the speech norms or ideals shared by a community. As a result of differing contact situations in history and conflicting values cherished by certain sections within the community, former dialects of the same language pull apart as distinct languages.

Historically, Konkani has been regarded as a dialect of Marathi (a South Indo-Aryan language). But during recent times many Konkani speakers have been asserting an identity independent from Marathi, as a result both of different norms of standardization established under Portuguese rule in Goa and of heterogeneous interaction with Dravidian (Kannada, Tulu, Malayalam) speakers farther south, often leading to diglossic complementation with these languages.

3. Shift in the nucleus of speech norms resulting in the emergence of a new model for a supradialectal communication network. Changes in the ideals as well as in the elite pressures in a community often lead to a shift in speech standards and hierarchical patterning of speech variations (Friedrich, 1966).

It is only during the past one hundred years that the development of creative prose writing in Khariboli has promoted that language as the main standard for the Hindi speech community; this has occurred at the expense of the Braj and Awadhi literary standards, which flourished until the end of the nineteenth century. Similarly, the Illyrian movement among Croatians in the Balkans during the last century prompted the "Kajkavian"-speaking elite to patronize the centrally located "Štokavian" variety as a literary norm of the Croatian language in order to pursue the unifying identity of the South Slavs, thus voluntarily reducing the Kajkavian variety, which had a rich literary heritage, to a vernacular status.

4. Compromise between independent and equally strong language traditions (which must necessarily be covering a narrow linguistic spectrum) by pushing them together as a single "polycentric" language (Kloss,

1967b) for the sake of promoting a "composite identity" among two (or more) speech groups.

Efforts to amalgamate Hindi-Urdu in undivided India and Serbian-Croatian in Yugoslavia are good examples of promoting a "composite" linguistic identity. During the Independence movement in India, various efforts were made by Mahatma Gandhi and others to elevate the status of Hindustani (to be written in both Devanagari and Perso-Arabic scripts) to pacify the growing animosity between the Hindu and Muslim pressure groups expressed through Sanskritized Hindi and Perso-Arabized Urdu.

In Yugoslavia, Serbo-Croatian (or Croato-Serbian, as insisted on by some Croatians for the sake of parity) represents a complex case of bimodal standardization as a "composite" linguistic identity, though still maintaining Serbian (in Cyrillic script) and Croatian (in Latin) literary standards as expressions of distinct cultural identities.

Fluctuations in the language responses of the census returns for the North-Central region of India reveal that speakers' claimed mother tongues are not based on their actual performance but are mainly guided by the trends of social identification at a particular time. In such situations, individuals' declarations are made out of the conviction that their mother tongue is part of a particular "tradition."

NOTES

1. "Hindi" (proper) as a mother tongue is one among 43 mother tongues classified as a "Hindi dialect," covering a total of 129 million speakers in the 1961 census. Other prominent dialects of the "Hindi language," though claimed by very small populations, are Bangru (subsuming 4 mother tongues), Braj Bhakha (5 mother tongues), Bundelkhandi (12), and Kanauji (1). (The 1961 census also classifies Awadhi and Chhatisgarhi, which were regarded as separate languages in Grierson's *Linguistic Survey of India* (1903-1928), as dialects of the Hindi language.)

2. Grierson, in the *Linguistic Survey* (1903-1928), classified 849 mother tongues (Mitra, 1964:213-220). Only 622 of them were attested to in the 1961 census. In addition, over 900 new "languages," which find no mention in Grierson's *Survey,* cropped up in the 1961 census as mother tongues. A high rate of birth and mortality of mother tongues in such a short span of time itself explains the instability of language identification among less rigidly defined speech groups.

3. Distinct characteristics of Serbian and Croatian literary standards are explicitly listed in various manuals based on the Novi Sad *Dogovor* (agreement) and a fair amount of vigilance is maintained among publication circles regarding its implementation through the "lektor" system, by which all writings presented in Serbian or Croatian are appraised according to the prescribed norms (Khubchandani, 1972c).

CHAPTER 6

Language Ideology in Education

THE ROOTS OF THE INTENSE LANGUAGE CONTROVERSIES in South Asia can be found in the "schizophrenic" handling of education by the British rulers. Various "native" pressure groups championing the cause of different languages were mobilized during the nineteenth century mainly because of the rulers' policies of arbitrarily distributing favors or expressing prejudices through language concessions or constraints (awarding or withdrawing recognition to one or another vernacular or writing system) to bring some order out of the "chaotic" diversity or, at times, to serve imperial interests. Various instant, but often vacillating, decisions with regard to language education on the part of the British rulers have played a vital role in shaking the traditional fluid modes of language loyalty in South Asia. The great debate about language policies between colonial administrators and the "native" elite, which lasted for over a century, has left a deep imprint on the contemporary language ideologies of different nations in the subcontinent (Das Gupta, 1970; Khubchandani, 1973e).

The Education System before the British

Language used in formal communication is conditioned by the administrative and educational systems prevailing in a society. Before the consolidation of British rule on the Indian subcontinent at the turn of the nineteenth century, there were two competing systems of education:

1. the *pāṭhaśālā* (school) and *gurukul* (residential school) system of the Brahmins;
2. the *maktab* (school) and *madrasseh* (college) system of the Muslims.

In medieval Europe, the language of education was Latin, the language of sacred literature; in India until the early decades of nineteenth century, the privileged languages of education were Sanskrit for the Hindus and Arabic-Persian for the Muslims. Under Muslim rule, certain Hindu elites made themselves conversant with both systems of education. Significant characteristics of the traditional educational establishment in India can be described as follows:

1. Education was regarded as an extension of the "primary" socialization process imparted through the immediate environments of family, caste, creed, and tradition; it provided a superstructure within the society in which an individual operated. It emphasized the "disciple-master" relationship between pupil and teacher. Education was restricted to members of the classes that provided the priests, the rulers, and the merchants. Two patterns, shaped by vocational relevance, were prominently recognized in the education system:

   a. *ordinary tradition,* representing the "practical" education provided to aspiring administrators and merchants to cope with the day-to-day needs of society (e.g., for use in lower courts, for maintaining accounts) through locally dominant vernaculars;
   b. *advanced tradition,* representing the "elegant" education provided to the elite (sons of priests, ruling classes, and high officials) by the reading of scriptures and historical texts in Sanskrit or Arabic-Persian.

2. The education system was oriented to preserving segmental identities in the society through language hierarchy by catering to the needs of the "ordinary" and "advanced" traditions. A built-in hierarchical structuring of linguistic skills in the society promoted a chain of mutually intelligible speech varieties—from local dialects, to subregional dialects, to a superregional network of dialects or languages and "highbrow" styles —in different diglossic situations.[1] The education system provided a measure of fluidity in the use of language according to the propriety considerations of context and purpose, which is a characteristic strength of a plural society.[2] Sanskrit and Arabic-Persian-speaking elites acted as liaison between the rulers and the masses. To some extent, Hindustani in the North, Tamil in the South, and Bengali in the East also served this purpose for some of the princely states while catering to the needs of the "ordinary" tradition.

3. Many regional systems of writing were used for the same language, varying according to locality and professional group. Besides the regional varieties of *Devanagari,* and the *Naskhi* and *Nastalik* characters of the Perso-Arabic script, many variants of *Mahajani* writing prevailed among

merchants. Scholars, drawn from the privileged few, had to be acquainted with a variety of writing systems, distinguished according to locality, social group, and domain of use.[3] Sanskrit of the "advanced" tradition was in vogue in more than one writing system. Apart from the Devanagari writing system, Sanskrit records are found in Grantha, Malayalam, and Telugu characters in the South; in Bhoti script in Tibet; in Sharada script in Kashmir; in Bengali and Maithili variations of Nagari writing in the East; and other regional variations of Devanagari script in different areas.

Language in Colonial Education

With the consolidation of British rule on the Indian subcontinent at the turn of the nineteenth century, the rival British education system known as *schools* soon eclipsed the traditional *pāṭhaśālā* and *maktab* education systems in large sections of British India, though many princely states continued their patronage of traditional educational institutions. For over one and a half centuries the colonial education policy went through different phases, depending on the political expediency of the times.

Initially, the change in the content of education from "traditional" to "Western" knowledge represented little more than a continuation of the earlier system, as far as the spread and the medium of education was concerned. But soon a sharp contrast developed between the missionary system and the government system of education over the questions of the spread and the medium. The missionaries were keen to set up rural schools with local vernaculars as the medium, in opposition to the "advanced" tradition of education; whereas the rulers' stress on education through the medium of English was aimed at attracting "respectable" members of Indian society to fill administrative positions (Document 5, Sharp, 1920).

At the same time, the British administrators themselves remained divided—the Orientalists represented by Princep and the Anglicists represented by Grant and Macaulay—over the basic issues of the education policy for Indian subjects (Documents 22, 30, and 34, Sharp, 1920). With the accruing privileges of economic status and social stratification, the Hindu and Muslim elites were lured to accepting English as their liaison language, abdicating or curtailing the use of Sanskrit and Persian for such purposes. Many Indian elites had realized that English was their gateway to the outer world. Hindu reformers and educationists like Raja Ram Mohan Roy and Ishwar Chandra Vidyasagar saw the incompatibility between the medium and the content of education. Hence they pleaded with the rulers to provide the English system of education to Indians. In 1823 Raja Ram Mohan Roy, citing the merits of the Baconian philosophy which displaced the system of classical schools—"the best calculated to perpetuate ignorance"—petitioned Prime Minister William Pitt to abolish the Sanskrit system: "[It] would be the best calculated to keep this country in darkness if such had been the policy of the British Legislature" (Document 26, Sharp, 1920: 98-101).

British administrators could not resolve the three basic issues of education: the content, the spread, and the medium (Dakin, 1968:5-12). Macaulay's hard line concerning the triple question was echoed in the education program of the British throughout their stay on the subcontinent. In his famous "Minute" of 1835, Macaulay recommended a policy of imparting Western knowledge through a Western tongue (English), and then only to a minority:

> It is impossible for us with our limited means to attempt to educate the body of the people. We must at present do our best to form a class who may be interpreters between us and the millions whom we govern—a class of persons Indian in blood and colour, but English in tastes, in opinions, in morals and in intellect. (Sharp, 1920:116)

Arguing with pungent rhetoric the intrinsic superiority of the English language, Macaulay claimed: "We have to educate a people who cannot be educated by means of their mother-tongue. We must teach them some foreign language. The claims of our own language it is hardly necessary to recapitulate. It stands pre-eminent even among the languages of the West . . . What the Greek and Latin were to the contemporaries of More and Ascham, our tongue is to the people of India" (Sharp, 1920:110-111).

In the same year, Governor General Bentinck, concurring in the sentiments of Macaulay, made it explicit that the "the great object of the British Government ought to be the promotion of European literature and science among the natives of India; and that all the funds appropriated for the purpose of education would be best employed on English education alone" (Sharp, 1920:130-131). Princep, however, favored the retention of the traditional education system. Registering his protest against the Bentinck Resolution, he called it "a rash act" and "a declaration of the mischievous and injurious tendency" (Document 34, Sharp, 1920: 139).

The Hardings Proclamation of 1844 further divorced the objectives of education from the environment by spelling out preferential treatment in recruitment for service in public offices "to those who were educated in English schools" (India, 1953:8).

During a later phase of the colonial period, British rulers modified their policy by accepting the responsibility for the education of the whole population, as recommended in the 1854 Wood Despatch (Richey, 1922: 367–392). It suggested the use of a vernacular medium "to teach the far larger class who are ignorant of, or imperfectly acquainted with, English." But the introduction of vernacular education was extremely slow, since in its actual implementation, when resources were allocated, the priority continued to be given to English secondary schools in cities and towns to the neglect of vernacular schools in villages. Though the rulers frequently proclaimed their policy of secular and vernacular education, individual administrators at the district level were often enthusiastic in lending direct or indirect support to promoting English education under missionary patronage.[4]

With the establishment of Calcutta, Bombay, and Madras universities in 1857, primary and secondary education became merely a step to fulfilling the requirements of entry to the university. These universities adopted English as the exclusive medium of instruction, and the study of Oriental learning as well as of the modern Indian languages remained largely neglected.

The Hunter Commission, reviewing in 1882 the implementation of the 1854 Despatch, recommended that priority should be given to primary education (through vernaculars) and that it should be made the responsibility of provincial governments. A shift in the rulers' policy—to run their administration at the lower level in the vernacular—also required setting up committees to develop a single script and to establish a single standard variety of the Indian langauges for use in formal communication. In 1902 the Education Commission recommended the mother tongue as the proper medium of instruction for all classes up to the higher secondary level.

In fact, the British recognized three types of education:

1. the English medium, in urban centers for the education of the elite, right from the primary stage;
2. the two-tier medium, vernacular for the primary stage and English for the advanced stage in towns;
3. the vernacular medium, in rural areas for primary education.

Thus, by the turn of the twentieth century, "although the official policy was that of the Despatch of 1854, it was Macaulay's policy of selective higher education in English that had achieved comparatively the greater success" under the plea of devoting the inadequate financial resources to improving the quality of education (Dakin, 1968:8).

During the long struggle for Indian independence, the selective education structure was vehemently criticized by the leaders of the Indian National Congress. Gokhale and other intellectuals, influenced by the Western literature of the eighteenth-century Enlightenment, saw the need for universal elementary education, and also put forward arguments for the use of the mother tongue in administration. Pleading for a self-governing India on Western lines, Gokhale, leader of the moderates in the Congress movement, argued: "the quality of education assumes significance only after illiteracy is liquidated" (Saiyidain, Naik, and Husain, 1952:65). The 1929 Hartog Report, on the other hand, emphasized "a drastic re-organization of the elementary system" before introducing "any wide application of compulsion."

During the 1930s, Mahatma Gandhi proposed a schema for "basic education" which was practically the antithesis of Macaulay's policy concerning the questions of content, spread, and medium. It attempted to resolve the conflict between educational quality and quantity by proposing to bring education into a closer relationship with the child's environment, and to extend it throughout rural areas without increasing the cost by integrating it with rural handicrafts. Nobel laureate Rabindranath Tagore also rejected both the manner and the content of English education.

Though Gandhi's self-supporting rural education was seriously contested by many Indian educationists, it found eventual acceptance in the 1944 Sargent Report which envisaged universal, compulsory, and free education for children between the ages of six and fourteen. "But the gap between the ambitions and achievement of British administration on the eve of Independence [in 1947] was immense. Though nearly every Province had passed a compulsory education bill, only one quarter of the school-age population was actually attending the school in 1948-49" (Dakin, 1968:9).

As is evident from this review, the British policies had a significant impact on the concept of education itself and also on the role of language in education for plural societies of the subcontinent.

Contrary to the "modern" values attributed to humanism, India was rather confronted with a deliberate policy of selective higher education to train an elite class to mediate between the masses and the British—a technologically superior "caste" or class. The English language, which was largely responsible for injecting "modern" thought into Oriental life, took over the dominant position hitherto enjoyed by "classical" Sanskrit and Persian. The British system of education in India thus perpetuated the dichotomy of the privileged language (English) versus vernaculars, whereas in Europe the accelerating modernization processes during the periods of the Renaissance and the Enlightenment had resurrected modern European languages from the dominance of the classical languages of Latin and Greek.

At the same time, the Western Enlightenment, absorbed through English contact, radically changed the concept of education for the Indian elite. The "modern" conviction of the supremacy of the mother tongue brought about demands from the language elite for the use of Indian vernaculars for formal communication (i.e., administration, academic achievement, etc.). Dayanand Saraswati (toward the end of the nineteenth century), Tagore (1906), and Gandhi (1916) were among the leading champions of the struggle for vernacularization in education. This trend, to a certain extent, shook the dichotomous structure of the liaison between the elites and the masses which existed in the medieval period and which was perpetuated by the English rulers. But, by and large, after a century and a half of colonial history, Macaulay's famous "Minute" advocating the filter-down approach to education shows prophetic validity.

The diversification of language use prevailing in the traditional educational system of South Asia was regarded by colonial rulers as a handicap (cf. Chapter 3). As was already discussed, the British rulers axiomatically correlated their own values of social homogenization and laid great emphasis on clear-cut categorization and monistic solutions concerning languages and scripts. Many administrators engaged in standardizing a single writing system and in prescribing a standard grammar for each language so as to bring order out of a "chaotic" situation. For example, immediately after their conquest of Sind in 1843, the British rulers set up a committee to decide upon a single script for Sindhi in the midst of diverse usage. Though philologists like Stack and Trumpp agreed upon a modified version of Devanagari to suit the needs of the Sindhi language, owing to political considerations the rulers ultimately decided in favor of a modified Perso-Arabic script. But even today Sindhi settlers in India continue to be divided over the formal recognition of one or another script.

Indian languages have traditionally been characterized by "loan proneness" from classical as well as from spoken languages. Bilingual contacts with English have been greatly instrumental in developing various styles of expression in Indian languages to cater to the needs of modern society. The Anglicization tendency in many languages is evident in the "highbrow" spoken styles among urban speech communities, which are markedly different from the "highbrow" written styles.

The introduction of the printing press also played a significant role in developing Indian prose through the publication of reference works, grammars, dictionaries, encyclopedias, and translations of creative literature and works of knowledge from different European languages.

The Mother Tongue as Instructional Medium

The politicization of the language issue in India during the struggle for independence dominated the medium controversy, pushing into the background the ideological issues concerning the content of education. The native elite's demand for vernacularization was associated with cultural and national resurgence, and eventually with the growth of democracy, promoting equality of opportunity through education (Tagore, 1906; Gandhi, 1916). All the maladies of "ineffective" education—lack of responsiveness, imitative goals, poverty of original thinking, prevalence of rote learning—and other imbalances in the traditional societies which were generated by the alien system were romantically attributed to the alien (i.e., English) medium.

One of the most intricate characteristics in the medium debate in many developing nations has been the uncritical acceptance of the Western theories of education of the early twentieth century, which were largely derived from the experience of dealing with issues of relatively more homogenized societies, and were developed when the thrust of technology was less pervasive than it is in present times. Many modern education experts regard it as axiomatic that the best medium for teaching a child is his mother tongue. Several psychological, educational, sociopolitical, and historical arguments have been advanced in support of this contention. In this vein, a UNESCO report (1935:11) recommended:

> Psychologically, it [the mother tongue] is the system of meaningful signs that in his mind works automatically for expression and understanding. Sociologically, it is a means of identification among the members of the community to which he belongs. Educationally, he learns more quickly through it than through an unfamiliar linguistic medium.

The Indian Secondary Education Commission (1956) also endorsed this view: "Learning through the mother tongue is the most potent and comprehensive medium for the expression of the student's entire personality."

In the midst of debating the use of the mother tongue as medium, education experts did not fully comprehend the plural character of Indian society, where a child's earliest firsthand speech experiences do not necessarily resemble the formal "school version" of his mother tongue. As discussed earlier, in societies where speech habits are not consistently identified with a particular label, esteem for a particular ideal of speech or a sociopolitical belief may lead individuals to identify with a prestigious major language group which need not necessarily be one's native speech (cf. Chapter 5).

Many sociopolitical and psychological generalizations about the supremacy of the mother tongue made during the Independence movement have, to a great extent, obscured the picture. The issues concerning the facility of expression in the mother tongue have been highlighted in rather simplistic terms by juxtaposing the mother tongue with the foreign language—English. Within this context, it is taken for granted that a foreign medium hampers the growth of creativity and talent. In this conflict, anti-Hindi lobbies regard even Hindi, along with English, as a foreign language. The supporters of the mother-tongue ideology have not cared to define the bounds of the concept of mother tongue, nor have adequate efforts been made to account for the diverse patterns of language hierarchy prevailing in multilingual plural societies.

In the postindependence period, in spite of severe criticism that the content of present education is not well-integrated with society, no formidable challenge has been posed to the white collar-oriented, urban-biased education. Gandhiji's program of basic education, catering to the needs of rural masses, has not seriously been tried by the national elite, still wedded to the lofty values of "elegance" in education.

The dichotomy perpetuated by the education system between those who have and those who do not have education continues to prevail in the form of urban-elite standards, as far as the medium and the content of education are concerned. One notices several inhibitions among educationists concerning the problems of the wide gap between the hinterland varieties and the urban-based standards of literary languages being imposed in schools as mother tongue.[5] In several elementary education curricula one often notices an overemphasis on careful drilling in the "correct" forms of standard regional speech and pronunciation. Thus, the acquisition of literacy in languages like Hindi, Urdu, Panjabi, Marathi, and Tamil resembles learning a "second" language.

So far, there does not seem to be much awareness of the difficulties the rural population faces because of the unintelligibility of the instant "highbrow" standards projected by textbooks in the mother tongue. This lack of recognition of the problem results in considerable waste and stagnation in literacy programs. Most standardization devices in Indian languages today serve only to extend the "tradition-inspired" value system of a few elites (mostly derived through literature) over all domains in the entire speech community. The language leaders' pleas to develop puristic "academic," "official" standards of language—along the lines of the nineteenth-century Latinized English and the Sanskritized or Perso-Arabized "highbrow" literary styles of Indian languages—put a heavy strain on the users of language and themselves contradict their concern with students' development of facility of expression through education in the mother tongue. The catholicity of the elite-acceptable diction of one's speech often makes native speakers "alien" and "handicapped" in their own surroundings. The new values and norms proclaimed for their speech behavior, especially in the domains of public communication—administration, education, mass media, and so forth (cf. Table 8, Chapter 4)—disable them in their efforts to cope with even simple communication needs.

Plural Media

The heterogeneity of communication patterns in many regions, the unequal cultivation of different languages for use as media, the demands of "highbrow," elegant versions of school mother tongue, the nonavailability of personnel with adequate command over the textbook language, and the switching over to another medium in the multitier media system without adequate preparation are some of the difficulties faced by learners who are initiated to education through the medium of the mother tongue.

As has already been discussed, the content, the spread, and the medium of instruction have been matters of great concern to educationists for a long time. Contemporary thinking on the subject has come a long way, from the early phase of selective education through the media of classical languages (such as Latin, Greek, Sanskrit, Persian, Arabic) and colonial languages (such as English, French, Spanish, Portuguese) to the later phase of universal education through the medium of the student's mother tongue. But the multiplicity of languages in various regions has led to a reexamination of the value of the supremacy of the mother-tongue medium stretched over the entire education career. In recent years, many political and academic agencies have lent their support to the claims of imparting education either through a single dominant language in the region or through some sort of compartmentalized or selective bilingual media, in order to keep pace with the socioeconomic demands of rapid modernization.

Against the background of a multiple-choice media policy, the three stages of education have acquired distinct patterns of choice in the Indian system:

1. *Primary stage*
   Dominant regional language
   Pan-Indian languages—English/Hindi
   Other major languages *or*
   Newly cultivated languages (mostly tribal and other minority languages as preparatory media)
2. *Secondary stage*
   Dominant regional language
   Pan-Indian languages—English/Hindi *or*
   Other major languages
3. *Higher education stage*
   English as developed medium *or*
   Hindi and regional languages as emerging media

In recent years some multilingual states, mostly in eastern India, have introduced as a state policy bilingual education in which a "developing" language in a region is used as a partial medium, together with English, Hindi, or the neighboring regional language as the major medium. Some states are initiating bilingual schooling for their tribal populations; various minority communities, particularly in urban areas, also prefer bilingual media, as is shown in Table 18.

In informal settings, one notices a good deal of code-switching and hybridization of two or more contact languages. There are many multilingual institutions with multilingual teachers who cater to the needs of diverse populations spread through every state. Many minority institu-

Table 18. Bilingual Media

Bilingual Media at the Primary Stage	State
A. Manipuri—English	Manipur
Khasi—English	Meghalaya
Garo—English	Meghalaya
Mizo—English	Mizoram
Assamese—English	Arunachal Pradesh
Hindi—English	Andaman and Nicobar Islands
B. Santali—Elementary Hindi	West Bengal
Tibetan—Elementary Hindi	West Bengal
Kui—Oriya	Orissa
C. Kashmiri—Urdu	Jammu and Kashmir
Urdu—English	Jammu and Kashmir
Sindhi—English	Maharashtra
Sindhi—Hindi	Delhi
Panjabi—Hindi	Chandigarh
Malayalam—English	Lakshadveep Islands

tions in every state impart education through minority languages, and/or through pan-Indian languages like English and Hindi, depending upon the availability of textbooks, teachers, and the trends of language maintenance in the community.

Types of media are very diversified. Though many states prefer to promote the "exclusive" use of the regional languages as the medium of instruction, in practice many students experience a shift in language medium at one or another state of their education career, depending upon context, domain, and channel:

1. *passive and active media:* students listen to lectures in one language and write answers in another;
2. *formal and informal media:* formal teaching in the classroom is conducted in one language, but informal explanations are provided in another language;
3. *multitier media:* elementary education is initiated through the mother tongue as the preparatory medium, but when a student moves upward in the education ladder he has to shift to a more "cultivated" medium.

In the present system of education, a majority of students, mostly after the high school stage, face the problem of switching over from their mother tongue to a common existing medium—English or, in a few cases, Hindi, at the university stage. The success of the multitier system lies in adequate preparation for shifting from one medium to another; to achieve this it will be useful to formally introduce bilingual education at the higher secondary stage (classes XI–XII), based on a combination of the mother tongue and common language(s)—English or Hindi—the proportion of the latter gradually increasing until English, Hindi, or both become the media at the postgraduate stage (Khubchandani, 1967).

Apart from positive attitudes to speech variation, bilingual and bicultural education require a degree of planning, a proficiency in the language of the classroom and in the language(s) of learners, and a high level of skill in teaching. The validity of these assumptions for a complex plural society, such as India, needs to be assessed, and the differential roles of mother tongues and nonnative languages as media of instruction also need to be elaborated. A critical appraisal of the programs of bilingual education in the United States (for Chicano, American Indian, and Micronesian bilingual programs); Canada (for English and French); the Soviet Union; Yugoslavia (for Serbo-Croatian, Hungarian, and Albanian programs); the Philippines (for Tagalog and English); and other countries can also provide a useful perspective regarding the apportionment of and procedures for using the available languages as media of instruction.

As has already been pointed out, in India one notices a wide gap between the language policies professed and actual classroom practice. In many institutions there exist anomalous patterns of communication where the teacher and the students interact in one language, classes are conducted in another, textbooks are written in a third, and answers are given in a fourth language or style. Thus, one finds that the linguistic needs and the capacity of learners are the greatest casualties in the present language-education system.

Identity versus Communication

Language identity in India today is characterized by the demands of language privileges in different walks of life, and consequently the "highbrow" content of privileged language is cherished for its "ornate" functions, particularly in the school system. As an illustration, many Hindi, Urdu, and English teaching programs in the South Asian subcontinent usually ignore local interactional opportunities and are devised as if they were to be conducted in totally alien environments. Students within the Bombay metropolis learn one version of Hindi (Sanskritic Khariboli) in schools, while functioning actively in quite a different version of Hindi (known as Bombay Hindustani), which is stigmatized as "inferior" or "corrupt" Hindi in the elite-value system. At the same time, one is surprised to find that many native speakers of Khariboli (standard Hindi) settled in Bombay themselves acquire Bombay Hindustani as a mark of prestige and to signal their links with the region. Thus Sanskritic Khariboli (officially sponsored Hindi) remains largely dysfunctional outside the corridors of school. No wonder, then, that a large number of students quite at ease in their Bombay Hindustani consider school Hindi to be very tedious, and fail to score good marks in the subject. On the other hand, the Bombay metropolis abounds in instances where many illiterate migrants from different regions acquire a good command over one or more subsidiary languages (Hindi, Marathi, Gujarati) without much strenuous effort by participating in natural "language events" (in other words, by "doing" a language).

Present second and foreign language programs seem to be operating in a vicious circle of selecting teaching and curricular matrices and then assessing the proficiency of pupils on the basis of the same materials. These programs, whether conducted through reading-based systems (inherited from the tradition of teaching classical languages) or through the oral-aural system, regard the classroom (often extended to the language laboratory) as the sole reservoir of language learning. Language in such situations is taught as an "exercise" or as a preparation for eventual utilization goals, but with no immediate plans whatsoever for reinforcement outside the classroom. As a result, the task of the students demands strenuous effort and intense motivation. In such programs, classroom "exercises" in the target language become an end in themselves. No communicative task is actually performed.

Many linguists are now turning their attention to the notion of effectiveness in communication, that is, making one's language actually *do* things. Language as a means of communication and of social mobility in a plural society acquires significantly different characteristics under the pressures of modernization. It is the rural and working class learners who bear most of the brunt of the imbalance arising from the lopsided emphasis on language privileges and language elegance at the cost of effective communication.

Many language-standardizing agencies (such as school), in evaluating effectiveness of communication, tend to be concerned exclusively with the homogeneous grasp of language skills. Yet this is only one factor, although no doubt a significant one, in human communication. In the reality of everyday life, one does not find the pedantic dichotomy of "right" versus "wrong" (acceptable-unacceptable) utterances in a language. Deviations from the "norm" in specific situations could be more appropriate, purposeful, amusing, pejorative, offensive, ambiguous, hazardous, unintelligible, socially neutral, or revealing of a group (characteristic of a region, strata, class, etc.) than so-called normative language.

In cross-purpose encounters as well as in cross-cultural settings one often notices that although some message is communicated, it is perhaps not the one intended. Barriers to communication are often highlighted through the difficulties people have in understanding one another if they do not have a language (dialect, register) or experience in common; in other words, it is alleged that there is lack of reciprocity of language skills among the communicators. But one generally fails to identify the miscues in communication that arise from the lack of common interest and discordant values and attitudes in an interaction (i.e., the mutuality of focus), even though the communicators possess ample reciprocity of language skills.

In the school value system, nonstandard varieties have been rated grammatically as "incorrect" and "bad," conceptually as "deficient," and sociologically as "deprived." In school-lore, the educational disadvantage experienced by rural and poor children is often thought to have its origins in the language deprivation the child suffers at home in the preschool years and afterward (Bernstein, 1971).

Under the influence of progressive theories, many educators are now coming around to the view that the child's perception of reality should be accepted on its own terms rather than be treated as a sort of "deficiency" in his system. These developments throw doubts on the exclusive concentration upon elite culture in schools where the majority of students has to struggle to catch up with the Joneses in their linguistic competence (for an interesting account of this race between Upper and non-Upper usage in British English, see A. Ross, 1959). Labov's studies show in definitive terms that language differences among blacks in the United States can be specific and of equal value; they handle abstract and logical arguments effectively:

> " 'Cause, you see, doesn' nobody really know that it's a God, y'know, 'cause I mean I have seen black gods, pink gods, white gods, all color gods, and don't nobody know it's really a God. An' when they be sayin' if you good, you goin't' heaven, tha's bullshit, 'cause you ain' goin' to no heaven, 'cause it ain't no heaven for you to go to . . . I'll tell you why. 'Cause the average whitey out here got everythin', you dig? An' the nigger ain't got shit, y'know? Y'unnerstan'? So-um-for-in order for *that* to happen, y'know it ain't no black God that's doin' that bullshit." (Labov, 1972: 194–196)

During the past few decades a significant shift in modern linguistics has drawn attention away from the "prescription" of language toward "relativism" in speech, refusing to make absolute value judgments about human communication. Current sociolinguistic studies accept speech variation as a "natural" process of verbal behavior, and lend powerful support to the view that "there is actually no such thing as a slovenly dialect or accent" (Halliday et al., 1964:103).

Questioning the theory of deprived culture (assessed by means of I.Q. tests and other such devices), these studies assert that the so-called poor culture does have educational skills which are not exploited in the conventional school system: ". . . in many ways working-class speakers are more effective narrators, reasoners and debaters than many middle-class speakers who temporize, qualify and lose their argument in a mass of irrelevant detail" (Labov, 1972:193).

How far do the differences in speech behavior we observe in our population reflect differences in *adequacy* as opposed to *acceptable* variation? This inquiry raises certain fundamental issues that need to be probed in an interdisciplinary perspective. How does language structure reality—both in the child's "innocent" view of his universe, and in the adult's "culturally determined" view of phenomena? "How far a child's ability to think internally is related to the external evidence of this thinking, by words? A standard language use is often equated with good standard thoughts; but this may not be the case" (Wilkinson, 1975:ii–iii). In what manner do the "highbrow" values of speech, taken for granted in the education system, actually meet the demands of adequacy and effectiveness in everyday communication among rural and working-class children? "To elaborate is not necessarily to clarify; it is sometimes more likely to complicate and often to confuse" (Searle, 1973:136). In this respect, Whitehead's (1932) remarks on "hard-headed" clarity merit serious attention: "Insistence on clarity at all costs is based on sheer superstition as to the mode in which human intelligence functions. Our reasonings grasp at straws for premises and float on gossamers for deductions" (1948 ed.:91).

The present-day goals of teaching a mother tongue or a second language, being primarily conditioned by the criterion of excellence in the normative sense, have, in a way, been instrumental in leading to the erosion of some of the humanistic qualities in everyday life communication. The classroom provides a situation typically of unequal language exchange both in type and in balance. The Barbiana *Letter* (1970), raising an accusing finger at the teacher who represents the higher-class values of speech, points to the fundamental rights of individuals: "All citizens are equal without distinction as to language . . . But you honour grammar more than constitutions."

Classroom language is characterized by its rational usage, which is only one of the sociolinguistic variables in actual speech activity. Classroom interaction generally puts a premium on explicit, unambiguous, overt manifestation through language. Teachers' stress on normative standards in the classroom demands "appropriate" language behavior from pupils, and rejects indirect, side-tracking, witty, or mischievous answers. Such schooling promotes "empty verbalism" among cunning pupils, behind which there is no real understanding. We need to look at a student's speech in everyday life and his interpretation of the classroom situation, in the light of the demands made by the teacher. There is no intrinsic advantage in holding to the superiority of adult communication in the classroom.

Various impediments to the spread of education are attributed to the multiplicity of languages, whereas the real issues are the confrontation between "tradition" and "modernity" concerning the role of language in education, and dogmatic rigidity in claiming privileges for different languages in educational curriculum in the thrust for "autonomy." When dealing with education in plural societies, we shall do well to realize the risks involved in attempting uniform solutions.

NOTES

1. For a detailed account of the patterns of hierarchy in language loyalties in the broad Hindustani region, see Gumperz and Naim (1960) and Khubchandani (1972a, 1974a).

2. The Collector of the Bellary district (presently in Karnataka State) in 1823 reported that out of 533 schools in the district, 235 schools employed Carnataca (Kannada), 226 Teloogoo (Telugu), 23 Maharatta (Marathi), 21 Persian, 4 Tamil, and one the English medium; moreover, 23 schools were exclusively for Brahmins, teaching "some of the Hindoo sciences, such as theology, astronomy, logic and law, still imperfectly taught in the Sanscrit language" (Sharp, 1920:65).

3. Burton (1851:134-157) gives an elaborate account of the multilingual pattern of education in Sindh before its conquest by the British in 1843. According to him, a Hindu child started by learning the Devanagari script from a Brahmin teacher to study religious texts in Sindhi, and also acquired the rudiments of Sanskrit. He also learned Gurumukhi characters to read the *Guru Granth*—a sacred text of the Sikhs and Hindus in northern India. An *Amil* boy (belonging to the "courtly" Hindu class) then moved to an *Akhund* (a Muslim or Hindu pedagogue under the *maktab* system) and was introduced to popular Persian poetry. A few studied Arabic also. The *Amil* boy is "then taken to some *daftar* (secretariat) by a relation to be initiated in the mysteries of *arzi* (petition writing in Persian), simple calculation, etc." (p. 149).

4. Johnstone, the Political Agent of Nagaland (1873-1874), opposed the adoption of the "effeminate ways and religious characteristics of the Assamese [language]" and wanted the Nagas to be instructed in the English language and the Christian religion under the clergy of the Church of England (Barpujari, 1973:24-30).

5. The Central Advisory Board of Education in its 1938 annual meeting accepted the literary language of the region as the medium of education and made it quite clear that dialects were unacceptable as media of instruction (India, 1960: 39-40).

CHAPTER 7

Pressures from Language Elites

DURING RECENT DECADES in many developing countries, language-loyalty pressures have increased sharply in political and educational systems; consequently, language is emerging as one of the most important elements in identifying with a "group"—an emblem of national or group solidarity.

Considering the linguistically heterogeneous composition of nearly half of the districts in India, the numerical majority of twelve regional languages in the respective regions does not necessarily correspond with the language communication patterns in those areas (cf. Chapter 1). The demands for the use of regional languages as media during the struggle for independence signified, to a large extent, assertive attitudes of the pressure groups aligned with the numerically dominant language in a region.

Group Dynamics

During the past three decades, with the politicization of language pressure groups, attention has increasingly focused on legislating the role of languages in public spheres of communication, that is, administration, education, mass media, and so on (Nayar, 1969; Das Gupta, 1970). In this regard, national leaders show great mastery in tightrope walking, recognizing the strengths and weaknesses of diverse pressure groups in language politics. With a view toward resolving the highly sensitized issues of language privileges, several language labels—such as home language, regional language, link language, national language, official language, literary language, library language, world language—have acquired political salience in educational and other developmental programs. A cursory glance at the patterns of group dynamics as projected through confronting language elites in India draws our attention to some of the complexities involved in determining a language policy for multilingual societies.

The Hindi-Urdu struggle on the Indo-Pakistan subcontinent provides a typical example for understanding the nature of the conflict that was simmering between the two pressure groups well before the forces of "modernization" came to play any significant role on the Indian scene. The conflict came to the surface mainly as a consequence of the simultaneous decline of the Persian language in the Mughal court and elevation of Persianized Khariboli (called Hindvi, Rekhta, Urdu, Dakhini) in its place, at the time when the influence of the Mughal rulers was itself on the decline. In this regard, the role played by the British rulers in aggravating conflicting loyalties, which eventually were utilized as effective weapons for political mobilization, needs to be critically assessed. The failure of the Hindi and Urdu particularist elites to agree to Mahatma Gandhi's proposal to elevate the "composite" Hindustani language to a national status reflected the rigid political postures (for the sake of influencing the higher echelons of authority) during the period of colonial rule. This contributed, in a significant way, to the partition of the country. Immediately after independence, no doubt, the Sanskritic Hindi elite succeeded in installing Hindi (not Hindustani) as the official language in constitutional provisions by means of the adversary principle instead of the accepted consensus tradition prevailing in the Indian National Congress party. But they could not escape accommodating the "composite" attributes of Hindustani (namely, international numerals, borrowings from the languages listed under the Eighth Schedule), although with many reservations and conflicting interpretations. The result is the constitutional directive for the development of Hindi (Article 351), which provides a unique specimen of the most intricate and ambiguous "language engineering" ever envisaged through legislation. "These conflicts, more often than not, have proved to be the schools of bargaining and negotiation" (Das Gupta, 1970:269).

As discussed earlier, the dominance of English during the period of British rule caused a reaction to the other extreme: a feverish campaign for a total switch from English to indigenous languages in the post-British period. The demand for the immediate expulsion of English in favor of Indian languages (though it might generate a "vacuum" in transition) is generally voiced out of concern for optimal development of latent talent through the full use of a mother tongue. But at the same time it is, to a great extent, motivated by the issues of employment and economic opportunities. Alienation of the established elite from the masses has been a great source of irritation to the newly rising democratic forces in the country. The revolt against the English language, apart from havng overtones of national pride, is primarily the symptom of the revolt against the established, privileged "caste."

The established elite, on the other hand, has a vested interest in maintaining the predominance of English in all spheres of life, and has been clamoring for the status quo in the name of Indian unity and stressing the advantages to a nation in possessing a "world" language. The clash of interests between regional languages and Hindi and the "underdevelopment" of Indian languages for modern needs are cited as factors necessitating the retention of English. The task of language transition could be somewhat smoother if the "established" English elite were to give up the notion of "exclusive dominance" and work in "partnership" with Indian languages in the field of public communication. There is a good deal of truth in the charge that the Westernized intelligentsia do not care to address their own people but seek an international audience and, within the country, stay within the "clubs" of their self-restricted elite. The English-educated elite in India develop a kind of "dual personality." Their personal life is virtually sealed off from their drawing room behavior, acquired through education in "a kind of linguistic polythene bag" (Le Page, 1964:20).

The battle over the role of language in education and other privileges has been fought largely in the political arena. Often language has been used as a weapon in the struggle for political power. During the Independence movement, local languages were used as a means of arousing the masses against the "alien" system. "What Hindi was to be on the national scale, the regional languages were on the provincial scale: a rallying cry, and a means of ruling" (Dakin, 1968:31). After independence, the language elites, equipped with the verbal affluence of multilingual societies, continued to engage in the manipulative game of settling their scores on the sociopolitical front. While many governmental agencies under the pressure of democratization may be eager to discard English in favor of regional languages, the agencies engaged in trade and technology still judge an individual's achievement orientation and merit on the basis of English. The masses in general, lured by the "magnetic" pull of modernization, also do not show as much disenchantment with English, or hostility toward it, as is evident from a section of the leadership. English-medium schools are still very much sought after by the social elite or by those who want entry into the ranks of the social elite through their children.

The solution to the controversy of English versus Indian languages lies neither in discarding English altogether nor in reducing it to a barely minimal functioning in Indian society because of an inferiority complex, but in changing the colonial domination role of English so that it has equal participation with the developing Indian languages in the multilingual communication network.

Privileges of Language Study

In this light, a critical review of the processes involved in arriving at amicable decisions concerning language policy in education would provide useful insights into the characteristics of group dynamics among plural societies in a federal democratic polity.

Amid sharp controversies concerning the role of different languages in education, a broad consensus has been arrived at in the three-language formula, which provides a basis of policy for prescribing languages in school education (Khubchandani, 1967). The definition of a mother tongue and the feasibility of teaching a mother tongue to linguistic minorities in different states on the grounds of practicability have dominated the thinking of policymakers in assigning a language the first place for study during the primary and secondary stages of education. The introduction of second and third languages at the lower and higher secondary stages has remained bound up with the issues of language privileges, cultural prestige, and socioeconomic mobility.

The University Education Commission in 1949 first considered the teaching of a regional language, a general language (Hindi), and English in schools. In 1953 the Secondary Education Commission, in a rather generous mood, suggested the teaching of five languages: mother tongue, regional language, two "federal" languages—Hindi and English—and also optionally a classical language, Sanskrit, Pali, Prakrit, Persian, Arabic. The Council for Secondary Education (1956) settled down to the three-language formula, recommending mother tongue, Hindi, and English for the non-Hindi-speaking population; and Hindi, any other Indian language, and English for the Hindi-speaking population. The Central Advisory Board of Education in 1957 also endorsed the formula. But the struggle between the Hindi and English lobbies continued over the issue of second place in the education curriculum under the three-language formula.

In 1966 the Education Commission recommended a liberalized version of the formula, according to which it is expected that a student, on the completion of the lower secondary stage, will have acquired sufficient control over three languages: mother tongue and two nonnative modern languages, broadly, Hindi as an official medium and a link language for the majority of people for interstate communication, and English as an associate official medium and a link language for higher education and for intellectual and international communication. The choice of determining the second or third places for Hindi or English was left to the individual states.

According to the modified formula: (1) mother tongue or regional language will be studied for ten years (classes I-X, ages six to fifteen years); (2) the official language—Hindi, or the associate official language of the

Union, English—will be taught for a minimum of six years (classes V–X, ages ten to fifteen years); and (3) a modern Indian or foreign language—not covered under (1) and (2) and not used as the medium language—will be studied for a minimum of three years (classes VIII–X, ages thirteen to fifteen years).

But the formula has been differently interpreted by different states. On the one hand, Hindi states like Uttar Pradesh, Rajasthan, and Himachal Pradesh provide "classical" Sanskrit as the third language, in place of a "modern" Indian language; on the other hand, West Bengal and Orissa also favor Sanskrit at the cost of Hindi as the third language.

Because of the prevailing antagonism over the language issue, many state institutions dodge the compulsory provision of teaching second and third languages (Hindi and English) by making "passing" (securing credits) in these languages optional. Two states—Tamil Nadu and Mizoram—have backed out of the compulsory provision of the third language as envisaged in the formula, thus avoiding the teaching of Hindi.

For several linguistic minorities, it has become virtually a four-language formula, as many state governments insist on the compulsory teaching of a regional language. Confined to small pockets in almost all states there are many minority languages, the speakers of which comprise nearly 24 percent of the nation's population (1961 census). Some of these languages are widely spread within a state or are spread over more than one state: for example, Bhili is found in Madhya Pradesh, Maharashtra, and Rajasthan; Santali in Bihar, West Bengal, and Assam; Kurukh in Bihar, Orissa, and West Bengal; and Garo in Meghalaya and Tripura.

Some states, such as Andhra Pradesh, Karnataka, and Maharashtra, are experimenting with teaching "composite" courses by combining a modern Indian language, usually the mother tongue, with a classical language (Sanskrit, or Urdu along with classical Arabic) to be offered as first language after the primary stage.

Generally the number of languages provided for teaching at the elementary stage is higher, and the number is reduced as a student moves upward on the educational ladder. Various criteria are applied in different states for selecting languages as a subject of study: number of speakers, spread of the speakers in different areas, cultivation of language, and so on.

In addition to the compulsory teaching of three languages under the formula, many states provide for the teaching of one or two additional languages on an optional basis. Optional languages are usually the additional regional language(s) for linguistic minorities; or they may be a classical language (Sanskrit, Pali, Ardhamagadhi, Avestha, Persian, Arabic, Hebrew, Greek, Latin); Hindi; English; or any other modern Indian or foreign language (French, German, Italian, Spanish). These are usually studied at the terminal stages of school education, stretching from three to six years. Some institutions manipulate the choice of other subjects in favor of studying optional languages; for example, Rajasthan allows the study of three optional languages at a time. The most popular options among the classical languages are Sanskrit, Arabic, and Persian. In the eastern states, Maithili, Nepali, Santali, Khasi, Garo, Manipuri, Mizo, and Bodo are also offered on an optional basis. Khasi is offered as a subject of study up to the bachelor of arts degree in Meghalaya. Recently Dogri has also been introduced as a subject of study in the Jammu and Kashmir State.

Different weight is assigned to different languages in the total instructional program. Different states assign between one-fourth and two-thirds of the total teaching periods to the teaching of languages. The percentage of the time allotted to compulsory (and optional) language teaching is shown in Table 19 (Chaturvedi, 1976).

In spite of the heavy weight given to language learning in the education system, one notices a general devaluation of language instruction due to the lack of motivation and also to the lack of coordination. So far the general structure of language instruction has not been studied objectively and the linguistic content has not been spelled out adequately. The allotment of more or less time to the teaching of a particular language is judged as a prestige or status issue for that language. In the absence of a clear objective in learning a language, one notices many political pressures—literary prestige of a language, sociopolitical privileges of language speakers—being applied for incorporating specific languages in the curriculum. At certain places language programs are allotted an out-of-proportion share in the total teaching load in order to suit the climate of language privileges.

Struggle over the University Language Medium

When the British left the country in 1947, there were many schools in which education up to the primary and secondary stages was given in the major Indian languages of the respective regions. But at the higher education stages, the universities recognized only English as the medium, with no alternatives. Osmania University, located at Hyderabad in the Telugu-speaking princely state of Nizam, was an exception in introducing the Urdu medium to maintain the traditional Muslim education.

During the independence struggle, in the thrust for language autonomy and language privileges, many political and educational organizations had exerted strong pressures to extend Indian languages as media at the university level. The All-India Universities Conference in 1939 had recommended that the mother tongue of students should be the medium

Table 19. Time Allotted to Language Instruction in Different States, Class X (1974)

Schools in State or Union Territory	Percentage of Periods Assigned to Compulsory Language Teaching	Total Periods per Week	Periods Allotted to Compulsory Languages	Periods Allotted to Optional Languages
Jammu and Kashmir	61.1	54	33	—
West Bengal	59.0	39	23	—
Assam	56.4	39	22	5
Manipur	53.8	39	21	—
Tripura	48.7	39	19	5
Haryana	47.7	44	21	5
Uttar Pradesh	45.8	48	22	5
Chandigarh	45.8	48	22	—
Kerala	45.7	35	16	4
Panjab	43.8	48	21	5
Goa, Daman, and Diu	42.9	42	18	5
Lakshadveep Islands	42.5	40	17	—
Dadra and Nagar Haveli	42.2	45	19	—
Delhi	41.7	48	20	—
Orissa	41.0	39	16	4
Bihar	41.0	39	16	—
Arunachal Pradesh	40.0	40	16	—
Himachal Pradesh	38.1	42	16	4
Madhya Pradesh	37.5	48	18	6
Rajasthan	37.5	48	18	—
Andaman and Nicobar Islands	37.5	48	18	—
Maharashtra	36.4	44	16	6
Gujarat	34.0	50	17	12
Andhra Pradesh	33.3	48	16	—
Karnataka	32.5	40	13	—
Tamil Nadu	31.5	35	11	—
Mizoram	28.9	38	11	—
Nagaland	26.5	49	13	—
Meghalaya	26.2	42	11	—

of instruction at different stages of education up to degree courses. This recommendation was again endorsed by the fourth Conference of Indian Universities in 1943 and by the Central Advisory Board of Education in 1946 (India, 1960:156).

Initially, the new Congress government showed a good deal of enthusiasm for rapid change in the language-medium policy, and some universities expressed their willingness to introduce Hindi, Urdu, and other regional languages as media in five years' time (India, 1948). The University Education Commission in 1949 also endorsed the view that the switchover to education in the mother tongue should be achieved within the next five years in all universities so as to promote cultural renaissance and social integration. But soon it became evident that due to ideological conflicts among the national leaders and to the unenthusiastic response of the education experts who operated within the "established" system, the government had to face an uphill task as far as the fulfillment of such aspirations was concerned.

In this struggle for leadership among the "established" and the "rising" power elites, various language interest groups adopted rigid stands regarding language policy at the university stage:

1. the supporters of English claimed the virtues of having an "advanced" medium for technological and scientific progress;
2. the supporters of Hindi were motivated by the interests of cultural regeneration and cohesion at the national level;
3. the supporters of regional languages emphasized the facility of expression for students and were guided by the claims of equal privileges and autonomy for their languages.

National leaders like Jawaharlal Nehru, Maulana Azad, and Zakir Hussain (1950) were the early champions of the common medium. Trying to moderate the rigid postures in the medium controversy, they suggested the alternate media policy, in which Hindi, serving the national interests, could be adopted as the university medium along with English as a universally developed medium of knowledge. But the Tarachand Commission (1948) rejected Hindi as the common medium for universities and suggested regional media in the states for administrative and academic purposes, restricting the common medium to the federal government.

The Official Language Commission in 1956 spelled out the criteria for the choice of medium at the university stage on the basis of the facility of expression and the usefulness of the medium for students. It endorsed the alternate media policy, with regional language as the major medium. A variety of solutions emerged from the dissenting notes:

1. English with alternatives (Hindi, or dominant regional language);
2. Hindi with alternatives (English, or regional language);
3. Hindi the sole medium;
4. Regional language the sole medium.

The latter two suggestions were later dubbed as expressions of "Hindi imperialism" and "language chauvinism," respectively, by the opponents of these solutions in the controversy.

During the 1950s many sociopolitical and legal battles were fought over the university medium issue as it concerned Bombay, Gujarat, and Madras universities. The enthusiasm of the respective state governments for switching over to Hindi (for Bombay University), Gujarati (for Gujarat University), and Tamil (for Madras University) was frustrated by professional bodies. Hence, by and large, the states had to compromise and leave largely unimplemented the program of switching over in the universities. At the time of the linguistic reorganization of the states in 1956, it was strongly felt throughout the country that language tensions were undermining national unity. The demand for a nationwide common medium gained momentum on the strength of the argument that national loyalty required free and rather intense communication within the nation and that regional languages as the sole media would damage the country's administrative, judicial, and academic integrity and scientific pursuits.

The University Grants Commission (UGC) in its 1960 report pointed to the difficulties of students when moving from a school using a mother tongue as instructional medium to the English-medium university education, leading to rote learning and the crippling of original thought. It strongly argued that the sole dependence on English was widening the gulf between the educated few and the uneducated masses, which could not be nourished in a democratic society. Earlier the Official Language Commission (1956) had also emphasized the detrimental effects of English-medium education, characterizing it as "a wearisome burdening of the memory, a sacrifice of the faculty of independent thinking, and a blunting of intellect" (p. 89).

Hence, from early stands in sole support of English, Hindi, or a regional language, by 1961 a new approach promoting a link language had gained favor among national leaders. English and Hindi enthusiasts again seized the opportunity for claiming the "new" link status. Some southern and eastern states showed a preference for English in place of Hindi as a common medium. The *link language formula* was evolved by the Central Advisory Board of Education in 1962, suggesting that a regional-language medium would be necessary to remove the gap between the masses and the elites and that English as the "transitional" and Hindi as the "eventual" link language would promote national unity, mobility among teachers and students, and the standards of education. The timing of the switchover to the new system was left open. Concerning the eventual adoption of Hindi as the link language, a veto was given to the states and also to the professionals to ensure a gradual and well-prepared change from English to regional languages and Hindi, on lines similar to the 1835 Macaulay doctrine of "refining the vernacular dialects" (cf. Chapter 2).

After the unsuccessful attempts of the 1950s, the forces of hypersensitive language chauvinism are now considerably weakened, and rapid change in shifting the media of education at the university level is ruled out. The status quo of English as a compulsory medium for some time to come is now being widely accepted on most university campuses, on the grounds that knowledge is more important than the medium, and standards are more important than timetables. By hard struggle the Indian languages are now proving themselves increasingly practicable and acceptable for a wider range of study in the "elitist" framework of education. Today, after the lapse of more than a quarter century, the citadels of higher learning have yielded only in providing an alternate medium of regional language, usually associated with the "ordinary" tradition in education, for humanities and commerce courses up to the graduate level.

The quality and prestige of the "advanced" tradition still rests with the English medium. In a survey conducted at Nagpur University, it was found that although Hindi and Marathi were compulsory media for undergraduate arts and science courses, 88 percent of the science students in 1955 obtained "special permission" to study through the English medium. Failures in both arts and science faculties were higher among the regional-medium students. These findings reveal that the better students prefer English and are able to cope with it (Dakin, 1968:28-29).

There were more than twenty universities in the mid 1970s which still maintained their unilingual character and provided education only through English. These were the universities in the metropolitan areas—Bombay, Calcutta, Madras; many southern universities such as Bangalore, Kerala, Sri Venkateswara (Tirupathi); and also those imparting professional education, such as agricultural and technological institutions, where there is no alternative to English. At the same time, many universities of the Hindi and Bengali regions have been relatively more enthusiastic about providing regional language as an alternate medium along with English.

Thus the supporters of the English status quo won the battle of time, and the Hindi and regional-language supporters felt contented with the formal recognition of their viewpoint, and also with their claims to large funds for language development.

Linguistic Minorities

In a large nation committed to the gigantic task of eradicating illiteracy it is rather amazing to find that the intellectuals, with their political power and educational expertise, have become entangled in the web of language privileges at the university level under the pretexts of concern for the range and quality of education. During British rule the English medium indisputably remained a mark of a superior, "advanced" education, and the regional-language media were conceded the role of somewhat inferior, "ordinary" education in rural and urban areas.

With the professed policy of the Indianization of the "alien" education system, the administrators were soon confronted with demands from the linguistic minorities for education in mother tongues. Initially the administrators' approach was of "harassed bureaucrats trying to impose a workable system on linguistic chaos" (Dakin, 1968:31). Eighty-seven percent of the country's total population is aligned with twelve major regional languages: 76 percent residing in their home states and 11 percent staying outside their language regions (Khubchandani, 1972b). Once the dominant groups' right to education in a mother tongue was fully assured in their respective states, the new governing class did not lose much time in focusing its attention on the practical objectives of economy, utility, communication, and political cohesion, as far as they pertained to the demands of the remaining 13 percent of linguistic minorities, comprising a total of more than 50 million speakers (at the time of the 1961 census).

The first president of India, Dr. Rajendra Prasad, pointed out in 1961 that the costs of making separate arrangements for education in a mother tongue for different linguistic groups would be "colossal" and "feasible only if the linguistic group is of an appreciable size and forms a compact region. It cannot be reasonably demanded by those who are very small in number or are scattered in different parts of other linguistic regions" (India, 1961) . The secretary to the University Grants Commission also pointed out that "A child bred in an area where the regional language is something other than its own mother tongue acquires the regional language with almost the same facility as that with which he acquires [his] mother tongue" (Mathai,1959: 9–10).

After initial reluctance, the narrow interpretation of mother tongue (cf. Chapter 3) was conceded in favor of linguistic minorities who identified with a major language outside the region—languages which "transcended provincial barriers" (Azad, 1949). But major languages without any specific region, such as Urdu and Sindhi, had to face initial discrimination in certain states like Uttar Pradesh in getting the facilities for education in a mother tongue. Concessions to tribal and other minority languages were slow in coming. The All-India Language Development

Pressures from Language Elites

Conference in 1953 and the Congress Working Committee in 1954 accepted tribal languages as media in the primary school stage. The second Five-Year Plan in 1956 also mentioned, under tribal welfare programs, facilities for preparing special textbooks in different tribal languages (pp. 589-590). In 1956, Articles 350A and 350B were inserted in the Constitution by the Seventh Amendment Act, according to which "It shall be the endeavour of every State to provide adequate facilities for instruction in the mother tongue at the primary stage of education to children belonging to linguistic minority groups." But as the constitutional provisions for safeguarding the interests of the linguistic minorities are recommendatory and not mandatory, one notices a lack of enthusiasm on the part of state authorities in implementing such programs. The authorities, by and large, still have not given up the hope that in practice the linguistic minorities will come to accept the advantages of the regional languages (cf. Chapter 4).

Polarization of Issues

Many of the issues generating acrimonious debates at the national level, sometimes erupting into campus skirmishes, do not seem to have much relevance to the quality of education. Prominent axes over which the medium controversy has become polarized during the past 150 years are shown in Table 20.

In the long-drawn-out sociopolitical and legal squabbles over the language medium, one notices various shades of opinions between the two extremes. Eventually the experts upholding the status quo seem to have temporarily succeeded in their strategy in insisting that the Indian vernaculars should first be cultivated through translations from advanced languages and, even before undertaking this task, they must equip themselves with the scientific terminologies appropriate for different subjects. Because of the "highbrow" elegant values in formal language behavior, the task of cultivating urban-based standards has been the prerogative of the so-called purists of language. Ironically, in elite parlance, the modern languages saturated with "instant" derivative terms from nonnative classical and neoclassical stocks—Sanskrit, Perso-Arabic, or classical Tamil—are regarded as *śuddha* (pure) languages, but those mixed with everyday terms borrowed from other living languages—such as English, Bengali, and Marathi, matching the newly acquired concepts from different cultures—are regarded as *khichRii* (hotchpotch, potpourri) languages (Khubchandani, 1968).

The preparation of textbooks to teach technical subjects at the higher education stage is guided by the values set by ideological and literary leadership, and not by the exigencies of individual subjects, of professionals, and of the recipients of education. Thanks to the purists' antago-

Table 20. Polarities in the Language-Medium Controversy

Conflicting Issues	Extreme Stands Professed by the "Established" Elites	Extreme Stands Professed by the "Emerging" Pressure Groups
1. Objectives of education	universal values of knowledge	knowledge in consonance with cultural background
2. Role of language in education	autonomy for mother tongue as a full-fledged medium (from primary to advanced stages)	language hierarchy with multitier media (preparatory, auxiliary, and major media—linked with the relevance of education)
3. Choice of medium	common medium (national or universal)	plural media (regional and minority languages)
4. Requirements qualifying medium languages	(a) advanced languages, with "tradition-inspired" literary standards (b) cultivated with "elegant" terminologies and translations	vernacular languages, with prevailing "situation-bound" implicit propriety controls endowed with uninhibited convergence resulting from pidginization, hybridization, code-switching, etc.
5. Pace of change	status quo or, if any change, only after adequate preparation	rapid change from dominating language(s) by creating "vacuum" in favor of vernacular languages

nism toward endowing new concepts with expressions borrowed from real life, many scholars in various fields, finding the lofty coinages forbidding, are discouraged from making meaningful contributions through their native language (cf. Chapter 2).

Various programs of change in the medium policy pay little regard to the reorientation limitations of the professionals, who in turn adopt an "obstructionist" attitude in implementation. Teachers, who could play a pivotal role in implementation programs, are consequently reluctant to join in the processes of language shift, as most of them believe the issues concerning language policy are politically motivated and are not very practicable. One often notices a strong bias among them toward rigid political stands concerning the functions and the content of different languages in the education curriculum. Against this background, teachers, particularly of the advanced stages of education, who are themselves the product of a select education system, remain, by and large, uninvolved in the developmental processes of language media, demanding the cultivation of Indian languages on a platter and waiting until the "developed" textbooks are conveniently produced by the language experts. At the annual conference in 1952, university teachers in Madras State expressed their reluctance to make any change until "a large variety of books and journals in the national and regional language become available."

The actual beneficiaries of this game seem to be the multilingual elites who adopt language postures according to the ideologies preferring cultural resurgence, language autonomy in education, a common medium, elegant styles, and the "vacuum" theory; but in practice, they feel at home in the prevailing patterns in education—cherishing universal knowledge, the language hierarchy, alternate media, hybridization, code-switching, and the status quo. One is confronted with an interesting characteristic of regional "neo-elites" in the emergent power structure who have succeeded in manipulating the colonial education system to their advantage by aligning themselves with the masses through the demands of cultural resurgence and rapid change in the education system while at the same time professing the "elitist" values of language autonomy, uniform medium, and elegant styles of "school" language. Hence in everyday verbal communication one notices an enormous diversity of and fluidity among codes dealing with informal situations, whereas in the formal situations, particularly in the written form, one demands compartmentalized "appropriate" and "correct" usage according to the professed language policy.

One of the serious handicaps in implementing language-education policies by different education agencies at the central and state levels is the continuance of the inherited dichotomies of "ordinary" and "advanced" traditions, and the urban-biased system of education as shaped during the period of colonial rule. From the administrative point of view, "language diversity, differentiation, distribution, and development all intensify difficulties of eradicating illiteracy" (Dakin, 1968:18). Amid the conflicting ideologies concerning language, the administration tends to sidestep the difficulties by means of shortcuts and promoting ad hoc solutions. On the grounds of feasibility, many programs remain unimplemented because of the paucity of monetary and human resources, and the administrators content themselves with plugging the holes in the functionally outdated system, all of which does not show much consonance with the growing aspirations of the masses.

CHAPTER 8

Directions of Language Planning

FROM THE NARROW LINGUISTIC CONCERNS of "intellectual" fostering of the standard languages (Prague School, 1932; Tauli, 1968) the canvass of language planning is now enlarged to include language as an "object of human manipulation," introducing the "cost-benefit" and "decision-making" models from economics and political science (Rubin, 1973). But one cannot deny that the basic character of many language-planning agencies and the major concern of many investigators in this field have remained largely normative. In this sense, the deliberate change envisaged for a language is in actual terms "manipulation by the elite."

The cost-benefit models regard language as a "societal resource," and the success of planning is evaluated in terms of operational policies: targets (based on ideologies), strategies of action, legislative authorization, implementation by executive agencies, and periodic evaluation (Jernudd and Das Gupta, 1971). In the entire process the common man—the "consumer" of language-planning programs—is present only by proxy, carrying the elite "cross." It is mainly the custodians of language who loftily decide what is "good" for the masses, by the virtue of their position of power in the sociopolitical or literary scene.

In the enthusiasm for benefiting from the economic and political experiences of planning, we do not seem to give due consideration to the constraints of human sensitivities in defining the targets of language planning. Planning for deliberate changes in human behavior cannot be equated with planning for the development of natural resources or of technology. Economic planning in many developing countries has itself fallen short of grasping the human complexities involving behavioral changes, which result in various sociopsychological problems not predicted at the time the targets were defined.

Given the linguist's preoccupation with the study of language as a "formal" system, we have not yet seriously probed into various contours of speech behavior as such. As an example, the persistent notion among the Hindustani population in North-Central India of relating mutually distant speech varieties with one language based on different traditions— Hindi, Urdu, or Panjabi—signifies the sociolinguistic reality of complex heterogeneous societies (cf. Chapter 5). The present theoretical framework in language planning does not account for the plurifunctional characteristics of language. Thus, from the top to the bottom, language-planning processes are presumed to be elite conditioned. In this respect, Gorman's (1973) account of language allocation in Kenya draws attention to some of the complexities involved in language-policy adoption. It reveals that our present concern in language-planning theory with the surface targets of "determination-development-implementation" (Jernudd, 1973:17) could be inadequate to explain the language-planning processes in many developing societies. Along with Kenya, India and Ireland provide insights into distinguishing the processes of language allocation from those of language implementation. As such, language-policy adoption should be regarded as mere "communicative conduct" in the realms of language allocation rather than as a program for implementation.

Human Sensitivities

The sociolinguistic upheaval in several newly independent nations in Asia and Africa during the past three decades vividly portrays the limitations of the language elite in programming changes in the language behavior of the masses. The South Asian experience of shift in language policies brings to the fore certain basic tenets for introducing deliberate changes in the communication patterns of a speech community, such as: (1) the changes envisaged have to be in tune with wider social trends; (2) the switchover in language functions needs to be phased appropriately; and (3) there has to be a functional justification for learning a skill (Khubchandani, 1969b):

1. *Changes in tune with social trends.* A living language takes shape by the will of the people; it survives in the usage of the people; and its status or identity is located in the interactions among the people. Changes in the content or functions of a language can be actualized only by social acceptance and not by any decree. All governmental and elitist educational institutions can accelerate or slow down the tempo of certain trends concerning the content or functions of a particular language, but the ultimate authority lies with man as a social being. The colonial experience of the past shows that imperial powers can impose a language for certain

functions against the wishes of the people, but that language is usually cast away as soon as the situation changes.

In the context of South Asia, we notice two remarkably different trends regarding the use of language for formal communication. On the one hand, in response to democratic pressures, local governmental agencies are keen to discard the use of English, a vestige of the colonial era, and to switch over hastily to their respective regional languages. On the other hand, many agencies of trade and technology in the private sector, which compete among themselves in spearheading the modernization process, still judge an individual's achievement orientation and merit on the basis of knowledge of English, as they feel that by giving up the international media altogether their economic goals will be adversely affected (see Group Dynamics, Chapter 7).

In such circumstances, the educational system has to cater to the needs of all sectors of society. States have to consider providing such socioeconomic opportunities and incentives that learners are motivated to opt for the subject or medium of instruction required for national purposes. Psychologically, compulsion of any kind, even for the benefit of an individual, is met with resistance, which defeats the very purpose of education.

One of the complications in the language issue of India has been rather too much reliance on the legislative prerogatives of introducing changes in language behavior and of granting privileges to different languages through legal decrees, instead of taking measures to justify the functional load of these languages and providing incentives for reeducating the population. Readership in a language can be attracted only through literature of quality, which would thus raise the stature of that language in its competition with other languages. Imposition or censure of certain language functions would only invite fanatic reactions from other speech groups and would generate a climate of mistrust and hostility among different speech groups.

2. Phasing of language shift. Habits establish firm roots at an early age. With regard to bringing about any change in the functions of a language (in administration, education, etc.), individuals can be induced to convert their language habits only optionally. Compulsory and hasty displacement of existing language functions adds only insecurity to certain segments of the population in respect of their role in society. Consequently, such displacement promotes antagonism toward the change itself, which defeats the very purpose of the envisaged change. A gradual shift in language functions causes minimal disruption in an individual's capabilities. Language replacement or language reforms are often the results of the shift in language loyalty in the ever changing political history of the world. Demands for a changeover in language functions often represent political or socioeconomic threats to the established elite by a rising group.

3. *Functional justification for language learning.* Language learning is an aspect of socialization. One may study languages other than one's mother tongue either focusing on utilitarian purposes (occupational advancement; scholarly interest in literature, history, technology, etc.) and/or on integrative purposes (e.g., cross-cultural synthesis and appreciation, a liking for other cultures and people). By internalizing the linguistic behavior of another stratum of society, an individual attains mobility—the ability to move from one group to another. He enjoys the fruits of sharing in the group speaking the same language. Often elements of prestige, art, and cultural affiliations become more prominent than the principal use of the language for ordinary communication, as do Sanskrit for Hindus, Arabic and Persian for Muslims in South Asia, and French for artists. The factors of social identification through a language determine the attitude of learners.

To arrive at an amicable settlement of language functions in a multilingual society, it is necessary to take into account all subjective factors (such as language attitudes and spontaneous trends among different social groups) as well as objective factors concerning demographic, social, economic, and political conditions of a nation. One must measure the consequences of the shift over both short-term and long-term periods.

Therefore, it becomes essential to pay due attention to the "consumer," to his linguistic requirements, in order to enable him to participate effectively in modern communication systems. The linguistic skills the urbanized Parsees, immigrant Sindhis, Mysorian Urdu speakers, rural Santalis, and Madurai Saurashtrians need for effective communication in different parts of the Indian subcontinent cannot be identical. Equally different are the needs of a Marathi child in rural Vidarbha, in urban Poona, and in metropolitan Bombay in relation to education in a mother tongue. Isolated "language-development" agencies, insulated from each other by sharp boundaries, cannot do justice to the complex needs of various plural speech communities.

Situation-bound Planning

The issue of language development merits close scrutiny in considering the chances of success of the present aspirations of language elites in newly independent nations, shaped in the "language autonomy" mold, to meet the needs of their heterogeneous pluralistic communities. The contemporary values of autonomy and standardization (Ray, 1963) have lured many language reformers toward the exclusive development of the dominant languages in each region. But in spite of the diverse speech patterns, Indian society as a whole has a kind of "organic unity" resting in its pluralistic model of speech behavior (Chatterjee, 1945).

Various developmental actions aimed at transforming the convergent, "situation-bound" patterns of speech behaviors into divergent, pseudo-autonomous, puristic, "tradition-inspired" languages—and associated societies—are leading the new nations into serious problems in relation to national integration. Consequently, the harmonious mutual accommodation of heterogeneous speech communities has given way to a tense and rigid insistence on different normative systems and a pervasive competition for language privileges in different domains and regions. In pluralistic nations such as India, the principles of "situation-bound" language planning can provide a sound basis for bringing dynamic adjustments in response to real-life communication settings. A brief outline of certain concrete measures in the Indian context is presented below.

1. The basic unit for language planning should be a speech area *(Sprachbund)* rather than one or another language in its entirety. Work on languages, including that in schools, should respond to the communication patterns among different speech communities prevailing in the region.

2. If we accept the pedagogic principle of proceeding from "known to unknown," we must evolve flexible programs which widen the students' linguistic experience by progressive differentiation from local speech to supradialectal varieties, culminating in a sophisticated grasp of standard and literary styles for the community's motivated specialists. These programs would have to be attuned to the great variation in linguistic usage with the characteristics of the social situation. A liberal and flexible approach to linguistic usage in education can potentially release new energy among the neoliterates, enable different elite layers to act as models of supradialectal varieties, and thus break the monopoly of small urban elite, far removed from the common man's speech, as the sole custodians of language.

3. Similar strategies for teaching contact languages in different regions can respond to both the immediate and the long-term societal needs. In devising the learning system for a second or third language, it is essential to coordinate the instructional strategies (work in the classroom and with laboratory aids) with interactional strategies (graded and controlled interactional programs outside the classroom focusing attention on "events" rather than on "expressions") (Khubchandani, 1975a). A pragmatic approach in this regard will help in avoiding anomalous situations such as the treatment of Hindi and Urdu (two social variants of Khariboli) as two distinct "autonomous" systems in the context of second language teaching. For a native speaker of Hindi to acquire mastery over Urdu, it will suffice to learn another script (Persian writing system)

and add to his repertoire some "highbrow" vocabulary of Perso-Arabic origin. The insistence on teaching "highbrow" Sanskritic Khariboli as a second language in Bombay schools, where its "grass-roots" version (Bombay Hindustani) is in active use in everyday life, is another instance (cited earlier, cf. Chapter 6) of not taking into account the sociolinguistic parameters within which learners operate. An efficient teaching system for nonnative languages should devise opportunities to participate in natural "language events"; it can help the student to acquire formal linguistic competence and situational performance capability (sensibility) simultaneously.

4. Linguistically heterogeneous areas may be encouraged to provide bilingual schools that are flexible regarding the proportions of, and the procedures for, using the available languages as media of instruction. To promote early active bilingualism, contact languages can be employed as media of instruction, auxiliary to the mother tongue, for certain "demonstrative" subjects such as geography, science, and technology. This practice will induce the reinforcement of the functions of such contact languages outside the classroom and help in reducing the teaching effort required for attaining any particular level of proficiency in these languages (Khubchandani, 1967, 1968, 1969e; Widdowson, 1968).

When both nonnative languages, Hindi and English, have significant functional value in the normal activities of a literate citizen, it does not appear to be a sound principle that the student should be conditioned strictly to a single medium throughout his long career of education (from the age of six to twenty-one or so, roughly fifteen years), and for two nonnative languages to be taught in school simply as an exercise for eventual use in the student's adult life but with no immediate bearing on his day-to-day communication needs (just as classical and foreign languages are taught for limited functional value). Particularly at the postgraduate stage, the aim of education is constantly to advance the boundaries of knowledge to new horizons by maintaining active professional coordination across language boundaries, to compete in terms of international standards, and also to develop ability among students to think and make original contributions in their native language and the link language. It would do much to raise the standards of education if the discourse between teacher and student were to be conducted through the bilingual media of the native language (or the language of primary communication in the region) and a cultivated language in the field of specialization (mostly English; in certain cases it might be Russian, French, German, etc.).

Such an approach would also remove, to a great extent, the handicaps faced by the nation, at least at the postgraduate stage, by promoting economy, efficiency, mobility of teachers and students from one part of the country to another, easier communication among academic and professional people and administrators, and intellectual coordination among universities and exchange of research knowledge published in various Indian languages.

The auxiliary media will also be useful as alternatives for smoothing the switchover from one medium to another in case facilities for higher education are not available at certain places in the mother-tongue medium.

5. It will be useful to distinguish between "language" skills and "literature" courses in contact-language teaching programs. The former, with utilitarian aims, need to be taught on a wider scale; "literature" courses can come later for those adequately skilled in the "language." For efficient operation of "language" courses, we need to train pedagogically and linguistically oriented teachers rather than to recruit scholars with literary sophistication, as has been the practice hitherto in the case of teaching English.

6. No one would deny the value of standardization for ensuring efficiency and precision in communication, but most of the standardization devices in Indian languages today serve only to extend the "tradition-inspired" value system of small elites over all domains in the entire speech community. Language-standardization processes ought to proceed naturally from real-life norms, and not through arbitrary "instant standards" imposed by an urban, literary elite upon educational programs.

In standardizing languages for a pluralistic society such as India, then, it is essential to inculcate an entirely different set of values in order to build on the resources inherent in the wide range of speech settings characteristic of the intricately segmented communities in the country. The "tradition-inspired" norms as professed by grammarians are also valuable in broadening the range of one's intellectual experiences and in sharpening one's awareness of the various societal expectations of verbalization. These are, thus, complementary to the community's implicit "situation-bound" propriety controls in speech.

7. Of the newly coined words, a majority has no sanction in *prayoga* (usage), and therefore these remain dysfunctional. The terms can be standardized after they have withstood the test of *prayoga*. A language develops through usage, not through ivory-tower coinages. Official efforts in this direction so far have put the cart before the horse. The use of such terms serves not so much to promote communication between the author and the reader as to declare publicly the author's pride in the new pedantry, as discussed in Chapter 7.

The "highbrow" *tatsamized* styles, fed on neologisms arbitrarily derived from nonnative classical stock, have been a major drag on the effective use of Indian languages in higher learning and in any serious communication. Instant derivation of terms from the classical or neoclassical stocks on a large scale can only enlarge the gulf between the speech of the masses and of the intelligentsia in the same linguistic region. To make the public communication channels more intelligible to the masses, expressions from live situations for new experiences should receive priority over artificial coinages, even if this tends to hybridize a language system.

Grass-roots Approach

Education in the elitist model has been projected as society's investment for "eventual" returns—preparing the younger generation for adulthood. Conventional education, in this sense, tends to be bookish, unproductive, and alienated from "immediate" needs. These attributes are reflected in an undue stress on the rational and overt use of language in the school, as pointed out earlier. Language in such situations is treated as an "artifact" in which pupils remain detached and uninvolved from the communication point of view; only rehearsals are conducted for eventual confrontations with the unknown (i.e., future) reality. In contrast, speech outside the classroom, as a living phenomenon, is very much a "fact" in which participants are directly involved (cf. Table 6).

Linguists, convinced about the central role language plays in the development of the child as a social being, profess a new approach to language teaching. A new order in education envisages the language teacher "to serve a language environment which makes sense" (Britton, 1970), and provides opportunities for learners to learn "how we use language to live." A grass-roots approach to education supports the value of encouraging children's creativity by starting with their experiences and "keeping the flow going without fussing about grammar and spelling." Waismann (1962), a noted philosopher, has rightly remarked: "Correctness is useful but a negative virtue. . . . Grammatically streamlined language is only good for saying things that are no longer worth saying" (p. 117).

The grass-roots approach emphasizes making education more meaningful, useful, and productive to work-experience. Sensitivity to speech variation and a grasp of the communication ethos prevailing in the society is, no doubt, enhanced by "doing" verbal events in natural settings. In this regard, an elaboration of Gandhiji's thinking concerning basic education could provide a useful focus. Gandhiji (1956) laid stress on integrating education with experience and language acquisition with communicability (as advocated in his approach to Hindustani).

In recent years these trends have led toward strong reaction against the elitism of a literary approach to teaching languages. The present stress upon literature in schools in the U.K. is regarded as the contemporary version of the nineteenth-century approach to the classics. The majority of English teachers are working on the principle that if a pupil reads the best literature it will "rub off" on him and enable him to write the "best English" (Doughty, Pearce, and Thornton, 1972). Following the pattern of the English curriculum in the Indian education system, the teaching of literature in modern Indian languages has also acquired the central position (see Language and Education, Chapter 4). A grass-roots approach suggests studying literature through "themes" and "projects" to enable the learner to extend his range within a language and to adapt to a variety of roles in everyday life.

In the implementation of these programs, however, one notices an increasing gap between the supporters of oral work who encourage the children's "personal" use of language across the curriculum, and those promoting the "bonding" character of a standard language through its use in textbooks. Halliday, McIntosh, and Stevens (1964:229) point to the danger of separating the written and spoken language in children's schoolwork: "(It) puts a brake on children's self-expression and leads ultimately to the listlessness of some classroom essays."

We need to look into how to tackle varying demands in the spoken and written forms of the same language. It is necessary to adopt a pragmatic approach to linguistic usage in education, taking into account the mechanisms of standardization of language in plural societies as well as the values attached to such a process.

Deliberate Behavioral Change

Studies prompted by language-development programs such as devising orthographies, technical terminologies, and other such issues dealing with language planning in newly emerged nations have, no doubt, had a significant impact on the formulation of sociolinguistic theories. The problems of language modernization and of language shift away from the colonial goals in newly independent countries, the tension relating to white and black English in the United States, the "language-engineering" processes on the Indian subcontinent as well as in Israel and Indonesia-Malaysia, making demands on language from computer and mass communication agencies and other, similar challenges can certainly sharpen the understanding of language activity in different dimensions.

Sociolinguistics as a discipline can count upon certain advantages from the relatively high degree of formalization and rigor achieved in "formal" linguistics. So far, however, the social and behavioral sciences have not developed the conceptual tools with which to evaluate social-planning strategies. With closer scrutiny of the language-planning processes, one can gain insights into deliberate behavioral change, patterns of areal and social propagation of linguistic innovations, as well as the motivational or rationalizing behavior behind decision-making processes for language development.

Before the introduction of radical changes in the patterns of speech behavior in the developing world through these stereotyped emphases, the underlying notions about language, as well as oral mass communication needs of the twentieth century (discussed in Chapter 4), should be examined.

No one would doubt the complex, multidimensional character of language activity. But, at the same time, one finds that in "formalistic" studies of language, the linguist confines himself solely to the cognitive dimension of communication. The affective and identificational dimensions of language have not received much attention in linguistic studies (Khubchandani, 1973b).

So far, linguists have been on the fringe in contributing to actual language-planning processes in individual countries. Until recently in the studies concerning language change, linguists have been more occupied with such questions as how language changes rather than how to effect deliberate changes in the speech activity of a group to meet the challenges of rapidly changing societies. One needs to look at language use as a basic instrumental factor of social change as well. Because language use is inseparable from such activities as planning, propaganda, and evaluation, it plays a crucial role in the reorganization of institutions. Developmental programs are to be equipped with "linguistic material" (built out of symbols, formulas, and rules of syntax and semantics) in order to accomplish diverse communicative tasks. The Asian scene, because of its complex multiplicity, can be of special interest for a study of this kind. To successfully implement developmental programs such as family planning, we need to devise ways and means of optimizing the persuasive powers of language for different kinds of media.

One observes markedly varied persuasive techniques in the conduct of election campaigns—delivering speeches, conducting debates, organizing publicity, and so on—in such different countries as India, Britain, and the United States. Reluctance to adopt the family-planning and agricultural-promotion campaigns carried by radio and television in "poor" Oriental societies could be attributed to the importation of "affluent" Occidental techniques of persuasion, which do not have much effect on the Oriental masses. Language for such purposes is not only to unfold specific thought processes (such as inference), or to integrate facts with other facts; it has at the same time to be productive and effective as transmitted through a particular communication ethos. Studies on language focus as a crucial factor in reorganizing institutions by devising optimal ways and means of bringing about social change in the country should provide many useful insights into the "modernistic" demands on speech communities.

Language-planning theory at this stage seems to be largely concerned with language problems, paying little regard to the language assets in "traditional" speech communities. Many studies seem to imply the handicap model to achieve the determined targets of development. One general concern of language planners seems to be to adjust the speech behavior of a community to the demands of modernization. Language studies, being heavily biased in favor of "elitist" written cultures, put a high premium on "highbrow" values of speech, and assume without question that standardization, elegance, and other such demands of "sophisticated" communication are essential for development. No serious attempt is made to justify these elitist values in the context of changed situations and changed times. The educated elite construes change as "replacement" of values instead of as an "increment" in the existing order. It is time we start looking at the possibility of adjusting the values of communication and not just at the adjustment of human beings to fit the new demands. It might be more fruitful to consider the adaptation model and to take into account the given assets as well as handicaps in meeting the new challenges. In order to counter the fractionalizing tendencies in these societies, it is essential to draw upon the traditional virtues of language tolerance promoted through language hierarchy, grass-roots multilingualism, and fluidity in speech behavior.

In the formative stages of a theory, one would expect more debate on the perspectives of language planning as a human phenomenon and on the basic tenets with which the planning agencies concern themselves. Surprisingly, one does not find much attention being given to the rationale for various processes undertaken under the head "language planning," such as the need for standardization and for coining elaborate terminologies, and the mechanisms of language choice in actual behavior. As far as the basic concepts of language "manipulation" are concerned, too much seems to be taken for granted.

EPILOGUE

Epilogue

> Everyday language is a part of the human organism and is no less complicated than it.
>
> *Wittgenstein, 1961*

THE PRESENT STUDY has attempted to unravel some of the "organic" characteristics of language activity in South Asia. These characteristics, though manifested through plurality of languages and cultures, are enmeshed in an integral whole. An evaluation of language as a "social institution," no doubt, leads to a better understanding of communication patterns in an area, and such an approach has been preferred here to a conventional account of the genealogical relationships of diverse language structures in a specific territory.

Concept of Language

In a way, this study departs significantly from the prevailing concept of language as a "cognitive" system, by bringing into focus the "conditioning" and "regulative" processes in verbal repertoire, which to a large extent shape a language system. The contours of identity and innovation (also treated as "manipulations") at macro- and micro-levels help us to understand the rich diversity of speech communications. Various ecological factors such as contact environment (heterogeneity, mobility, urbanity, density of population, and so forth), interactional patterns, and reference-group pressures, and along with them, the functional load of speech communication and creative faculties of speakers, constitute social reality "here and now" for a group or individual, and these intermix with language activity in everyday life. Hitherto, the impact of such "echo" systems has been treated peripherally when describing a language system. The theory concerned with the formalization of "ideal" language, the speech of "an ideal speaker-listener in a completely homogeneous speech community," regards such elements in the language system as "deviant" or "trivial" (Chomsky, 1965).

Studies in linguistics during the past one hundred years have been overshadowed by a rather narrow view of language, that is, treating it as a homogeneous signalling system and weaving "the gossamer of well-formed 'productions' on the basis of rules of formation and transformation" (Mahulkar, 1981:16 ff.). In this process, modern linguists have confused the "natural" language with the "formal" language and thus misconceived the very object of their investigation (cf. Table 6). In their vigorous efforts to fit into the shoes of "exact" science, they tend to misuse the notions and techniques of logical formalization when they talk of natural language. "An extended, often unexamined analogy underlies the whole concept of scientific linguistics" (Steiner, 1975:110).

One wrong step leads to another, and we find present-day transformationists "formalizing" the natural language by restricting their data to a rigid "standard," or inventing one if need be, in midst of the diverse usage of speech in a community. In this regard, the warning sounded by logicians over fifty years ago does not seem to have made much of an impact on contemporary linguists: "It may, however, be doubted whether the language of everyday life, after being 'rationalized' in this way, would still preserve its naturalness and whether it would not rather take on the characteristic features of the formalized language" (Tarski, 1956: 267).

When we focus attention on everyday life communications through speech, it becomes apparent that natural language is structured both temporally and spatially. Both the temporal and the spatial structures of speech have social correlates. A historical study of language provides an understanding in depth of the phenomena of speech in a group on the time scale. On the other hand, an account of the organization of speech and patterns of speech diversity prevailing in a society presents a perspective in terms of the breadth of the range of a speech spectrum on the space scale. In a small and relatively homogeneous speech group, speech diversity can be confined to a narrow spectrum, whereas in a complex plural society, made up of fluid speech groups, this linguistic spectrum can extend to overlapping language "boundaries."

In both synchronic and diachronic studies in linguistics, one notices more emphasis on the time scale; for example, reconstructing histories of distinct languages, tracing their genealogies, classifying languages on the basis of genetic affinities, determining language boundaries in a speech continuum according to historical branching, explaining chronological stages of proto-language(s) and of language change.

In relation to the time dimension, the space dimension has not received adequate attention. Bias toward the time scale, probably taken from the philological tradition of language "families," has been so pervasive that

Epilogue

even studies of various spatial aspects of speech behavior, such as regional dialects, bilingualism, diglossia language contact, and borrowings, are framed in terms of temporality.

To gain a clear perspective of the role of language in the lives of individuals and in society, it is necessary to examine the "tradition" and "echo" systems available to a speech community. One cannot brush aside spatial characteristics such as situational norms, and heterogeneity and inherent fluidity in the speech spectrum, as mere interferences in the "ideal" language system, as has been implied in many language-planning programs.

The lacuna of the "space" dimension in linguistic studies is significantly felt when considering the problems of language development for heterogeneous plural communities. In order to attain a proper perspective of the role of language standardization in a speech community, it is essential to examine the entire speech matrix as it becomes modulated according to the propriety controls imposed on the interlocutions of participants, settings, and channels of communication; and also as it is conditioned by the interplay of ecological and socioeconomic factors and various cultural traits like schooling opportunities, economic strata, occupation, and so on. Elsewhere I have discussed at length some of the dynamic characteristics of language, treating the case of Indian Sindhi as a "transplanted" language being nurtured in urban multilingual settings in India since 1947, when about a million Sindhi speakers migrated from Sind at the time of the partition of the country (Khubchandani, 1963).

In language activity one finds characteristics of different dimensions (formal, institutional, pragmatic) flowing simultaneously into one another, responsive to differences of density as in osmosis (for an application of the three-dimensional model of language activity, see the discussion about the address and reference system of Hindi-Urdu, Chapter 2). Often it is difficult to isolate elements as belonging exclusively to one or the other dimension. This approach casts serious aspersions on the general assumption in linguistics that language is a "self-contained" autonomous system.

Language can be better understood as a part of the human organism, as pointed out by Wittgenstein, and we need to evolve "organic" models to treat the structure of living languages. Recent discoveries in the field of molecular biology leading toward the deciphering of the DNA code as a genetic language point to the fruitful application of linguistic concepts in the research of life sciences (Jakobson, 1973). An evaluation of such "continuous" or "developmental" systems should provide the necessary stimulus to develop a comprehensive theory to account for diverse dimensions of language activity. In this regard a critical probe into the communication devices generated among heterogenous speech communities in India, interacting over "fuzzy" language boundaries, can cast significant light in our efforts to understand "natural" processes of language activity.

Language and Communication

Communications at the humanistic level utilize language as an infinitely subtle, flexible, and powerful instrument to cope with the endless variety and diversity of facts. At this level communication generally transpires through the evocation of mental imageries in a dyad. There is no mechanistic transfer of information as such, that is, "sending and receiving" of the message like a postal delivery. But, more appropriately, one can describe the process as the "releasing and catching" of the message, regulated by the vagaries of space and time and by indeterminacies, attitudes, and backgrounds of the participants.

On the inferential plane, it can be claimed that a communication never starts with a clean slate: every message is prevalued (to begin with) and revalued (after the event). In the reality of everyday life, what transpires from a speech event matters more than what it signifies. As early as two thousand years ago, Bhartrhari's philosophy of *sphoṭa*, "plosion", that is, the ultimate in language, stressed this reality, that verbal and nonverbal signals evoke a situation of reality, just as throwing a pebble in a pond causes ripples (Subramania Iyer, 1963).

Communication in its rudimentary sense is built on multiple and overlapping signalling devices, so that its interpretation does not have to be tagged with one and only one signalling system. It is primarily a "synergistic" system in which numerous elements operate in an independent and intricate fashion, adjusting to the imperatives of time and space. The multifaceted character of a communicative act can, at best, be compared to an orchestra. All symbolic subsystems in such an orchestra—verbal (and nonverbal) cues, roles and identities of participants, conscious attitudes, unconscious moods, value structures, intensity of involvement, and so on—play their part in realizing a message.

Every speech act is endowed with an intrinsic purpose. Speech is noteworthy for what it conceals as much as for what it reveals. As was pointed out earlier, language in everyday life is characterized by implicit imperatives of reference or peer groups and covert suggestions. The Japanese people are known to value highly keen sensitivity about nurturing the concept of *amae* in interpersonal and group communications, that is, seeking to protect a relationship (through mutual desire for a smooth, congenial transaction; cf. Doi, 1974). In the "implicative" sense, speech

Epilogue

evokes ideas, images, and other introspective experiences in the mental system of the hearer that often remain vague and indeterminate. Time, distance, and disparities in outlook or assumed reference make a speech message an operation of "interpretative decipherment" (Steiner, 1975). Ambiguity becomes a virtue in such communication settings: for example, "He didn't say in so many words what he meant." But in contemporary societies many modernization processes have been undermining the multidirectional, interactive, participatory processes in humanistic communication, as revealed from the present-day targets of language standardization and language teaching.

Patterns of Plurality

The South Asian experience provides a unique model of plurality in verbal and nonverbal communications which has withstood the test of time over the centuries. At this stage it will be worthwhile to recapitulate some of the salient characteristics over which the edifice of linguistic plurality has been built through the ages:

1. *relativity:* The verbal repertoire is organized in relation to identity and purpose of interaction leading to functional heterogeneity, as discussed in Chapter 2. This characteristic is in sharp contrast to the prevailing tendency in homogenized societies, where a high premium is placed on the cultivation of an "absolute" standard of language through positive or negative attitudes to specific usages in the verbal repertoire.
2. *hierarchy:* A system of linguistic stratification forms the basis for channeling the promotion (or even cultivation) of speech diversity in the everyday repertoire through bilingualism, diglossia, and so forth. The concept of a selective development of one or a few languages (or speech varieties) on the basis of certain societal and projectional dimensions (cf. Table 5) goes against the grain of harmonious patterning of variation in the verbal hierarchy of plural societies.
3. *instrumentality:* Speech variation in everyday settings is explicated as an instrument of an ongoing redefinition of relationships, crisscrossed by the imperatives of context and purpose. In this process affiliations with a particular language as mother tongue, with a regional language, or with a language of superior culture are treated as "given" or ascribed, and their manifestation in a repertoire is marked by a certain degree of flexibility and manipulation in adjusting to situational needs. In contrast, many homogenized nationality

groups, as in Europe, regard affiliation with one's mother tongue as a "defining" characteristic, leaving not much room for manipulating the primary group identity. In this context, any departure in its verbal manifestation is regarded as an "outward" shift; in a way, one is aspiring to entry into another club.

A plural society as an "organic" whole is strengthened by a measure of fluidity in the use of language according to considerations of relativity, hierarchy, and instrumentality. In the context of language "content," this fluidity is experienced through the processes of language hybridization, pidginization, code-switching, and so on. In the context of language "loyalty," fluidity is revealed through the fluctuating claims of language identity, lack of clear-cut categorization of language boundaries, and so forth. The North-Central region of the subcontinent presents a sharp characterization of these processes (cf. Chapter 5). The case of the vernacularization of Braj and Awadhi (cited earlier), relinquishing their role as literary languages in favor of projecting Khariboli as a literary base of the "Hindi amalgam" only a hundred years ago, exemplifies the extent of fluidity in language domains prevailing among plural speech communities.

The foregoing discussion of diverse characteristics of Indian plurality in the context of speech communication convinces us that assertions of language identity vary at different times and in different places. In the traditional Indian order, affiliation with a particular mother tongue has been regarded merely as an instrument to accentuate identity. Language identity as such cannot be universally regarded as a "defining" feature for belonging to an "exclusive" group.

Very few populations in the world can be considered totally homogeneous in terms of ethnic affiliations. There are, however, many forces at work promoting cultural homogenization among different groups. In an ethnographic account, Said and Simmons (1976) observe that out of 892 distinct ethnic groups covering 132 nations throughout the world, only 9 percent of the groups are considered to be totally homogeneous, and 19 percent are considered to be 90 percent homogeneous; in 30 percent of the cases there is no single group comprising a majority of population, and in over 40 percent of the cases there are 5 or more significant groups.

Pluralism in South Asia is marked by a stratificational network of primary groups governed by a varying degree of boundedness signifying lineage, occupation, and religion. Different identity groups, crisscrossing in more than one manner, are involved in a complex web of relationships with one another, presenting a kind of mosaic, and are averse to their be-

Epilogue

ing rigidly identified with a particular "insulated" group. Diverse groups thus related to a whole under the label "we" can be characterized as

$$1 \times 1 \times 1 = 1$$

This phenomenon can be identified as a case of "organic" pluralism, where two identities are simply two sides of the same coin. Heterogeneity in speech, marked by implicit "etiquette" and flexibility, can best be viewed within an overall "organic unity" of communications.

In contrast, different identity groups, when combined under the umbrella of a common structure sharing the same space and/or same interests, characterize the label "we" as

$$1 + 1 + 1 = 3$$

Pluralism in Western societies is generally based on the coexistence of different primary groups structurally separated by ethnic/nationality boundaries insulated through traits such as color, religion, and language territory (in the case of migrants, their ancestral languages). This phenomenon has been referred to as "structural" pluralism. In such a society, harmony among diverse primary groups is sought by containing their rival aspirations through safeguards provided within the parameters of equality and social justice.

In the context of racial and ethnic relationships, Gordon (1981) distinguishes two patterns of structural pluralism—liberal pluralism and corporate pluralism—and enumerates six prominent dimensions to evaluate their pros and cons for American society, namely, (1) legal recognition and differential treatment, (2) individual meritocracy and equality of opportunity versus group rewards and equality of condition, (3) structural separation, (4) cultural differences, (5) area exclusivism, and (6) institutional monolingualism versus institutional bilingualism or multilingualism.

The two models of pluralism—organic and structural—are sharply distinguished by their relation to the whole:

- "integral" relation (signified by ×), where diverse primary groups form an integral part of the whole;
- "combined" relation (signified by +), where diverse primary groups are proportionately balanced in a structural whole.

One further notices two major cross-currents characterizing both models of pluralisms, one favoring conditions for homogenization, and the other promoting the processes of differentiation. These cross-currents affect, in a significant manner, directions in the maintenance or shift of sociocultural diversity.

Under organic pluralism, we get the pattern of "melting pot" pluralism favoring homogenization; it accepts variations within universal ideals. Another pattern is of "stratificational" pluralism, where differentiation of sociocultural traits is functional, and is integrated through superconsensus. Under structural pluralism, liberal pluralism is an example of favoring conditions for voluntary homogenization, where diversity is subtly tempered with individual preferences and personal rights. Corporate pluralism, on the other hand, contributes to the accentuation of sociocultural identities through mandatory safeguards for "group" rights.

This schema gives us a "plurality square," where the distinction between organic and structural pluralism is regarded as of primary order and the distinction favoring homogenization versus differentiation is treated as of secondary order.

	Homogenizing	Differentiating
Organic	"Melting Pot"	Stratificational
Structural	Liberal	Corporate

It will suffice here to informally present a few salient features of four major types of pluralism (Table 21) to gain some understanding of how the manifestation and organization of speech, and external pressures (geographic, political, and others) on speech, are differentially treated in a society.

Diverse profiles of speech communication in different countries and at different times make us realize the futility of pursuing illusionary goals of universal order in the name of "efficient" communication. India, China, and Japan represent typical cases of stratificational pluralism; the United States and Latin American countries can be cited as examples of "melting pot" pluralism; Luxembourg and the Scandinavian countries can be identified as examples of liberal pluralism; and the U.S.S.R. and Belgium typify corporate pluralism. Recent trends in India, Canada, and the United States point to the processes favoring corporate pluralism.

Epilogue

Pangs of Transition

Since World War II, many countries in Asia have been going through the trauma of language transition (shedding the dominance of colonial languages and assigning new roles to indigenous languages). Issues of identity and development at national, regional, and social levels have led political thinkers and planners to examine afresh the role of language in pluralistic societies so as to respond to the apparent crisis in an adequate manner.

Not only have these issues been focal points among the intellectual and political elite on the national and international scenes, but they have also found frequent expression through mass participation at the grass-roots level in these societies. The roles and privileges of different languages and the clashing loyalties they have aroused in these regions acquired political salience during the struggles for independence from colonial powers (cf. Chapters 6 and 7).

With the new forces of modernization penetrating all walks of life, the subcontinent has been acquiring a new order of pluralism in its cultural and linguistic expression. Most of the formal organizations in the realm of education and sociocultural activities are modeled on the modern Western pattern. This study has dealt at length with some of the significant characteristics of this impact, namely:

- allegiance to "absolute" language standards promoted through schools;
- commitment to the "autonomous development" of certain languages, mostly selected on the basis of demographic pressures in specific regions (e.g., languages listed under the Eighth Schedule in the Constitution);
- emphasis on the "exclusiveness" of language identity and on sharp boundaries through legislative and administrative intervention (e.g., delineating the state boundary between Haryana and Panjab on the basis of the 1961 language census);
- empowering administration to codify language use in public domains by coining technical terminologies, etc.

So far, the Indian response to the onslaught of modern (mostly alien) institutions has been to accept divergence between the "folk" reality in communications and the formal postures for claiming privileges through language affiliations. The Indian situation vividly illustrates the apparent paradox generated by a pronounced difference in speech as a "folk" reality and language as an "ideal" (cf. Table 6). The paradox is expressed in a widening gulf between the "highbrow" content of language utilized for

Table 21. Major Types of Pluralism

	Organic Pluralism		"Melting Pot" (homogenizing)	Structural Pluralism	
	"Stratificational" (differentiating)			"Liberal" (homogenizing)	"Corporate" (differentiating)

I. *Manifestation of Speech*

	"Stratificational" (differentiating)	"Melting Pot" (homogenizing)	"Liberal" (homogenizing)	"Corporate" (differentiating)
1. Total repertoire	superposed homogeneity in valuing speech variation	favoring homogenization among varieties	heterogeneity tolerated in individual domains	heterogeneity supported through institutional provisions
2. Content	cultivation of functionally heterogeneous varieties (dialects/languages)	convergence of different varieties	partial convergence (particularly in public domains)	emphasis on maintaining divergence
3. Domains	variation maintained through diglossia, code-switching, multilingualism, etc.	shift-oriented (based on aptitude, proficiency of codes)	cleavage between private and public domains	privileges specified through mandatory provisions
4. Categorization	language boundaries remain in flux as per communication needs at the "grass-roots" level (through language hybridization, creolization, etc.)	total loss or pidginization of ancestral languages	efforts to minimize effects of acculturation on languages	stress on maintaining sharp language boundaries and exclusiveness of tradition, as per the dicta of language elites

II. *Organization of Speech*

5. Loyalty toward mother tongue	instrumental, partial (guided by other-than-language affiliations)	transient ("nostalgic" for some)	individual-oriented	defines affiliation to a group
6. Identity through language	relevant, flexible, (context-bound)	favoring merger	relevant (based on discretion)	absolute as an element of the primary group membership (e.g., nationality groups in Europe)
7. Status	speech variation placed on a hierarchy-scale (dependent on communication ethos)	minority languages become marginal	language privileges based on the equality of opportunities	assertion of language rights based on the equality of conditions
8. Controls	guided by "ascriptional" identity, adhering to implicit "etiquette" system	aspiring to entry in the dominant group through language shift	favoring maintenance of ancestral language(s) for ethnic domains	safeguards through legislative and administrative guarantees; allegiance to explicit standards along lines determined by the custodians of language

(Continued)

Table 21. (Continued)

	Organic Pluralism		Structural Pluralism	
	"Stratificational" (differentiating)	"Melting Pot" (homogenizing)	"Liberal" (homogenizing)	"Corporate" (differentiating)

III. "Eco-pressures" on Speech

9. Territory	communities comprising "concentrating" patterns of speech varieties	correlation of a speech variety to a territory not regarded as significant	languages marked by degrees of dominance (majority/minority languages)	communities relating "exclusive" allegiance to territory
10. Impact of technology	widening gulf between human versus mechanical channels of communications	accelerating the processes of assimilation	preference for languages favorably placed in a politico-economic structure	proliferation of technology helps in asserting "autonomy" of diverse communication systems
11. Democratization processes	continuous reshaping of communication ethos through consensus	the dominant group determining values in communication	individual choice (depending on positive or negative attitudes)	minorities asserting their rights in communication systems through pressure lobbies, language posture, etc. (e.g., bilingual education in the United States)
12. Government machinery	encourages multiple choice, reflecting communication needs of diverse groups	indifference, or indirect support to the processes of assimilation	neutral to the individual choice, laissez faire policy	committed to execute mandatory provisions concerning language use and to regulate conflicting demands of language pressure groups

Epilogue

the purposes of identity and pragmatic considerations of language as a means of communication. A classic example is of lingua franca Hindustani on the one hand, and pedantic Hindi and Urdu for formal domains on the other (cf. Chapter 6). The differences lead to inherent anomalies in the patterns of language use, and also to discrepancies in conscious and unconscious attitudes about speech activity, that is, language images and language postures, as discussed in Chapter 3.

The interplay of such centripetal and centrifugal factors explains, to a large extent, the conspicuous gap between the perceptions about language among everyday users and among language elites (those who control the formal channels of language use or of its promotion, including grammarians, lexicographers, language teachers, copy editors, language reformers, and policymakers). The modern language elite, in his role as a liaison between Western language values and indigenous language patterns, has appropriated for himself the gatekeeper's privilege of approving or disapproving various shifts being introduced in verbal repertoire. Mostly the elite cartels manage interactions among themselves, very little realizing the indifference of the masses to such endeavors in their everyday speech activity (cf. Chapter 7).

Recent agitations concerning the identity assertions of minority groups in many Western countries (the United States, Canada, Belgium) also confirm the fact that the dominance of technology in a society does not necessarily lead to cultural homogenization. With the growing organized conflict over sociocultural identities in the modern West, many social scientists are now questioning the treatment of ethnic/racial loyalties as "cultural residues characteristic of premodern societies ... that will erode with modernization and increased social mobility" (Lambert, 1981:191).

India is very fast turning into an institutionally multilingual nation, with issues concerning language having a very high order of saliency. The implicit consensus over stratificational hierarchy of language use is giving way to the explicit provisions of legislative hierarchy (cf. Chapters 6 and 7). "Grass-roots" pluralism is being replaced by "mandated" bilingualism through education and other systems of acculturation.

One of the most radical turnabouts in recent history, transforming the concept of language pluralism on the subcontinent, has been the explicit recognition of language claims over "exclusive" territory. This recognition has given rise to the questions of numerical majority and minority in a particular territory based on language. The implicit inclination of the colonial rulers to recognize the claims of religion over exclusive territory (as revealed from their unsuccessful attempt in 1905 to bifurcate the then Bengal Province by carving out "Muslim" Bengal, under the pretext of administrative convenience) were counterchallenged by the secular leadership in the national struggle, who committed themselves to the principle of rationalizing provincial boundaries on the basis of language. A lot of sociopolitical pressure was built up over the implementation of this principle, as is seen in the separation of Orissa from the then Bengal Province and of Sind from the then Bombay Province in 1935-1936. The language principle temporarily lost its momentum when the claims of religion over "exclusive" territory acquired political prominence during negotiations for the country's independence. But immediately after partition in 1947, one of the first tasks carried out was the reorganization of states on a linguistic basis in 1956. In this process, dominant language groups in different regions emerged as significant political lobbies on the national scene. The "Mumbai amchi" (Bombay is Ours) protest movement during 1956-1960, which succeeded in reversing the States Reorganization Commission's recommendation of making the Greater Bombay district a Union territory, is a case in point.

In the past, the colonial provinces and princely states comprised many distinct language "concentration areas" with no exclusive claims of one language over a specific territory. The process of correlating language with "exclusive" territory has led to the upsurge of language identity from a low-key "instrumental" role in the framework of stratificational pluralism to the "defining" characteristic in the new emerging order of pluralism. The emotional stresses and strains in the new order are evident in the unresolved boundary disputes between states as well as in agitation for safeguarding or granting economic and sociocultural privileges to the "sons of the soil." The Jharkhand movement in Bihar and the "aliens" issue in Assam are instances of such concerns.

Resolutions of these controversies are still being attempted. One notices a good deal of "adhocism" in response to pushing and pulling by divergent language and sociocultural lobbies. A serious probe aimed at understanding the role of democratization processes, mass communication technology, and economic mobility in the communication patterns of contemporary societies—developed as well as developing—will significantly contribute to a long-range view of the issues involved in such fundamental changes. In the same vein, questions of the changing role of the government, and of the elite as custodians of the interests of their people, also are raised.

Apparent contradictions on the pluralistic South Asian scene make us aware of the challenges ahead. In the midst of conflicting elitist and progressive theories, it is essential to investigate the fundamental issues in the linguistic reconstruction of reality, and through such an investigation form sound judgments for the transcendental interests of mankind.

Appendix

Languages Used as Media

Language	Genealogical Affiliation	Mother Tongues Grouped under the Language*
A. *Principal Media*		
1. Hindi	Indo-Aryan—Central	279
2. Bengali	Indo-Aryan—East	15
3. Telugu	Dravidian—South	36
4. Marathi	Indo-Aryan—South	65
5. Tamil	Dravidian—South	22
6. Urdu	Indo-Aryan—Central	9
7. Gujarati	Indo-Aryan—Central	27
8. Malayalam	Dravidian—South	14
9. Kannada	Dravidian—South	32
10. Oriya	Indo-Aryan—East	24
11. Panjabi	Indo-Aryan—Central	27
12. Assamese	Indo-Aryan—East	2
13. Sindhi	Indo-Aryan—Northwest	8
14. English	Indo-European—Germanic	1
B. *Foreign Media*		
1. Persian	Iranian	
2. Portuguese‡	Indo-European—Romance	
3. French	Indo-European—Romance	
C. *Partial Media*		
1. Santali	Austric—Munda	11
2. Kashmiri	Indo-Aryan—Dardic	5
3. Nepali/Gorkhali	Indo-Aryan—Pahari	4
4. Manipuri/Meithei	Tibeto-Chinese—Kuki Chin§	3
5. Khasi	Austric—Mon Khmer	6
6. Garo	Tibeto-Chinese—Bodo	3
7. Lushai/Mizo	Tibeto-Chinese—Kuki Chin	2
8. Tibetan	Tibeto-Chinese—Tibetan	14
D. *Preparatory Media* (recognized by the state[s])		
1. Maithili‡	Indo-Aryan—East	9
2. Sadan/Sadri‡	Indo-Aryan—East (pidgin)	1
3. Konkani	Indo-Aryan—South	16
4. Kurukh/Oraon	Dravidian—North	9
5. Mundari	Austric—Munda	2
6. Ho	Austric—Munda	2
7. Bodo	Tibeto-Chinese—Bodo	2
8. Tripuri	Tibeto-Chinese—Bodo	6
9. Kharia	Austric—Munda	5
10. Ao	Tibeto-Chinese—Naga	3
11. Konyak	Tibeto-Chinese—Naga	3
12. Angami	Tibeto-Chinese—Naga	2

Total Speakers, 1971 (in thousands)†	Percentage to Total Population	Dominant State(s)
208,514	38.0	Hindi-Urdu-Panjabi (HUP) region, and urban centers
44,792	8.2	West Bengal, Tripura
44,757	8.2	Andhra Pradesh
41,765	7.6	Maharashtra
37,690	6.9	Tamil Nadu, Pondicherry
28,621	5.2	HUP region, Andhra Pradesh
25,865	4.7	Gujarat
21,939	4.0	Kerala, Lakshadveep Islands
21,711	4.0	Karnataka
19,863	3.6	Orissa
14,108	2.6	Panjab
8960	1.6	Assam
1677	0.3	Maharashtra, Gujarat, Rajasthan, Madhya Pradesh, Delhi
192	0.04	Urban centers
11		
6		
—		
3787	0.69	Bihar, Orissa West Bengal
2495	0.46	Jammu and Kashmir
1420	0.26	West Bengal, Sikkim
792	0.14	Manipur
479	0.09	Meghalaya
412	0.08	Meghalaya
272	0.05	Mizoram
49	0.01	West Bengal
[figures grouped under Hindi]		Bihar
[figures grouped under Hindi]		Bihar
1508	0.28	Goa, Daman, and Diu
1236	0.23	Bihar
771	0.14	Bihar
751	0.14	Bihar
557	0.10	Assam
373	0.07	Tripura
191	0.04	Bihar
75	0.01	Nagaland
72	0.01	Nagaland
69	0.01	Nagaland

Languages Used as Media (Continued)

Language	Genealogical Affiliation	Mother Tongues Grouped under the Language*
13. Sema	Tibeto-Chinese—Naga	1
14. Ladakhi	Tibeto-Chinese—Tibetan	5
15. Hmar	Tibeto-Chinese—Kuki Chin	1
16. Lotha	Tibeto-Chinese—Naga	1
17. Kuki	Tibeto-Chinese—Kuku Chin	3
18. Naga	Tibeto-Chinese—Naga	2
19. Mishmi (Digaru Taron)	Tibeto-Chinese—NEFA	4
20. Sangtam	Tibeto-Chinese—Naga	3
21. Yimchungre	Tibeto-Chinese—Naga	2
22. Phom	Tibeto-Chinese—Naga	2
23. Nicobarese	Austric—Mon Khmer	1
24. Chang	Tibeto-Chinese—Naga	1
25. Khiemnungan	Tibeto-Chinese—Naga	1
26. Rengma‡	Tibeto-Chinese—Naga	2
27. Chakhesang‡	Tibeto-Chinese—Naga	3
28. Karen‡	Karen (foreign)	1

E. *Elementary Media* (promoted by private institutions)

Language	Genealogical Affiliation	Mother Tongues Grouped under the Language*
1. Bhili	Indo-Aryan—Central	36
2. Gondi	Dravidian—Central	13
3. Halabi	Indo-Aryan—Central (pidgin)	1
4. Korku	Austric—Munda	4
5. Nissi/Dafla	Tibeto-Chinese—NEFA	5
6. Apatani‡	Tibeto-Chinese—NEFA	1
7. Adi-Mishing	Tibeto-Chinese—NEFA	14
8. Tangkhul	Tibeto-Chinese—Naga	1
9. Kabui	Tibeto-Chinese—Naga	1
10. Thado	Tibeto-Chinese—Kuki Chin	19
11. Dimasa	Tibeto-Chinese—Bodo	1
12. Mao	Tibeto-Chinese—Naga	1
13. Lepcha	Tibeto-Chinese—Himalayan	1
14. Paite	Tibeto-Chinese—Kuki Chin	1
15. Nocte	Tibeto-Chinese—Naga	1
16. Koch	Tibeto-Chinese—Bodo	1
17. Tangsa	Tibeto-Chinese—Naga	1
18. Lakher	Tibeto-Chinese—Kuki Chin	1
19. Vaiphei	Tibeto-Chinese—Kuki Chin	1
20. Mech‡	Tibeto-Chinese—Bodo	1
21. Anal‡	Tibeto-Chinese—Kuki Chin	2
22. Kom‡	Tibeto-Chinese—Kuki Chin	1
23. Zemi‡	Tibeto-Chinese—Naga	1
24. Gangte‡	Tibeto-Chinese—Kuki Chin	2
25. Singpho‡	Tibeto-Chinese—Kachin	1
26. Khampti‡	Tibeto-Chinese—Thai	1

* According to the 1961 census, annexture III, Mitra (1964).
† Census of India: 1971, Social and Cultural Tables, Part II-C (i), A. Chandra Sekhar (1976:4–86).
‡ Listed separately in Provisional Tables, 1971 census—Mother Tongues, Appendix II, R. C. Nigam (1972:333–339).

Total Speakers, 1971 (in thousands)†	Percentage to Total Population	Dominant State(s)
65	0.01	Nagaland
60	0.01	Jammu and Kashmir
38	0.01	Manipur, Assam
37	0.01	Nagaland
33	0.01	Nagaland
23		Nagaland
22		Arunachal Pradesh
20		Nagaland
20		Nagaland
18		Nagaland
18		Andaman and Nicobar Islands
16		Nagaland
14		Nagaland
9		Nagaland
—		Nagaland
—		Andaman and Nicobar Islands
3399	0.62	Gujarat
1688	0.31	Madhya Pradesh
346	0.06	Madhya Pradesh
307	0.06	Madhya Pradesh
115	0.02	Arunachal Pradesh
[grouped under Nissi/Dafla]		Arunachal Pradesh
99	0.02	Arunachal Pradesh
58	0.01	Manipur
51	0.01	Manipur
51	0.01	Manipur
40	0.01	Assam
35	0.01	Manipur
33	0.01	West Bengal
27	0.01	Manipur
25		Arunachal Pradesh
14		Assam
13		Arunachal Pradesh
12		Mizoram
12		Manipur
[grouped under Bodo]		West Bengal
7		Manipur
7		Manipur
7		Assam
6		Manipur
—		Assam
—		Arunachal Pradesh, Assam

§ The language family referred to as Tibeto-Chinese in this study is widely known among linguists as Sino-Tibetan. The use of the term "Tibeto-Chinese" in Indian census publications is based on Grierson's pioneering work, *The Linguistic Survey of India* (1903-1928).

Bibliography

Austin, John L. 1962. *How to Do Things with Words.* Cambridge, Mass.: Harvard University Press.
Azad, Maulana A. 1949. "Inaugural address." In *Proceedings of the Educational Conference.* New Delhi: Ministry of Education.
Barbiana, School of. 1970. *Letter to a Teacher.* Harmondsworth: Penguin.
Barpujari, S. K. 1973. "Naga education in the nineteenth century." *Highlander* [Kohima] 1(1):24-30.
Berger, Peter L., and Luckmann, T. 1966. *The Social Construction of Reality: A Treatise in the Sociology of Knowledge.* New York: Doubleday, Anchor Books.
Bernstein, Basil. 1971. *Class, Codes and Control.* London: Routledge and Kegan Paul.
Black, Max, ed. 1962. *The Importance of Language.* Ithaca: Cornell University Press.
Bose, Ashish. 1969. "Some aspects of the linguistic demography of India." In A. Poddar, ed., pp. 37-51.
Braga, Giorgio. 1972. "Norme e comportamento linguistico come dialettica fra aspettazione ed attuazione" [Linguistic norms and behavior: The dialectic of expectations and performance]. *Sociologia* [Rome] n.s. 6(1):7-58.
Britton, James. 1970. "Their language and our teaching." *English in Education* 4(2):5-13.
Brown, Roger, and Gilman, A. 1960. "The pronouns of power and solidarity." In *Style in Language,* edited by T. A. Sebeok. Cambridge, Mass.: The M.I.T. Press.
Burton, Richard F. 1851. *Sindh and the Races that Inhabit the Valley of the Indus with Notices of Topology and History of the Province.* London: W. H. Allens.
Chandra Sekhar, A. 1977. *Social and Cultural Tables: Census of India—1971.* Series 1, Part II-C (i). New Delhi: Registrar General and Census Commissioner of India.

Chatterjee, Suniti Kumar. 1945. *Language and the Linguistic Problem.* London: Oxford University Press.
Chaturvedi, M. G. 1976. *Position of Languages in School Curriculum in India.* New Delhi: National Council for Educational Research and Training.
Chomsky, Noam. 1965. *Aspects of the Theory of Syntax.* Cambridge, Mass.: The M.I.T. Press.
Cranston, Maurice. 1975. "Mother tongues." *The Sunday Times,* London, 2 February 1975.
Dakin, Julian. 1968. "Language and education in India." In *Language in Education: The Problem in Commonwealth Africa and the Indo-Pakistan Subcontinent,* by J. Dakin, B. Tiffen, and H. G. Widdowson, pp. 1-61. London: Oxford University Press.
Damle, Yashwant B. 1968. "Language problem: A sociological analysis." In L. M. Khubchandani, ed., pp. 27-31.
Das Gupta, Jyotirindra. 1970. *Language Conflict and National Development: Group Politics and National Language Policy in India.* Berkeley: Center for South and Southeast Asian Studies, University of California.
Davidson, T. T. L. 1969. "Indian bilingualism and the evidence of the Census of 1961." *Lingua* 22(2-3):176-196.
Deutsch, Karl W. 1953. *Nationalism and Social Communication: An Inquiry into the Foundations of Nationality.* Cambridge, Mass.: The M.I.T. Press.
Doi, Takeo. 1974. "Some psychological themes in Japanese human relationships." In *Intercultural Encounters with Japan: Communication—Contact and Conflict,* edited by J. C. Condon and M. Saito. Tokyo: Simul Press.
Doughty, Peter, Pearce, J., and Thornton, G. 1972. *Exploring Language.* London: Schools Council and Arnold.
Emeneau, Murray B. 1956. "India as a linguistic area." *Language* 32:3-16.
———. 1962. "Bilingualism and structural borrowings." *Proceedings of the American Philosophical Society* 106(5):430-442.
Ferguson, Charles A. 1959. "Diglossia." *Word* 15:325-340.
———. 1962. "The language factor in national development." In *Study of the Role of Second Languages in Asia, Africa, and Latin America,* edited by F. A. Rice, pp. 8-14. Washington, D.C.: Center for Applied Linguistics.
———. 1968. "Language development." In *Language Problems of Developing Nations,* edited by J. A. Fishman, C. A. Ferguson, and J. Das Gupta, pp. 27-36. New York: Wiley.
Ferguson, Charles A., and Gumperz, John J., eds. 1960. *Linguistic Diversity in South Asia,* special issue of *International Journal of American Linguistics* 26(3).
Fishman, Joshua A. 1974. "Language modernization and planning in comparison with other types of national modernization and planning." In J. A. Fishman, ed., pp. 79-102.
Fishman, Joshua A., ed. 1974. *Advances in Language Planning.* The Hague: Mouton.
Fodor, Istvan. 1966. "Linguistic problems and language planning in Africa." *Linguistics* 25:18-33.

Ford Foundation. 1973. *Language Planning Processes: Project Report.* Uppsala: International Conference on Language Planning.
Friedrich, Paul. 1966. "Structural implications of Russian pronominal usage." In *Sociolinguistics,* edited by W. Bright, pp. 214-259. The Hague: Mouton.
Gait, E. A. 1913. *Census of India—1911,* Vol. 1—India, Part I—Report. Calcutta: Government of India.
Gandhi, Mohandas K. 1916. "The present system of education." In *The Problem of Education (Collected Works:* 1962), by M. K. Gandhi. Ahmedabad: Navajivan Publishing House.
———. 1956. *Thoughts on National Language.* Ahmedabad: Navajivan Publishing House.
———. 1958. *All Men Are Brothers* (compiled by J. B. Kripalani). Ahmedabad: Navajivan Publishing House.
Garvin, Paul L. 1973. "Some comments on language planning." In J. Rubin and R. Shuy, eds., pp. 24-33.
Geertz, Clifford, ed. 1963. *Old Societies and New States: The Quest for Modernity in Asia and Africa.* New York: Free Press oy Glencoe.
Goel, B. S., and Saini, S. K. 1972. *Mother Tongue and Equality of Opportunity in Education.* New Delhi: National Council for Educational Research and Training.
Gordon, Milton M. 1981. "Models of pluralism." *Annals of the American Academy of Political and Social Science* 454 (March):178-188.
Gorman, T. P. 1973. "Language allocation and language planning in a developing nation." In J. Rubin and R. Shuy, eds., pp. 72-82.
Grierson, George A. 1903-1928. *Linguistic Survey of India.* 12 vols. Calcutta: Government of India.
Gumperz, John J. 1968. "Speech communities." *Encyclopedia of the Social Sciences,* Vol. 9, pp. 381-386.
Gumperz, John J., and Naim, C. M. 1960. "Formal and informal standards in the Hindi regional language area." In C. A. Ferguson and J. J. Gumperz, eds., pp. 92-118; also in Gumperz, 1971: *Language in Social Groups,* pp. 48-76. Stanford: Stanford University Press.
Halliday, M. A. K., McIntosh, A., and Strevens, P. 1964. *The Linguistic Sciences and Language Teaching.* London: Longmans.
Harrison, Selig. 1960. *India: The Most Dangerous Decades.* Princeton, N.J.: Princeton University Press.
Hartog, Philip Joseph. 1929. *Interim Report of the Indian Statutory Commission: Auxiliary Committee on Growth of Education.* London: H.M. Stationery Office.
Haugen, Einar. 1966. "Dialect, language and nation." *American Anthropologist* 68 (4):922-935.
Hertzler, Joyce Oramel. 1965. *A Sociology of Language.* New York: Random House.
Hutton, J. H. 1933. *Census of India—1931,* Vol. 1—India, Part I—Report. Delhi: Government of India.
India, Government of. 1948. *Report of the Committee on the Medium of Instruc-*

tion at the University Level. Pamphlet 57. New Delhi: Ministry of Education.

———. 1949. *Report of the University Education Commission.* New Delhi: Ministry of Education.

———. 1950. *The Constitution of India.* New Delhi: Ministry of Law.

———. 1953. *Secondary Education Commission Report.* New Delhi: Ministry of Education.

———. 1954. *Census of India—1951,* Language Tables. New Delhi: Registrar General of India.

———. 1956a. *Report of the Official Language Commission.* New Delhi: Ministry of Home Affairs.

———. 1956b. *Second Five Year Plan.* New Delhi: Planning Commission.

———. 1960. *Report of the University Grants Commission.* New Delhi: University Grants Commission.

———. 1961. *Silver Jubilee Souvenir.* New Delhi: Ministry of Education.

———. 1965. *Report of Standards of University Education.* New Delhi: University Grants Commission.

———. 1966. *Report of the Education Commission.* New Delhi: Ministry of Education.

———. 1972. *Pocket Book of Population Statistics, Census of India 1971,* Census Centenary Publication. New Delhi: Registrar General of India.

———. 1978. *Twenty Second Annual Report of the Registrar of Newspapers in India,* Part I. New Delhi: Ministry of Information and Broadcasting.

Jain, Dhanesh Kumar. 1973. "Pronominal usage in Hindi: A sociolinguistic study." Ph.D. thesis, University of Pennsylvania, Philadelphia.

Jakobson, Roman. 1973. *Main Trends in the Science of Language.* London: George Allen.

Jernudd, Björn H. 1973. "Language planning as a type of language treatment." In J. Rubin and R. Shuy, eds., pp. 11–23.

Jernudd, Björn H., and Das Gupta, J. 1971. "Towards a theory of language planning." In *Can Language Be Planned? Sociolinguistic Theory and Practice for Developing Nations,* edited by J. Rubin and B. Jernudd, pp. 195–215. Honolulu: University Press of Hawaii.

Katre, Sumitra M. 1961. *Introduction to Modern Indian Linguistics.* Gauhati: University of Gauhati.

Kelkar, Ashok R. 1968. *Studies in Hindi-Urdu.* Vol. 1. Poona: Deccan College Postgraduate and Research Institute.

Khubchandani, Lachman M. 1963. "The acculturation of Indian Sindhi to Hindi: A study of language in contact." Ph.D. dissertation, University of Pennsylvania, Philadelphia; Ann Arbor: University Microfilm Corporation.

———. 1966. "Bilingual interference in language learning." Seminar on Language Teaching, American Institute of Indian Studies, Poona.

———. 1967. "Education policy for a multilingual society: Comments on the Education Commission Report—1966." *Education Quarterly* 18 (January): 42–48. Reprinted, with discussion, in L. M. Khubchandani, ed., 1968:32–50.

———. 1968. "Planned change in the media of instruction: Problems of switch over." Proceedings of the Seminar on Historical Survey of Language Controversy, Shantiniketan (New Delhi: National Council for Educational Research and Training); also in *La Monda Lingvo-Problemo,* 1972:4: 142-152.

———. 1969a. "Sindhi." In *Linguistics in South Asia: Current Trends in Linguistics,* Vol.5, T. A. Sebeok, gen. ed., pp. 201-234. The Hague: Mouton.

———. 1969b. "Language planning in multilingual communication network: A study of Indian situation," *Actes du X Congrès International des Linguistes,* 1967, Bucharest, Vol. 1, pp. 591-597.

———. 1969c. "Functional importance of Hindi and English in India." In A. Poddar, ed., pp. 178-189.

———. 1969d. "Equipping major languages for new roles." In A. Poddar, ed., pp. 89-90.

———. 1969e. "Media of education of a multilingual nation." In A. Poddar, ed., pp. 304-309.

———. 1971. "Language education policy of British rulers in India." South Asia Seminar, University of Pennsylvania, Philadelphia.

———. 1972a. "Mother tongue in multilingual societies." In *Economic and Socio-cultural Dimensions of Regionalization,* A. Chandra Sekhar, gen. ed., pp. 427-450. Census Centenary Monograph No. 7. New Delhi: Registrar General of India.

———. 1972b. "Distribution of contact languages in India: A study of the 1961 bilingualism returns." Indian Census Centenary Seminar, New Delhi: Registrar General of India; also in J. A. Fishman, ed., 1978. *Advances in the Study of Societal Multilingualism,* Vol. 2, pp. 553-585. The Hague: Mouton.

———. 1972c. "Yugoslavia: In search for identity." Paper presented at the Indian Institute of Advanced Study, Simla; also in L. M. Khubchandani, 1981. *Theoretical Issues in Sociolinguistics: Collected Papers,* Vol. 1. Poona: Centre for Communication Studies.

———. 1973a. *Social Stratification and Language Behaviour.* Simla: Indian Institute of Advanced Study.

———. 1973b. "Aspects of cognition, propriety and compatibility in language activity: A study of Hindi-Urdu address and reference system." Workshop on Social Stratification and Language Behaviour, Indian Institute of Advanced Study, Simla; revised title: 1978. "Towards a selection grammar: Fluidity in modes of address and reference in Hindi-Urdu." *Indian Linguistics* 39:1-24.

———. 1973c. "English in India: A sociolinguistic appraisal." *International Journal of Dravidian Linguistics* [Trivandrum] 2(2):199-211.

———. 1973d. "Indian bilingualism and English: An analysis of the 1961 census data." *Demography India* 2(1):160-174.

———. 1973e. "Language policy: Review of Das Gupta (1970)." *Language in Society* 2(2):289-293.

———. 1973f. *South Asian Sociolinguistics: A Select Bibliography.* Simla: Indian Institute of Advanced Study.

———. 1974a. "Fluidity in mother tongue identity." In A. Verdoodt, ed., *Applied Sociolinguistics,* Vol. 2. Copenhagen AILA Proceedings. Heidelberg: J. Groos Verlag; also in R. R. Mehrotra and L. M. Khubchandani.

———. 1974b. "Language policy for a plural society." In *Towards a Cultural Policy for India,* edited by S. Saberwal, pp. 97–111. Delhi: Vikas Publishing House and Indian Institute of Advanced Study.

———. 1974c. "Language in a behavioural framework." *RELC Journal* [Singapore] 5(1):16–26.

———. 1975a. "Foreign language teaching: Instruction and interaction strategies." *RELC Journal* [Singapore] 6(1):1–5; also in R. R. Mehrotra and L. M. Khubchandani.

———. 1975b. "Dilemmas of language transition: Challenges to language planning in India." In *Topics in Culture Learning,* edited by R. Brislin, Vol. III, pp. 151–164. Honolulu: East-West Center.

———. 1978. "Multilingual education in India." In *Case Studies in Bilingual Education,* edited by B. Spolsky and R. L. Cooper, Rowley, Mass.: Newbury House Publishers.

———. 1981a. *Language, Education, Social Justice.* Poona: Centre for Communication Studies.

———. 1981b. "Face-to-face interaction: A probe into processes of communication." *Indian Philosophical Quarterly* 8(3):373–384.

Khubchandani, Lachman M., ed. 1968. *Linguistics and Language Planning in India.* Special issue of the *Bulletin of the Deccan College Research Institute* 27:1–2; also published in the Deccan College Centenary Series, N. G. Kalelkar, gen. ed.

Khubchandani, Lachman M., ed. forthcoming. *Language and Plural Society: Studies on Indian Sociolinguistics.* Simla: Indian Institute of Advanced Study.

Kirk, Dudley. 1946. *Europe's Population in the Inter-war Years.* Geneva: League of Nations.

Kloss, Heinz. 1967a. "Bilingualism and nationalism." *Journal of Social Sciences* 23(2):39–47.

———. 1967b. "Abstand and Ausbau languages." *Anthropological Linguistics* 9:29–41.

———. 1972. "A sociolinguist's approach to language statistics." Indian Census Centenary Seminar, New Delhi.

Kloss, Heinz, and McConnell, Grant D. 1974. *The Linguistic Composition of the Nations of the World.* Vol. 1. Quebec City: Presses de l'Université Laval.

Labov, William. 1970. "The study of language in its social context." *Studium Generale* 23:30–87.

———. 1972. "The logic of nonstandard English." In *Language and Social Context,* edited by Pier Paolo Giglioli, pp. 179–215. Harmondsworth: Penguin.

Labov, William, Cohen, Paul, Robins, Clarence, and Lewis, John. 1969. A Study of the Non-Standard English of Negro and Puerto Rican Speakers

Bibliography 189

in New York City: Final Report, 2 vols. Philadelphia: U.S. Regional Survey.

Lambert, Richard D. 1981. "Ethnic/racial relations in the United States in comparative perspective." *The Annals of the American Academy of Political and Social Science [AAPSS]* 454 (March):189-205.

Lavondès, Henri. 1974. "Language policy, language engineering and literacy in French Polynesia." In J. A. Fishman, ed., pp. 255-276.

Le Page, Robert B. 1964. *The National Language Question: Linguistic Problems of Newly Independent States.* London: Institute of Race Relations.

Levy, Paul M. G. 1960. *La Querelle du Recensement.* Bruxelles: Belgian Institute of Political Science.

Loflin, Marvin D. 1967. "A teaching problem in nonstandard Negro English." *English Journal* 56(9):1312-1314.

Lutze, Lothar. 1968. "Linguistic prospects of the emergence of an internal contact language for India." *South Asian Studies* 4.

Mahulkar, D. D. 1981. Language and Linguistic Methodology. Radhabai Katre Memorial Lectures. Poona: Linguistic Society of India (mimeographed).

Mathai, S. 1959. "The future of the Three Language Formula." *Secondary Education* [New Delhi], October issue, pp. 9-10.

Mehrotra, Raja Ram, and Khubchandani, Lachman M. 1975. *Studies in Linguistics: Occasional Papers.* Simla: Indian Institute of Advanced Study.

Mitra, Asok. 1964. *Census of India 1961,* Vol. 1—India, Part II-C (ii). Delhi: Government of India.

Myrdal, Gunnar. 1968. *Asian Drama: An Enquiry into the Poverty of Nations.* 3 vols. New York: Pantheon.

Naik, J. P. 1963. *Selections from Educational Records of the Government of India.* Vol. 2: Development of University Education, 1860-1887. New Delhi: National Archives of India.

Nayar, Baldev Raj. 1969. *National Communication and Language Policy in India.* New York: Praeger.

Neustupný, Jiri V. 1974. "Basic types of treatment of language problems." In J. A. Fishman, ed., pp. 37-48.

Nigam, R. C. 1972. *Language Handbook on Mother Tongues in Census, 1971.* Census Centenary Monograph No. 10. New Delhi: Registrar General of India.

Pandit, Prabodh B. 1964. "Indian readjustments in the English consonant system." *Indian Linguistics* 25:202-205.

———. 1969a. "Logistics of language development." In A. Poddar, ed., pp. 112-117.

———. 1969b. "Parameters of speech variation in an Indian community." In A. Poddar, ed., pp. 207-228.

———. 1972. *India as a Sociolinguistic Area.* Guné Memorial Lectures. Poona: University of Poona.

Pike, Kenneth, L. 1967. *Language in Relation to a Unified Theory of the Structure of Human Behavior.* 2d rev. ed. The Hague: Mouton.

Poddar, Arabinda, ed. 1969. *Language and Society in India.* Transactions, Vol. 8. Simla: Indian Institute of Advanced Study.

Prague School. 1932. "General principles for the cultivation of good language," trans. by P. L. Garvin. In J. Rubin and R. Shuy, eds., pp. 102–111.
Ray, Punya Sloka. 1963. *Language Standardization: Studies in Prescriptive Linguistics.* The Hague: Mouton.
Richey, J. A. 1922. *Selections from Educational Records of the Government of India, 1840–1859,* Part II. London: Bureau of Education.
Ross, Alan S. C. 1956. "U and non-U: An essay in sociological linguistics." In *Noblesse Oblige,* edited by Nancy Mitford. London: H. Hamilton; also in M. Black, ed., pp. 91–106.
Ross, Jennie-Keith. 1975. "Social borders: Definitions of diversity." *Current Anthropology* 16(1):53–72.
Rubin, Joan. 1973. "Language planning: Discussion of some current issues." In J. Rubin and R. Shuy, eds., pp. v–x.
Rubin, Joan, and Shuy, Roger, eds. 1973. *Language Planning: Current Issues and Research.* Washington, D.C.: Georgetown University Press.
Said, Abdul A., and Simmons, Luis R., eds. 1976. *Ethnicity in an International Context: The Politics of Dissociation.* New Brunswick, N.J.: Transaction Books.
Saiyidain, K. G., Naik, J. P., and Husain, S. Abid. 1962. *Compulsory Education in India.* Studies on Compulsory Education, Vol. 11. Paris: UNESCO.
Sargent, H. 1944. *Post War Educational Development in India.* Delhi: Manager of Publications.
Saussure, Ferdinand de. 1959. *Course in General Linguistics,* edited by C. Bally and Albert Sechehaye in collaboration with Albert Reidlinger. Translated from the French by Wade Baskin. New York: Philosophical Library.
Searle, Chris. 1973. *This New Season.* London: Calder & Boyars.
Sharma, R. K. 1971. "Tribal education in Nagaland." In *Proceedings of the Conference of Tribal Research Bureaus in India.* Mysore: Central Institute of Indian Languages.
Sharp, H. 1920. *Selections from Educational Records, 1781–1839.* Part I. London: Bureau of Education.
Shils, Edward A. 1961. *The Intellectual between Tradition and Modernity: The Indian Situation.* The Hague: Mouton.
Sledd, James. 1972. "Doublespeak: Dialectology in the service of Big Brother." *College English* 33(4):439–456.
Spolsky, Bernard. 1971. "The limits of language education." *Linguistic Reporter* 13(3):1–5.
Steiner, George. 1975. *After Babel: Aspects of Language and Translation.* New York: Oxford University Press.
Subramania, K. A. Iyer. 1963. *Vākyapadīya of Bhartrhari.* Vol. 1. Poona: Deccan College Postgraduate and Research Institute.
Tagore, Rabindranath. 1906. "The problem of education." In *Towards Universal Man (Collected Works:* 1961), by R. B. Tagore. Bombay: Asia Publishing House.
Tarski, A. 1956. *Logic, Semantics, Mathematics.* London: Oxford University Press.

Tauli, Victor. 1968. *Introduction to a Theory of Language Planning.* Uppsala: Acta Universitatis Upsaliensis.
UNESCO. 1953. *The Use of Vernacular Language in Education.* Series: Monographs on Fundamental Education. Paris.
Waismann, Freidrich. 1962. "The resources of language." In M. Black, ed., pp. 107–120.
Weinreich, Uriel, Labov, William, and Herzog, M. 1968. "Empirical foundations for a theory of language change." In *Directions for Historical Linguistics,* edited by W. P. Lehmann and Y. Malkiel, pp. 97–195. Austin, Texas: University of Texas Press.
Whitehead, Alfred N. 1932. *Adventures of Ideas.* Cambridge: Cambridge University Press.
Widdowson, H. G. 1968. "The teaching of English through science." In *Language in Education: The Problem in Commonwealth Africa and the Indo-Pakistan Subcontinent,* by J. Dakin, B. Tiffen, and H. G. Widdowson, pp. 115–177. London: Oxford University Press.
Wilkinson, Andrew M. 1975. *Language and Education.* London: Oxford University Press.
Winograd, Terry. 1974. "Artificial intelligence: When will computers understand people?" *Psychology Today,* May 1974, pp. 73–79.
Wittgenstein, Ludwig. 1961. *Tractatus Logico Philosophicus,* translated from German by G. F. Pears and B. F. McGuinness. London: Routledge and Kegan Paul.
Zakir, Hussain. 1950. *Convention on the Cultural Unity of India.* Bombay: T. A. Parekh Endowment.

Language Index

Ad Dharmi, mother tongue (MT) label, 47
Adi-Mishing, 180
Ahiri Hindi, MT label, 47
Albanian, 128
Altaic, language group, 39n.2
American Indian, language group, 128
Anal, 180
Andhra, MT label, 47
Angami, 178
Ao, 178
Apabhraṃsha, classical, 26
Apatani, 180
Arabic, classical, 14, 72 (Table 8), 77, 111, 126, 152
  teaching of, 72 (Table 8), 118, 137, 138–139
Ardhamagadhi, classical, 138
Aryan. *See* Indo-Aryan
Assamese
  bilingualism, 4, 127 (Table 18), 133n.4, 178
  press, 13
  speakers, 6 (Table 1), 10 (Table 2), 106 (Table 17)
Austro-Asiatic (Austric), language group, 3, 4, 17n.3, 178, 180
Avestha, classical, 138
Awadhi, 27, 57, 104, 109, 112, 116n.1, 168
  literature, 26, 111, 115
  speakers, 96 (Table 12)
  speaking elite, 27

Baghelkhandi, MT label, 96 (Table 12)
Bagri, MT label, 96 (Table 12)
Balti, 11 (Table 2)
Bangru, Hariani (Haryanvi), 104, 109, 111, 116n.1

Banjari, 104
  speakers, 92, 96 (Table 12)
Basque, 58
Bazaar Hindustani. *See* Hindustani
Bengali, 3, 4, 71, 73 (Table 8), 145
  bilingualism, 13
  education, 70, 119, 143, 178–179
  press, 15 (Table 3)
  speakers, 6 (Table 1), 105, 106 (Table 17)
Bharati, MT label, 47
Bhili, 10 (Table 2), 138, 180–181
Bhojpuri, 9, 26, 27, 104, 109, 112
  speakers, 11 (Table 2), 92, 94 (Table 11)
Bhotia, 11 (Table 2)
Bhumij, 93
Bihari, language group, 9, 58, 59, 73 (Table 8), 98 (Table 14)
  speakers, 11 (Table 2), 46, 92–94, 102–104
Bodo
  education, 139, 178–179
  language group, 178–179
  speakers, 10 (Table 2), 93
Bolti Zaban, MT label, 47
Braj, Braj Bhakha, 27, 29, 104, 109, 116n.1, 168
  literature, 27, 111, 115
Breton, 19, 43, 58
Bulgarian, 64n.4
Bundelkhandi, 96 (Table 12), 104, 109, 116n.1

Caranthian, 57
Carnataca. *See* Kannada
Celtic, language group, 43, 58
Chakhesang, 180

Chameali, 104
Chang, 180
Chhatisgarhi, 27, 57, 109, 112, 116n.1
  speakers, 10 (Table 2), 92, 96 (Table 12), 103, 104
Chicano, 128
Chinese, 37, 111
  language group, 24
Christian, MT label, 47
Coorgi, 10 (Table 2)
Croatian, 46, 56, 57, 113, 115, 116
Croato-Serbian. *See* Serbo-Croatian

Dafla. *See* Nissi
Dakhini. *See* Hindi
Danish, 46
Dardic, language group, 5
Darri. *See* Persian
Dehlvi. *See* Hindi
Deshi, MT label, 47
Deswali, MT label, 111
Dhundhari, 96 (Table 12), 104
Digaru Taron. *See* Mishmi
Dimasa, 180
Dogri, 5, 139
  speakers, 10 (Table 2), 93, 96 (Table 12), 108, 109
Dravidam, MT label, 47
Dravidian, language group, 3, 4, 5, 17n.2, 26, 37, 70, 115, 178
Dutch, 46

Eastern Hindi, generic label, 58, 104
English, 5, 14, 15, 17, 41, 67, 68, 70, 71, 72–73 (Table 8), 75, 78, 79, 84, 111, 119, 120, 122–128, 135–139
  AIR (All-India Radio) English, 82
  American English, 78, 80
  BBC (British Broadcasting Service) English, 82
  bilingual education, 128
  bilingualism, 9, 10 (Table 2), 12–15, 17, 38, 51, 53, 54, 75, 80, 81
  Black English, 43
  borrowings from, 38, 113, 114
  British English, 78, 80, 114, 131
  in British and Scottish census, 57
  as a "classical" language, 80, 122, 123
  consonant system of, 78
  during colonial rule, 65, 66, 77–81, 119–126, 135, 150, 151
  in the education system, 72–73 (Table 8), 76–80, 86n.5, 119–122, 128, 129, 135–139, 143–145
  elite, 78–80, 119, 136, 142
  functions of, 14, 17, 76–81, 119, 120, 154
  Indo-English, 78
  as instructional medium, 20, 22, 70, 78, 79, 119–122, 124, 126, 128, 133n.2, 136, 142–144, 178
  internalization of, 77
  Latinized English, 126
  as a link language, 142
  literature, 79
  "loan proneness" of, 37
  modernization associated with, 66, 68
  as mother tongue, 77, 111, 145
  NNE (Non-standard Negro English), 43
  press, 14, 15, 15 (Table 3), 16 (Table 4), 17
  Pressure Index, 51, 52, 53
  RP (Received Pronunciation), 49, 114
  South Asian English, 77–81
  speakers, 6 (Table 1), 53, 62, 79
  and Swahili, 41
  in Three-Language Formula, 137, 138
  White and Black English, 157

French, 41, 58, 65, 126, 138, 152
  bilingual education, 128
  as instructional medium, 70, 178
Frisian, 19

Gaelic, 57
Gangte, 180
Garhwali, 10 (Table 2), 47, 93, 96 (Table 12)
Garo, 10 (Table 2), 127 (Table 18), 138, 178
German, 37, 57, 138, 154
  Low German, 46
Germanic. *See* Indo-European
Gojri, 96 (Table 12), 104
Gondi, 10 (Table 2), 180
  Maria Gondi, 93, 98 (Table 14)
Gorkhali, *See* Nepali
Greek, 120, 123, 126, 138
Gujarati, 5, 34, 46, 97 (Table 13)
  bilingualism, 13, 14, 129
  press, 15 (Table 3)
  medium, 142, 178
  speakers, 6 (Table 1), 10 (Table 2), 105, 106 (Table 17)

Halabi, pidgin, 180
Hariani, Haryanvi. *See* Bangru
Hebrew, 37, 138
Himalayan, language group, 180
Hindi, 5, 7, 8, 14, 41, 51–54, 57, 59–61, 69–71, 82–84, 97 (Table 13), 103, 104, 107–112, 125, 127–129, 135–138, 143

Language Index

Ahiri Hindi, MT label, 47
amalgam, 26, 27, 168
Anglicized version of, 26, 111
as "associate" native speech, 111
as "Ausbau" language, 112
bilingual education, 127 (Table 18)
bilingualism, 13, 14, 17, 51, 57, 128
borrowing patterns, 112, 113
Dakhini Hindi, 27
Dehlvi Hindi, 27
and Devanagari script, 70, 109, 112
development of, 68, 83, 84
dialect and language, 116n.1
elite, 27, 67, 135, 142
in Fluid Zone, 105, 107, 109, 112
fluidity in census claims, 102–104
functions of, 93, 111–113, 154
generic label, 58, 59, 104
"grass-roots" Hindi (Bombay Hindustani), 154
"highbrow" and "lowbrow" styles, 26, 110, 111, 113, 114
and Hinduism, 60
and Hindustani, 90
"imperialism," 142
and Khariboli, 8, 47, 110, 111, 129, 153
linguistic features of, 34–37, 110–114
as a link language, 67, 142
literacy in, 125
literary centers, 111
literature, 26, 111, 112
medium policy, 68–70, 126–130, 139, 141–145, 178–181
Nepali Hindi, MT label, 47
Panjabi-ized Hindi, 27
press, 14, 15 (Table 3), 16 (Table 4)
"proper," 89, 109, 116n.1
registers, 26–29, 50, 72–73 (Table 8), 89, 90, 110–114, 127 (Table 18), 129, 152
Sanskritic Hindi (Sanskritized, neo-Sanskritic), 82, 90, 111–116, 135
speakers, 6 (Table 1), 10 (Table 2), 91 (Table 9), 92, 101 (Table 16), 102–105, 107–109, 153
teaching in, 72–73 (Table 8), 128, 137–139, 153, 154
in Three-Language Formula, 137, 138
tradition, 47, 53, 110, 150
translations in, 83
Hindi-Urdu, 26, 27, 35, 106 (Table 17), 111–114, 135
address and reference system, 35–37, 165
amalgam, "Hirdu," 5, 26, 27, 52, 112, 114
as "associate" native speech, 53, 111
bilingualism, 10 (Table 2), 12–14, 51–54

elite, 61
male-female distinction in address system, 36, 37
Pressure Index, 52
Sanskrit and Perso-Arabic permutation in, 26
speakers, 55 (Table 7), 111
styles, 111, 113, 114
Hindi-Urdu-Hindustani, 58–61
Hindustani, Hindostani, 12, 58–61, 72–73 (Table 8), 90, 110–116, 150
bazaar Hindustani, 26, 114
Bombay Hindustani, 27, 129, 154
as colloquial Hindi or Urdu, 90, 104, 110, 153
"composite" Hindustani, 90, 135
distinct from Hindi, 135
education in "ordinary" tradition, 118
Gandhi's approach to, 114, 135, 156
Grierson classification of dialects, 60
and Khariboli, 112
as lingua franca, 175
Nagpur Hindustani, 72–73 (Table 8)
speakers, 90, 91 (Table 9), 98 (Table 14)
Hirdu. *See* Hindi-Urdu
Hmar, 180
Ho, 72–73 (Table 8)
Hungarian, 128

Indian, MT label, 47
Indian Sindhi. *See* Sindhi
Indo-Aryan (Aryan) language group
Central, 5, 46, 178, 180
Eastern, 4, 112, 178
Dardic, 5, 178
North-Western, 5, 178
Pahari, 178
South, 5, 115, 178
Indo-European, language group, 3, 17n.3, 24, 25, 58
Germanic, 178
Romance, 58, 178
Iranian, language group, 112, 178
Irish, 57
Islami, MT label, 47
Italian, 138

Japanese, 34
Jatki, MT label, 111

Kabui, 180
Kachhi Sindhi, 3, 46
Kachin, language group, 180
Kajkavian, variety of Serbo-Croatian, 115
Kanauji, 104, 116n.1

Kannada, 4, 85, 94, 115, 97 (Table 13)
  bilingualism, 14
  "Carnataca" (in Bellary schools), 133n.2
  in education, 178
  press, 15 (Table 3)
  speakers, 6 (Table 1), 10 (Table 2), 105, 106 (Table 17), 115
Karen, 180
Kashmiri, 5, 37, 69–71
  bilingualism, 14
  in education, 127 (Table 18), 178
  speakers, 6 (Table 1), 10 (Table 2), 106 (Table 17), 107
Kerala, MT label, 47
Khampti, 70, 180
Kharia, 178
Khariboli, 8, 29 47, 110, 111
  as "associate" native speech, 115
  a basis for Hindi, 27, 47, 109, 111, 112, 168
  distinct from Hindi, 103
  genre for prose, 27, 115
  and Hindustani, 154
  Persianized, 135
  registers, 26, 109, 153
  Sanskritic, 129, 154
  scripts, 111
  social variants (Hindi and Urdu), 153
  speakers, 98 (Table 14), 110, 111
  under "Western" Hindi, 104
Khasi, 10 (Table 2), 127 (Table 18), 139, 178
Khiemnungan, 180
Khortha, 94 (Table 11), 104
Koch, 180
Kom, 180
Konkani, 5, 6 (Table 1), 10 (Table 2), 68, 93, 115
Konyak, 178
Korku, 180
Kshatri, MT label, 47
Kui, 10 (Table 2), 92, 94, 127 (Table 18)
Kuki, 180
Kuki Chin, language group, 178, 180
Kului, 104
Kumauni, 10 (Table 2), 93, 104
Kurukh, Oraon, 92, 98 (Table 14), 103, 138, 178

Ladakhi, 10 (Table 2), 180
Lahnda, 59, 109, 111, 112
Lakher, 180
Lamani, 93, 96 (Table 12), 104
Latin, classical, 126, 138
Lepcha, 180
Lotha, 180

Low German. *See* German
Lushai. *See* Mizo

Madrasi, MT label, 47
Magadhi, Magahi, 9, 11 (Table 2), 72 (Table 8), 92 (Table 10), 94 (Table 11), 102, 104, 109
Maharatta. *See* Marathi
Maithili, 9, 27, 29, 68, 69, 92, 104, 109, 112, 114
  in education, 139, 178
  as literary language, 111, 112
  registers, 26, 27
  speakers, 10 (Table 2), 72 (Table 8), 92, 93, 94 (Table 11), 102
  writing, 119
Makedonian, 64n.4
Malayalam, 3, 4, 85, 115
  bilingualism, 14
  in education, 127 (Table 18), 178
  press, 15 (Table 3)
  speakers, 6 (Table 1), 10 (Table 2), 105, 106 (Table 17)
Mao, 180
Marathi, 3, 5, 72 (Table 8), 85, 94, 97 (Table 13), 115, 145, 152
  bilingualism, 13, 14, 94, 105, 115
  Devanagari script, 70
  in education, 70, 72 (Table 8), 125, 143, 152, 178
  "Maharatta" in Bellary schools, 133n.2
  Nagpuri Marathi, 72 (Table 8)
  press, 15 (Table 3)
  speakers, 6 (Table 1), 10 (Table 2), 105, 106 (Table 17)
  Varli dialect, 10 (Table 2)
Maria Gondi. *See* Gondi
Marwari, 47, 96 (Table 12), 104, 106 (Table 17), 107, 109
Mech, 180
Medieval Telugu, classical, 75
Meithei. *See* Manipuri
Mewari, 96 (Table 12), 104
Mewati, 96 (Table 12)
Micronesian, language group, 128
Mishmi, Digaru Taron, 180
Mizo, Lushai, 10 (Table 2), 127 (Table 18), 139, 178
Moldavian, 57
Mon Khmer, language group, 4, 178, 180
Mongolian, language group, 24
Mughaliya, MT label, 47
Mulki, MT label, 47
Multani, 109
Munda, 4, 72 (Table 8)
Munda, language group, 178
Mundari, 178

Language Index

Musalmani, MT label, 47
Muslim Pahari, MT label, 47

Naga, 10 (Table 2), 180
Naga, language group, 178, 180
Nagpuri, MT label, 47
NEFA, language group, 180
Nepali, Gorkhali, 10 (Table 2), 92, 104, 139, 178
  Devanagari script, 70
Nicobarese, 10 (Table 2), 180
Nimadi, 96 (Table 12), 104
Nissi, Dafla, 180
Nochte, 180
Norwegian, 46

Old Tamil, classical, 75
Oraon. *See* Kurukh
Oriya, 4, 6 (Table 1), 10 (Table 2), 71, 72 (Table 8)
  bilingualism, 8, 13
  in education, 178
  press, 15 (Table 3)
  speakers, 105, 106 (Table 17)

Pahari, 10 (Table 2), 27, 58, 98 (Table 14), 104, 109, 112, 114
  language group, 178
  Muslim Pahari, MT label, 47
  Patiali Pahari, MT label, 47
Pahlwani, MT label, 47
Paite, 180
Pakistani, MT label, 47
Pali, classical, 137
Panchpargania, MT label, 94 (Table 11)
Panjabi, 5, 9, 54, 58, 59, 85, 97 (Table 13), 103, 107, 108, 109, 111–114
  bilingualism, 13, 46, 54
  in education, 125, 127 (Table 18), 178
  in Fluid Zone, 109, 113
  a generic label, 58
  Gurumukhi script, 54, 109
  Perso-Arabic and Sanskrit characteristics, 26
  press, 15 (Table 3)
  and Sikhs, 108
  speakers, 6 (Table 1), 10 (Table 2), 93, 96 (Table 12)
  tradition, 150
Parji, 93
Pashto, 109, 112
Persian, 70, 108, 118, 122, 133n.2, 178
  classical, 14, 36, 77, 126, 135, 137, 139, 152
  Darri (in Afghanistan), 108
  Perso-Arabic characteristics, 75
  literary tradition, 111, 112

sounds, 113
styles, 8, 126
vocabulary, 37, 113, 154
Phom, 180
Polish, 23
Portuguese, 65, 70, 126, 178
Prakrit, classical, 26, 137
Provencal, 43, 58

Rajasthani, 68, 69, 93, 108, 112
  Banjari dialect, 92
  Dingal, literary variety, 111
  speakers, 10 (Table 2), 93, 96 (Table 12), 98 (Table 14), 103, 104
Rajputi, MT label, 47
Reddi Bhasha, MT label, 47
Rengma, 180
Riyasati, MT label, 47
Roman, MT label, 47
Romance. *See* Indo-European
Rumanian, 57
Russian, 154

Sadan (Sadri), pidgin, 73 (Table 8), 94 (Table 11), 104, 178
Sangtam, 180
Sanskrit, 3, 5, 6 (Table 1), 8, 26, 50, 75, 122, 126
  bilingualism, 13
  code-switching in, 14
  in education, 118, 119, 133n.2, 137, 152
  influence on Indian languages, 8, 37, 60, 75, 113, 114, 145
  as mother tongue, 46, 50, 57
  writing systems, 119
Santali, 10 (Table 2), 68, 72 (Table 8), 93, 152
  in education, 72 (Table 8), 127 (Table 18), 138, 178
Sarnarthi, MT label, 47
Saurashtri, Saurashtran, 3, 18n.4, 93, 152
Savara, 93
Sema, 180
Serbian, 46, 56, 57, 113, 116
Serbo-Croatian (Croato-Serbian), Serbian-Croatian, 56, 57, 113, 115, 116, 128
  Kajkavian and Štokavian varieties, 115
Sindhi, 5, 37, 46, 54, 68, 85, 144
  in education, 70, 127 (Table 18), 133n.3, 178
  and Gurumukhi script, 54
  immigrant Sindhi, 152, 165
  Indian Sindhi, as a "transplanted" language, 165
  Kachhi dialect, 3, 46
  Perso-Arabic and Sanskrit characteristics, 26, 37

press, 15 (Table 3)
script controversy, 86n.2, 123
speakers, 6 (Table 1), 10 (Table 2)
Vicholi, standard, 46
Singpho, 180
Sirmauri, 104
Slovenian, 57
   Caranthian (in Austria), 57
Spanish, 126, 138
Štokavian, variety of Serbo-Croatian, 115
Surajpuri, MT label, 94 (Table 11)
Surgujia, MT label, 94 (Table 11)
Swadeshi, MT label, 47
Swahili, 41
Swedish, 46

Tagalog, 128
Tahitian, 41
Tamil, 3, 4, 37, 75, 85
   bilingualism, 13, 52
   classicalized Tamil, 37, 82, 145
   in education, 118, 125, 133n.2, 142, 178
   Old Tamil, 37
   press, 15 (Table 3)
   Pressure Index, 52
   speakers, 6 (Table 1), 10 (Table 2), 105, 106 (Table 17)
Tangkhul, 180
Tangsa, 180
Telugu, 4, 71, 75, 85, 93, 94, 139
   bilingualism, 14, 94
   in education, 70, 178
   medieval, classical, 75, 82
   speakers, 6 (Table 1), 10 (Table 2), 93, 105, 106 (Table 17)
   "Telogoo" in Bellary schools, 133n.2
Thado, 180
Thai, language group, 180
Tibetan, 70, 127 (Table 18), 178
Tibetan, language group, 178, 180
Tibeto-Chinese (Sino-Tibetan), language group, 3, 4, 10 (Table 2), 178, 180, 181
Tibia, MT label, 47
Travankorian, MT label, 47
Tripuri, 10 (Table 2), 178
Tulu, 10 (Table 2), 115

Ukranian, 23
Uralic, language group, 39n.2
Urdu, 3, 5, 46, 52–54, 58, 60, 61, 69–71, 84, 108–113, 144, 175
   as "associate" native speech, 111
   as "Ausbau" language, 112
   bilingualism, 12, 14, 17
   borrowing patterns, 113
   distinction from Hindi, 112
   in education, 69, 125, 127 (Table 18), 129, 138, 141, 178
   elite, 135
   generic label, 58
   "highbrow" and "lowbrow" styles, 113, 114, 153
   and Khariboli, 8, 110, 154
   linguistic features, 112–114, 152
   literary centers, 111
   and Muslims, 60, 61, 94, 95, 97 (Table 13), 108, 110, 139
   Perso-Arabicized, 82, 90, 116, 154
   and Perso-Arabic script, 109, 111, 112
   press, 15 (Table 3)
   registers, 26, 36, 50, 72 (Table 8), 90, 112–114
   speakers, 6 (Table 1), 9, 10 (Table 2), 90, 91 (Table 9), 94, 95, 98 (Table 14), 100 (Table 15), 102, 107–109, 152
   tradition, 53, 111, 150

Vaiphei, 180
Varli Marathi, 10 (Table 2)
Vedic, classical, 47
Vicholi Sindhi, 46

Welsh, 43, 57
Western Hindi, generic label, 58, 104

Yiddish, 57
Yimchungre, 180

Zemi, 180

Subject Index

aap, form of address in Hindi-Urdu, 36
"Abstand" (characterizing intrinsic distance), concept defining language, 112
Acculturation, 3, 7, 41, 175
  effects of language, 172 (Table 21)
Achieved and inherited roles in an interaction, 31
Active bilingualism, 75, 154
Address and reference systems, 34–37, 165
Adequacy, in speech, 131
Administrative languages, 5, 6 (Table 1), 62, 121, 122
"Advanced" tradition in education system, 118, 119, 143
Aesthetics, 77
"Affective" meaning in language activity, 31
Agglutination, in Mongolian languages, 24
Agricultural promotion campaigns, techniques of persuasion in, 158
Akhund, pedagogue under the *maktab* system, 133n.3
"Aliens" issue in Assam, 176
Alternate media policy. *See* Instructional medium
All-India Language Development Conference, *1953,* 144, 145
All-India Universities Conference, *1939,* 139
amae, Japanese concept in communication, 166
Ambiguity, in communication, 49, 57, 76, 167
American society, 169
Amil, "courtly" Hindu class among Sindhis, 133n.3

Analogy, 81, 164
Ancestral languages, 169, 172 (Table 21)
Anglicists' view, among British administrators, 119–121
Anglicization of Indian languages, 26, 111, 123
Annamalai University, 85
Anti-Hindi lobbies, 125
Arabic script, 54. *See also* Perso-Arabic script
Area exclusivism, dimension of structural pluralism, 169
arzi, petition-writing in Persian, 133n.3
Ascribed (or inherited) roles in an interaction, 31
"Associate" native speech, 53, 71, 111, 114
Associate official language, 137
"Ausbau" (characterizing independent development), a concept defining language, 112
Austerlitz, R., 39n.2
Austrian census, 57
Autonomous languages, 21 (Table 5)
Auxiliary media, 154
ayurved, Indian medicine, 76
Azad, Maulana, 141

Baconian philosophy, 119, 120
Bangalore University, medium issue, 143
Barbiana *Letter,* 132
Basic education, 122, 125, 156
bazaar languages, 21 (Table 5)
Bentinck Resolution, *1835,* 120
Bhakti poetry, in Hindi, 26
Bhartrhari's philosophy, *sphoṭa* 'plosion', 166

Bhoti script, 119
Bicultural education, 128
Bilingual/multilingual behavior, 110, 111
Bilingual communities. *See* Multilingual societies
Bilingual contact, experience, 51, 78, 122
Bilingual education,
 media, 126–129, 154
 programs in other countries, 128, 172 (Table 21)
 schools, 154
Bilingual identity, 51–54
Bilingual interaction, 54
Bilingual Muslims, 95
Bilingual poetry, 14
Bilingual press, 15 (Table 3)
Bilingualism, 25, 64n.5, 76, 80, 154, 167, 169, 176
 active, 75, 154
 census reports, 9, 13, 14, 53, 54, 66, 109, 110
 compound, 38
 and language standardization, 74, 75
 social aspects of, 75, 82, 165, 169, 176
Bi-modal standardization, 27, 116
Bombay University, medium issue, 121, 142
Borrowings, 37, 135
 from classical literature, 77
 from English, 38, 113, 114
 from Medieval Telugu, 37
 from Old Tamil, 37
 patterns of Hindi-Urdu and Serbo-Croatian, 50, 113
 from Perso-Arabic, 37, 113
 from Sanskrit, 37, 113
 spatial aspects of, 165
Braga, Giorgio, 39n.3
Brahmin system of education, 117
British census, *1931,* England, Scotland, and Wales, 57
British education system, 79, 117, 119–123. *See also* Colonial education policy
British rulers, 117, 176. *See also* Colonial administrators
 and Hindi-Urdu struggle, 61, 135
 standardizing Sindhi script, 123
Brown, Roger, 34
Burton, Richard F., 133n.3

Calcutta University, medium issue, 121, 143
Canada, bilingual and bicultural education programs, 128
Caste dialects, 8, 86n.3, 109

Brahmin and non-Brahmin, 26
Categorization, manifestation of plurality in speech, 172 (Table 21)
Categorization process
 concerning languages and scripts, 123
 in a speech community, 48
Census reports
 biases in tabulation of, 57
 of different countries, 56–58
 Indian, 3–18, 45–54, 55 (Table 7), 59, 62, 63, 89, 90, 91 (Table 9), 92–95, 96 (Table 12), 97 (Table 13), 98 (Table 14), 100 (Table 15), 101 (Table 16), 102–105, 107–109, 116n.1, 138, 144, 171, 178–181
 oscillations in declaration, 90
"Center-periphery" hypothesis of language development, 19, 20, 22
Central Advisory Boards of Education, *1938, 1946, 1948, 1957, 1962,* 71, 133n.5, 137, 141, 142
Central Schools system, 70
Chatterji, Suniti Kumar, 17n.2
Child's speech, 124, 130, 131, 156
Chomsky, Noam, 39n.3, 163
Clarity, in communication, 132
Classical languages, 14, 37, 47, 65, 75, 155
 influencing regional languages, 75
 in teaching, 72 (Table 8), 126, 129, 137, 138
Classical literature, 76
Classicalization
 trends of borrowings, 37, 75, 112–114, 155
Classification
 genealogical, genetic affinities, 58, 164
 sociolinguistic types, 24
Classroom language, 132. *See also* School language
Code, 28, 32 (Table 6), 147, 172 (Table 21)
Code-mixing, 7
Code-switching, 7, 9, 14, 25, 32 (Table 6), 77, 81, 114, 126, 146 (Table 20), 147, 168, 172 (Table 21)
Coinage of terms, 22, 23, 38, 50, 77, 80, 83, 113, 146 (Table 20), 147, 155, 156, 159, 171. *See also* Technical terms
Colonial education policy. *See* British education
Commissioner of Linguistic Minorities, 84
Common medium. *See* Instructional medium
Communicability, 67, 156
Communication, 14, 17, 32 (Table 6), 34,

Subject Index

45, 77, 89, 109, 132, 142, 144, 152, 156. *See also* Speech communication, Verbal communication
  barriers to, 25, 66, 74, 75, 130, 154
  characteristics, 23, 25, 32 (Table 6), 40, 47, 82, 130, 132, 152–156, 158, 163, 165, 170
  cognitive dimensions of, 158
  defined, 166
  devices, 22, 26, 29, 30, 32 (Table 6), 147, 166
  environments, 8, 10 (Table 2), 80, 109, 114, 137
  formal, 12, 23, 65, 69, 83, 86n.3, 109, 110, 114, 117, 121, 123, 151
  group and interpersonal, 166, 167
  homogeneity in, 47, 109
  informal, 26, 51, 109, 110
  intergroup, out-group, 12, 17, 51, 52, 72 (Table 8), 166
  intragroup, in-group, 17, 51, 72 (Table 8), 79
  matrix (channels, domains, settings, participants), 31, 53, 126, 134, 136, 153, 155, 165, 172 (Table 21)
  and modernization pressures, 72 (Table 8), 129
  networks, 27, 28, 85, 110, 115, 136
  oral and written, 82, 110
  "organic" unity of, 169
  patterns, 8, 9, 25, 27, 50, 51, 81, 103, 109, 112, 126, 129, 134, 150, 152, 153, 163, 176
  profiles of plurality, 170, 172 (Table 21)
  as "synergistic" system, 166
  tasks, 6, 30, 32 (Table 6), 35, 44, 75, 82, 130, 155, 158, 172 (Table 21)
  values, 23, 49, 159, 172 (Table 21)
  verbal and nonverbal, 166
Communication ethos, 28, 156, 158, 172 (Table 21)
Communication "field," 32 (Table 6)
Communication "sensitivity," 32 (Table 6)
Communicative act. *See* Speech act
Communicative competence, 25, 50
Communicative conduct, 150
Compartmentalization, through linguistic differentia, 32 (Table 6)
Compartmentalization of linguistic resources, in diglossia, 18n.6
Compatibility, as axis in Hindi-Urdu address system, 35
Compiling dictionaries, 32 (Table 6), 84, 124
Composite courses in language teaching, 138
Compound bilingualism, definition of 38
Compulsory languages in teaching, 137–139
Conceptualization, 76
Congress Working Committee, *1954,* 145
Congruence, between language and territory, 40, 58
Constitution of India, 5, 6 (Table 1), 69
  languages in the Eighth Schedule, 6 (Table 1), 135, 171
  Seventh Amendment Act, 145
Contact languages, 32 (Table 6), 51–53, 63, 71
  code-switching, 127
  in education, 152–154
  functions, 12, 36, 51, 75, 153
  listing by states, 10 (Table 2)
  ratios of claimants, 10 (Table 2), 13, 14, 55 (Table 7)
Contact propriety in use of Hindi-Urdu pronouns, 35, 36
"Continuous" or "developmental" systems, in life sciences, 165
Convergence of speech varieties, 32 (Table 6), 81, 146 (Table 20), 172 (Table 21)
Correctness, 156
Council for Secondary Education, *1956,* 137
Creativity of expression, an "echo" process of language use, 32 (Table 6), 125, 156, 163
Creoles, 71
Creolization processes, 81, 172 (Table 21)
Cross-cultural settings, 130
Cultivated languages, 21 (Table 5), 126, 146 (Table 20), 154
Cultural homogenization, 168, 175
Cultural identity, 116, 150
Cultural resurgence, 124, 141, 147
Cyrillic script, 113, 116

DNA, deciphering code of as a genetic language in molecular biology, 165
daftar, secretariat
  in the Muslim court, 133n.3
Decennial census. *See* Indian census
Deliberate change
  behavioral, 158
  linguistic, 146 (Table 20), 149, 158
Democratization, 135, 172 (Table 21), 176
Demographic investigations, 41, 171
Demonstrative subjects, 154
Derivational features, 113, 148
Despatch, Wood's, *1854. See* Wood Despatch
Deutsch, Karl W., 64n.1
Devanagari script, 54, 70, 109, 110, 112, 116, 118, 119

modified version for Sindhi, 86n.2, 123, 133n.3
"Developed" and "underdeveloped" languages, a dichotomy, 19, 20, 21 (Table 5), 127
Dialect, 21 (Table 5), 43, 44, 51, 74, 75, 89, 104, 110, 118, 130, 133n.5
  determining boundaries of, 43
  and language, 50, 56–60
  restoring dethroned dialects, 112
  surveys, 84
Diction, elite-acceptable, "highbrow," 25, 126
Differentiation processes, 170
diglossia (diglossic), 18n.6, 27, 81, 109, 118, 167, 172 (Table 21)
  communication patterns, 13, 25
  complementation, 7, 18n.6, 49, 75, 109, 115
  functions, 21 (Table 5), 110, 114
Dingal, literature in medieval Rajasthani, 111
District languages, 10 (Table 2)
Divergence, a characteristic of language maintenance, 172 (Table 21)
Domains, manifestation of plurality in speech, 172 (Table 21)
Dominant (dominating) languages, 126, 134, 147, 152, 10 (Table 2), 21 (Table 5), 106 (Table 17), 146 (Table 20)

"Echo" processes of language use, 81, 163, 165
Ecological dimensions of language, 21 (Table 5), 32 (Table 6), 172 (Table 21)
Education, 12, 69–71, 74–80, 114, 117, 134, 145, 156
  advanced, graduate, university, 75, 76, 80, 121, 127, 128, 136, 138, 139, 142, 146 (Table 20), 147, 154
  bilingual. See Bilingual education
  and child's environment, 122
  compulsory, 122
  curricula, 79, 123, 125, 132, 137, 147, 157
  dichotomy of "advanced" and "ordinary," 22, 118–123, 125, 143, 144, 147
  elitist framework of, 75, 82, 122, 125, 136, 143, 156
  "filter-down" approach in, 71, 123
  grass-roots approach to, 156
  Indianization policies in, 122, 133n.2, 144, 145
  and linguistic identity, 108
  medium, See Instructional medium
  and modernization, 51, 81, 126
  objectives, 118, 123, 146 (Table 20), 154
  and politics, 124, 136, 138, 144, 147
  primary, elementary, 72 (Table 8), 86n.5, 121, 125, 127, 137, 138, 145, 146 (Table 20)
  progressive theories in, 130
  role of language in, 125, 126, 132, 154
  secondary, higher secondary, 121, 127, 128, 137
  selective, 122, 126
  systems before the British, 117–120, 123, 133n.3
  tradition, 74, 120, 123, 125, 143, 144
  universal, 122
  Western theories of, 123, 124
Education Commission, *1902*, 121
Education Commission, *1966*, 70, 84, 137
Educational development, 58, 65, 70, 134
Educational subjects, categories of, 76
Educationists, educators, 78, 122, 125, 127
Eighth Schedule. See Constitution of India
Election campaigns, techniques of persuasion in, 158
Elementary media of education, 180
Elite class
  as mediators, go-betweens, 78, 118, 122
  Westernized and regional, 20, 41, 67, 136
Elite (elitist) culture, 129, 130, 147, 159
Emeneau, Murray B., 17n.2, 18n.4
Emerging media of education, 126
Encounters, cross-purpose, 130
English education, 78, 119, 120, 136, 141, 157
  elite, 79, 119, 136, 143
  literature and, 79
  and the press, 15
  Pressure Index, 52, 53
  status quo supporters of, 143
  and technologically superior "caste," 122
  as universally developed medium of knowledge, 141
Enlightenment. See Western Enlightenment
Ethnic affiliations, 168
Ethnic boundaries, 169
Ethnic languages, 41, 21 (Table 5)
Ethnic/racial loyalties, 175
Ethnocentric bias, among eighteenth-century Indo-Europeanists, 26
European censuses, 57
European languages, 24, 38, 65, 123
Exclusive identity of speech groups, 112

Subject Index

Exclusive territorial claims of language and religion, 175
Expectations (distinct from actual performance) in linguistic behavior, 39n.3

Family planning campaigns, techniques of persuasion in, 158
Federal languages, 137
Ferguson, Charles A., 18n.6, 19, 27, 48
"Filter-down" approach to education, 71, 123
Fishman, Joshua A., 19, 22-24, 26, 31
Fluid language boundaries, 8
Fluid speech groups, 164
Fluid Zone, 7, 27, 98 (Table 14), 105, 106 (Table 17), 107, 109, 110, 112
Fluidity, 168. *See also* Language/speech fluidity
  concerning "content" and "loyalty," 168
  contextual and functional, 28, 165
  in language claims, 7, 89, 92, 102, 103
  in language use, 32 (Table 6), 35, 118
Foreign language teaching, 79, 120, 125, 129, 138
"Formal" meaning in language activity, 31
Formal-informal media for education, 127, 128
Formalistic speech, 113
Formalization of "ideal" language, 163
Formalized language, 164
Four-language formula, 138
Fourth Conference of Indian Universities, *1943,* 141
French nationality, 62
Functional heterogeneity, 19, 25, 28, 167, 172 (Table 21)
Functions, "ornate," of privileged language, 129

Gait Report, *1913,* 59
Gallicization, 41
Gandhi, Mahatma,
  on basic education, 122-125, 156
  on Hindustani, 114, 116, 135
  on plurality in society, 18n.5
  on vernacularization, 123
Garvin, Paul L., 24, 83
Genealogical classification of Indian languages, 3, 29, 58, 59, 104, 178, 180
Genealogical development theory, 25
Genetic affinity, of languages, 164
Genre, in Hindi literature, 26
German nationality, 62
Gilman, A., 34

Gokhale, Gopal Krishna, 122
Gordon, Milton M., 169
Gorman, T. P., 150
Governmental agencies for language development, 83-86
Grammar, 9, 23, 45, 71, 76, 82, 123
Grammar and constitutions, 132
Grammarians, 155, 175
Grant, Charles, 119
Grantha script, 119
Graphization, 21 (Table 5)
Grass-roots multilingualism, 25, 38, 66, 71, 82
Grierson classification of Indian languages, 58, 104
Grierson, George A., 60, 84, 104, 116n.2
Grierson *Survey,* 93, 116n.1, 116n.2
Group dynamics of language elite, 134-136
Group identity, 37, 45, 71, 112
Group loyalty and mother tongue, 45, 90
Group propriety, in the use of Hindi-Urdu pronouns, 35, 36
Group solidarity, 28, 48
Gujarat University, medium issue in, 142
Guru Granth, a sacred text of the Sikhs and Hindus, 133n.3
gurukul, residential school system, 117
Gurumukhi script, 54, 109, 133n.3
  interpreted as Panjabi language, 54

HUP region. *See* Hindi-Urdu-Panjabi region
Halliday, Michael A. K., 131, 157
Hardings Proclamation, *1844,* 120
Harrison, Selig, 66, 85n.1
Hartog Report, *1929,* 122
Haugen, Einar, 58
Heterogeneity, in speech, 4, 6, 8, 17, 19, 25, 38, 51, 53, 66, 82, 114, 164, 165, 169, 172 (Table 21)
Heterogeneous performance of speech, 45, 115
Heterogeneous situations, 49, 52, 81, 154
Heterogeneous speech groups/communities, 28, 109, 150, 152, 166
Hierarchy
  language/linguistic. *See* Language hierarchy
  legislative, 171
  stratificational, 32 (Table 6), 171
"Highbrow" speech styles, 9, 37, 38, 50, 71, 75, 111, 113, 118, 123, 126, 129, 154, 171
"Highbrow" values of speech, 23, 26, 80, 125, 132, 159

Higher education, 74, 76, 80, 127, 137
Hindi
  elite, 27, 68, 112, 129, 135, 142
  and Hindus, 59–61, 108, 110
  "imperialism," 142
  in Indian census, 55 (Table 7), 89, 90, 91 (Table 9), 92, 93, 98 (Table 14), 101 (Table 16), 102–104
  literature, 26, 27, 111
  non-Hindi speaking population, 137
  press, 15, 16 (Table 4)
  promotion agencies, 83, 84
  speech community, 115
  Tarachand Commission, *1948*, 141
  "tradition," 47, 53, 110, 150
Hindi-Urdu
  amalgam, Hirdu, 5, 26, 27, 52, 86n.3, 112, 114
  Pressure Index, 52
  rivalry, 27, 60, 61, 135
Hindi-Urdu-Hindustani, semantic acrobatics, 61
Hindi-Urdu-Panjabi (HUP) region, 7, 27, 57, 93, 96 (Table 12), 103, 109, 112, 114, 133n.1. *See also* Hindustani region
"Hindoo" sciences, 133n.2
Hindu and Muslim elite, 114, 118, 119
Hindustani
  during Independence movement, 114, 135
  as liaison in "ordinary" tradition of education, 118
Hindustani region. *See* Hindi-Urdu-Panjabi region
Hispanic Americans, 39n.1
Historical associations, of a speech community, 29
Historical branching, for determining language boundaries, 164
Homogeneity in communication, 24, 27, 29, 32 (Table 6), 47, 107–112
Homogeneous-signalling system, a view of language, 164
Homogeneous speech groups/communities, 28, 163
Homogenized perception of speech, 45
Homogenized societies, 125, 167
Human behavior, 64, 85, 150
Human communication, 130, 166
Human sensitivities, in language planning, 150–152
Humanism, 122
Humanities, 22, 143
Hunter Commission, *1882*, 121
Hussain, Zakir, 122, 141
Hutton, J. H. 8, 60

Hybrid speech varieties/languages, 21 (Table 5), 71, 72 (Table 8), 127
Hybridization, 21 (Table 5), 29, 32 (Table 6), 38, 127, 146 (Table 20), 147, 168, 172 (Table 21)

IQ tests, 131
Ideal language, theory concerning the formalization of, 163
Identity, 168
  ascriptional, 172 (Table 21)
  segmental, 6, 7, 118
Identity affiliations, 104, 111, 168
Identity assertion, Konkani distinct from Marathi, 115
Identity pressures, 29, 49, 56, 90, 92–95, 102–104, 109
Illiteracy, 12, 122, 144, 148
Illiterate communities, 71, 82
Illyrian movement in Balkans, 115
Immigrant Sindhis, 54, 152
Independence movement, 116, 122, 136, 139
  medium controversy, 122, 139
  role of regional languages, 136
Indian Census
  genealogical classification in, 58
  Sindhi immigrants' claims concerning Gurumukhi, 54
  sociopolitical situation affecting language tabulation in northern states, 108, 109
Indian Census, decennial
  1881, 57
  1901, 104
  1911, 59
  1931, 8, 60, 90, 91 (Table 9)
  1951, 54, 56, 90, 91 (Table 9), 92, 95, 97 (Table 13), 98 (Table 14), 104, 108
  1961, 8, 9, 10 (Table 2), 13, 17n.3, 46, 47, 50–52, 55 (Table 7), 89, 90, 91 (Table 9), 92 (Table 10), 92–95, 96 (Table 12), 97 (Table 13), 98 (Table 14), 100 (Table 15), 101 (Table 16), 102, 103, 105, 107, 109, 116n.1, 138, 144, 171, 178–181
  1971, 5, 6 (Table 1), 64n.5, 89, 92 (Table 10), 93–95, 96 (Table 12), 97 (Table 13), 100 (Table 15), 101 (Table 16), 102, 104, 105, 107, 178–181
Indian communication patterns, sociolinguistic realities of, 8, 9
Indian Constitution. *See* Constitution of India
Indian elites, 22, 58, 119
Indian languages, 9, 12–14, 17n.2, 20, 35–38, 41, 123, 137–139, 155

Subject Index

development of, 75-78, 80, 83, 136, 147, 155
"highbrow" styles of, 125
as medium of instruction, 20, 69, 121, 139, 141-143
standardization of, 121, 125, 155
Indian literature, 68, 124
Indian National Congress, 122, 135
Indian newspapers and periodicals, 15
Indian Secondary Education Commission, *1956*, 124
Indian vernaculars, 121, 145
Indianization policy in education, 144
Indigenous languages, 67, 113, 135
Individual propriety
  in use of Hindi-Urdu pronouns, 35
Indo-English writers, 78
Indo-Europeanists, 24
Inference, 158, 166
Information processes, 76, 166
In-group communication, 72 (Table 8)
Innate capacity
  of learning language, 71
Innovations, 32 (Table 6)
Instructional medium/media, 20, 22, 69-71, 72 (Table 8), 76, 78, 118, 119, 120, 133n.5. *See also* Medium of instruction/education, Linguistic medium
  alternate media policy, 22, 70, 139, 141-143, 146 (Table 20), 147
  auxiliary media, 154
  controversy, 124-126, 139, 141-143
  a dimension of language development, 21 (Table 5), 130-139, 147
  formal-informal, 127, 128
  patterns of choice, 126
  plural (multitier) media, 126-128, 146 (Table 20)
  problems of switchover, 82, 83, 128, 141, 142
  two-tier, 121
  types of, 70, 83, 121, 126-128, 138, 141, 142, 146 (Table 20), 147, 151, 152, 154, 155, 180
  university language medium 121, 139, 141-143
Instructional strategies of language teaching, 153
Intellectualization, characteristic of language modernization, 24
Interaction(s), 31, 71, 130, 167
  in classroom, 132, 153, 156
Interactional strategies of language teaching, 153
Interference, an "echo" process in language use, 81

Internal reconstruction of language histories, 23-25, 38, 164
International communication patterns, 81, 163
International numerals, 134
"Interpretative decipherment," of speech message, 167
Intertranslatability, a scale of language modernization, 19, 24
Intrinsic distance ("Ausbau" characteristic) between speech varieties, 44
Irish census, 57

Japanese address system, 34
Japanese people, 166
Johnstone, Political Agent of Nagaland *(1873-74)*, 133n.4

Kajkavian elite and Illyrian Movement, 115
Katre, S. M., 17n.2
Kelkar, Ashok R., 112
Kenya, language allocation, 150
Kerala University, 85, 143
Khariboli
  belt/region, 35, 110
  for prose, 27, 115
  in Devanagari and Perso-Arabic scripts, 110
  social variants, 153
KhichRii (potpourri) languages, 145
Kirk, Dudley, 62, 64n.3
Kloss, Heinz 64n.2, 111, 112

Labov, William, 113, 131
Lahore Indian Association, *1876*, 22
Language
  affective and identificational dimensions of, 31, 158
  Chomsky's model, 39n.3, 163
  and communication, 23, 117, 130, 158, 166, 167, 170, 175
  concept of, 43, 56, 60, 63, 163-166
  distinguished from dialect, 43, 63, 110, 116n.1
  and education, 69-71, 72 (Table 8), 74, 75, 117-129, 130-132, 134-139, 145, 146 (Table 20), 147
  etic and emic approach, 39n.3
  as "fact" and "artifact," 30, 156, 165
  as a formal system, 35, 150, 164, 165
  malleability of, 112
  modernizing processes in, 19, 20, 22-24, 83, 157, 172 (Table 21)
  and nation, correlation, 38, 48, 57, 63
  as normative system, 24, 29, 30, 32 (Table 6), 63, 75, 115, 130, 153, 171

as an object of human manipulation, 63, 149, 155
as a part of human organism, 163, 165
and political mobilization, 61, 67, 68, 136, 139
pragmatic considerations of, 35, 37, 158, 165, 175
and primordial loyalties, 58, 61, 175
rational and reflexive use of, 34
and religion, 60, 94, 95, 97 (Table 13), 102, 108, 109, 113, 118, 119, 139, 175
as social institution, 24, 28, 29, 34, 35, 38, 42-47, 49, 51, 58, 85, 109, 113, 129-131, 134, 150, 151, 163, 165, 171, 175
as speech process, 29, 30, 32 (Table 6), 164, 170
and territory, 40, 58, 129, 163, 171, 172 (Table 21), 175, 176
theory of *language* and *languages,* 50
and thought processes, 92, 131, 158, 171
in time and space, 164
universalist/pluralist view of language, 50
use in press, 15, 16 (Table 4)
written and spoken, 21 (Table 5), 54, 60, 123, 157
Language acquisition by participation in "language events," 129, 156
Language activity, 31, 34, 75, 114, 156
identificational characteristics, 108
plurifunctional characteristics, 150
temporal and spatial characteristics, 164
three-dimensional model of, 34-36, 158, 164
Language affiliations, 48, 51, 168, 171, 172 (Table 21)
Language allegiance, 48, 107, 112, 171, 172 (Table 21)
Language allocation, 150
Language aptitudes, 172 (Table 21)
Language area. *See* Linguistic region
Language assertion, 92
Language assets in traditional societies, 159
Language attitudes, 51, 54, 89, 107, 114, 152, 166, 171
Language autonomy, 23, 29, 66, 72 (Table 8), 75, 77, 81, 83, 132, 139, 147, 152
Language behavior. *See* Speech behavior
Language borrowings. *See* Borrowings
Language boundaries (borders), 4, 5, 29, 32 (Table 6), 43, 46, 51, 59, 89, 154, 164, 168, 171, 172 (Table 21)
Language categorization, 45, 172 (Table 21)

Language census. *See also* Language statistics
information on speech behavior, 42, 44, 47
interpretation of, 42, 57, 59-61
as planning tool, 61-64, 171
universalists' and pluralists' approach to, 63
Language change, chronological stages of, 164
Language change, deliberate
colonial experience with, 150
manipulation by the elite, 146 (Table 20), 149, 150, 159
Language chauvinism, 68, 79, 111, 142. *See also* Hindi imperialism
Language choice mechanisms, 51, 159, 172 (Table 21)
Language claims (in census returns), 41-45, 47, 51, 57, 60, 66, 90, 92-95, 102-104, 105, 107, 116, 176. *See also* Linguistic claims
Language classification, 57, 63, 105, 165
Language codification, 23, 77, 171
Language competence. *See* Language proficiency
Language compromise, domains of, 115
Language concentration areas, 176
Language conformity, 32 (Table 6)
Language consciousness, 9, 56, 67
Language contact processes, 25, 163, 165
Language context, 118, 127
Language controversy, 51, 82, 117, 137-139
Language convergence, 81
Language cultivation, 21 (Table 5), 30, 31, 34-37, 51, 68, 76, 80, 83, 126, 138, 145, 146 (Table 20), 154, 167
Language curricula, 69, 82, 139
Language custodians, 114, 149, 153, 172 (Table 21), 175
Language data, 44, 54, 56-61, 89, 90, 92-95, 102-104, 105, 107, 116n.1
politicization of, 56-61
Language deprivation, 131
Language development, 19, 20, 21 (Table 5), 22-25, 65-69, 75, 80-86, 144, 145, 147, 152, 158, 165, 171
assumptions of, 22-25
dichotomous approach in, 20, 32 (Table 5)
governmental and voluntary agencies, 69, 81-85, 153, 157
Language displacement, 102, 110
"linguistic displacement," a demographic interpretation, 90
Language differentiation, 148

Subject Index

Language discourse, 25, 32 (Table 6), 80, 113, 155
Language distribution, 148
Language diversity, 66, 67, 148
Language domain, 21 (Table 5), 23, 42, 82, 85, 126, 167, 172 (Table 21)
  reshaping of (through expansion, shift, etc.), 114–116
Language elaboration, 23, 50, 75–77, 83
  processes and patterns, 36, 48
Language elegance, 113, 114, 129, 159
Language elite, 12, 27–31, 32 (Table 6), 67, 69, 71, 75, 79, 83, 135, 147, 155, 158. *See also* Language custodians
  "established" and "rising," 135, 136, 141, 152, 146 (Table 20), 172 (Table 21)
  expressions defined by, 28, 171
  group dynamics of, 61, 134–136, 141, 149, 155
  Hindu and Muslim, 61–114, 118, 119
  as liaison between rulers and masses, 78, 117, 122
  in the Serbo-Croatian context, 115
  Westernized versus regional, 20, 41, 67
Language engineering, 135, 157
  to develop Hindi, 135
  in various countries, 157
Language environment, 156, 163
Language etiquette. *See* Linguistic etiquette
Language events, 32 (Table 6), 129, 153
  "doing" a language, 129
Language expansion, reshaping language domain, 114
Language expression, 32 (Table 6), 76, 153
Language families, 3, 5, 17n.2, 44, 58
  philological tradition of, 165
Language fluency. *See* Language proficiency
Language fluidity. *See* Fluidity
Language functions, 48, 51, 68, 82, 150, 151
  functional heterogeneity, 19, 25–27, 167, 172 (Table 21)
  subjective and objective factors, 152
Language groups, 47, 61, 66, 67, 125, 144, 175. *See also* Linguistic groups
Language habits, 151
Language hierarchy, 23, 28, 49, 75, 113, 118, 125, 146 (Table 20), 147, 159, 168. *See also* Linguistic hierarchy
Language hybridization. *See* Hybridization in communication
Language identification, 43, 46, 51, 89, 115
Language identity, 4, 7, 20, 32 (Table 6), 41, 46, 54, 62, 69, 71, 90, 102, 129–132, 150, 168, 176. *See also* Linguistic identity
  "composite," 116
  exclusiveness of, 112, 171
  fluidity of, 8, 25, 168
  organization of plurality, 172 (Table 21)
Language ideology, 113, 117–132, 145
Language image, 41, 56, 62, 63, 67, 175
Language implementation versus allocation in language planning, 150
Language imposition, 150
Language information. *See* language data
Language innovation. *See* Linguistic innovation
Language instruction, 137–139, 140 (Table 19). *See also* Language teaching
Language interest groups. *See* Language pressure groups
Language label(s), 28, 46, 48, 49, 56, 89, 90, 125, 134
Language learning, 22, 71, 72 (Table 8), 83, 130, 138, 139, 151, 154, 155
  laboratory, 130, 153
Language legislation, 134, 151
Language lobbies. *See* Language pressure groups
Language loyalty, 9, 45, 48, 56, 58, 61, 108, 112, 115, 132, 134, 151, 168, 172 (Table 21)
Language maintenance, 44, 81, 108, 172 (Table 21)
Language manipulation, 61–64, 149, 159, 163
Language medium. *See* Instructional medium
Language modernization, 19, 20, 22–31, 34–39, 64, 66, 77, 81, 130, 157
Language norms. *See* Language standards
Language performance, 39n.3, 45, 47, 154
  versus expectations, 39n.3
  versus perception, 45
Language pidginization, 25, 32 (Table 6), 77, 81, 146 (Table 20), 168, 172 (Table 21)
Language planning, 23, 77, 149–159
  agencies, 25, 38, 81–86, 149, 159
  processes, 149, 157, 159
  programs, 74, 81–85, 150, 165
  situation-bound, 152–156
  theory, 23, 24, 31, 77, 150, 159
Language plurality, 5–9, 69, 167, 168, 175. *See also* Linguistic plurality
Language policies, 23, 41, 65, 67, 83, 117, 137, 138, 141, 147, 149–152, 172 (Table 21)
  and linguistic minorities, 66, 68, 145

Language politics, 61, 65–69, 84, 102, 134
Language posture, 40, 41, 56, 62, 64, 67, 172 (Table 21), 175
Language pressure groups, 62, 66–69, 117, 136, 138, 146 (Table 20), 172 (Table 21), 176. *See also* Language interest groups
Language Pressure Index
  English, 52, 53
  Hindi-Urdu, 52
  state language, 51, 52
Language prestige, 51, 139
Language privileges, 20, 41, 51, 56, 58, 59, 61, 65, 66 80, 83, 107, 129, 132, 134, 137, 139, 144, 153, 171, 172 (Table 21)
Language proficiency, 39n.3, 41, 42, 45, 48, 51, 52, 63, 78, 128, 154, 172 (Table 21). *See also* Language (linguistic) competence, fluency
Language projections, 21 (Table 5), 64n.1, 77
Language promotion activities, 65–86
Language propriety (controls), 32 (Table 6), 165, 172 (Table 21)
Language purity, 32 (Table 6), 50, 145
Language reformers, 30, 152, 175. *See also* Language visionaries
Language reforms. *See* Language planning
Language role(s), 24, 136, 155, 165, 175
  achieved and inherited, 31, 34
Language scene, 18n.6, 41–43, 62, 66, 67. *See also* Language situation
  in Belgium, 62
Language shift, reshaping language domain, 63, 81, 114–116, 147, 151, 157, 172 (Table 21)
Language split, reshaping language domain, 112, 114
Language standardization, 7, 9, 27–30, 47, 49, 81, 123, 130, 152, 155, 157, 159, 165, 167
Language standards, 126, 132, 145, 154, 164, 171. *See also* Language norms
Language statistics. *See* Language census
Language stereotypes. *See* Linguistic stereotypes
Language stratificational differences. *See* Linguistic stratification
Language structure, system, 23, 76, 155, 163
Language studies. *See* Linguistic studies
Language study privileges, 137–139
Language styles. *See* Speech styles
Language teaching, 12, 70, 76, 84, 128, 137, 139, 140 (Table 19), 154, 156, 167. *See also* Language instruction

an "exercise" for eventual use, 130
  literary approach, 156
  oral-aural system, 129
  reading-based system, 129
Language tolerance, 159
Language tradition, 29, 77, 80, 108, 115, 165, 172 (Table 21)
Language traits. *See* Linguistic traits
Language transition, 38, 67, 82, 109, 136, 171, 176
Language trends, 37, 38, 64n.1, 93, 96 (Table 12), 108, 111
  assertive and assimilative, 93, 96 (Table 12)
  contemporary, classicalization and Westernization, 37, 38, 113
Language usage, 7, 14, 40–43, 62, 63, 78, 113, 123, 132, 147, 150, 153–155. *See also* Linguistic usage
Language use (patterns), 22, 37, 40, 44, 75, 83, 117, 123, 125, 132, 150–152, 156, 158, 168, 171, 172 (Table 21), 175, 176
  interplay of centripetal and centrifugal factors, 30, 32 (Table 6), 175
  rationalized and reflexive, 34
Language values, 32 (Table 6), 69, 71 72 (Table 8), 129, 145, 175. *See also* Speech values
Language visionaries. *See* Language reformers
Languages
  acceptable to the elite, 20, 21 (Table 5), 22
  development of, 152
  diversity/plurality of, 66, 163
  European values of homogenization, 123
  legislating the role of, 134, 151
  reconstructing histories of, tracing genealogies of, 164
  transcending "provincial barriers," 144
  variants of Hindi-Urdu amalgam, 109–114
Language(s), according to content
  colloquial "bazaar," 21 (Table 5)
  creoles, 71
  cultivated, 21 (Table 5), 127, 146 (Table 20), 154
  "highbrow" and "lowbrow," 9, 36–38, 50, 71, 75, 110, 111, 113, 114, 118, 123, 125, 129, 154, 171
  hybrid, 21 (Table 5), 71, 72 (Table 8), 127
  pidgins, 178, 180
  polycentric, 115
  school/classroom, 75, 132, 147

Subject Index

slangs, 21 (Table 5)
standard, normative, 19, 21 (Table 5), 26, 28, 50, 64n.4, 71, 130, 149, 157
śuddha (pure) and *khichRii* (potpourri), 145
textbook, 128, 157
transplanted, 165

Languages, according to functions
administrative, 5, 6 (Table 1), 62, 122
associate official, 137
autonomous, 21 (Table 5)
classical, 14, 37, 48, 65, 75, 154
compulsory versus optional, in teaching, 137-139
contact, 10 (Table 2), 12-14, 32 (Table 6), 36, 51-53, 55 (Table 7), 63, 71, 75, 127, 154, 155
"developed" and "underdeveloped," 20, 21 (Table 5), 126
district, 10 (Table 2)
listed under the Eighth Schedule of the Indian Constitution, 5, 6 (Table 1), 135, 171
federal, 137
home, 58, 107, 134
instructional media, 20, 69-71, 72 (Table 8), 76, 78, 79, 118, 120, 121, 128, 133n.2, 138, 139, 146 (Table 20), 147, 151, 154, 180
liaison, 119
library, 75, 80, 134
lingua franca, 52, 71, 175
link, transitional and eventual, 67, 134, 137, 142, 154
literary, 21 (Table 5), 68, 103, 112, 118, 126, 133n.5, 134, 167
living, 165
national, 3, 5, 21 (Table 5), 67, 134, 147, 151
"near-dialectized," 109, 112, 116n.1
official, 5, 58, 67, 68, 108, 134, 137
for press, 14, 15 (Table 3), 16 (Table 4)
spoken, 54, 59, 123
state, 5, 81, 109
as subject of study, 137, 138, 150
subsidiary, 13, 53, 95, 129
target, in teaching, 130
vernacular(s), 121, 145
wider communication, 21 (Table 5)
world "library," 21 (Table 5), 75, 134, 136
written and unwritten, 19, 21 (Table 5), 157

Languages, identity-labels
ancestral, 169, 172 (Table 21)
classified, according to genealogical affiliations, 3, 29, 58, 60, 104, 164, 178, 180
classified, sociolinguistic types, 24
contemporary/modern, 4, 19, 21 (Table 5), 37, 38, 48, 138, 145, 146 (Table 20), 152, 165, 169
dominating/dominant, 10 (Table 2), 21 (Table 5), 106 (Table 17), 127, 134, 146 (Table 20), 147, 152
ethnic, 21 (Table 5), 41
European, 24, 38, 65, 123
of Fluid Zone, 109-114
foreign, 56, 70
Indian, 9, 12-14, 17n.2, 20, 35, 37, 38, 41, 123, 137, 156
indigenous, 67, 113, 135
major, 7, 127, 144
majority and minority, 7-9, 19, 21 (Table 5), 52, 57, 71, 74, 128, 138, 146 (Table 20), 172 (Table 21)
native and nonnative, 38, 154
Oriental, 34
pan-Indian, 14, 70, 127, 129
privileged, 115, 122
regional, 14, 41, 70, 75, 83, 84, 95, 105, 107, 108, 127, 134, 136, 137, 146 (Table 20), 147
traditional (primitive), 19, 25
tribal, 68, 70, 71, 144, 145
Western, 113
Langue (and parole), Saussure's dichotomy, 39n.3
Latin script, 113, 116
Learning through mother tongue, 124-126
Legendary convictions, in identifying mother tongue, 47
Legislative hierarchy, 171
Legitimization, a dimension of language development, 21 (Table 5)
"Lektor" system, in Yugoslavia, 116n.3
Liaison language, 119
Library language, 75, 80, 134
Lingua franca, 52, 71, 175
Linguistic approach in defining mother tongue, 43
Linguistic behavior
expectations and actual performance, 39n.3
and social mobility, 152
Linguistic chaos, 144, 147
Linguistic code, 53, 111, 113
Linguistic claims. *See* Language claims
Linguistic competence. *See* Language proficiency
Linguistic differentia, 32 (Table 6)
"Linguistic displacement." *See* Language displacement

Linguistic etiquette, 28, 32 (Table 6), 169, 172 (Table 21). *See also* Language etiquette
Linguistic groups. *See* Language groups
Linguistic heterogeneity, time and space dimensions of, 164, 165
Linguistic hierarchy. *See* Language hierarchy
Linguistic homogeneity, 8, 68
Linguistic identity. *See* Language identity
Linguistic instrumentality, 167
Linguistic innovation, 24, 32 (Table 6), 158, 163. *See also* Language innovation
Linguistic medium. *See* Instructional medium
Linguistic minorities, 3, 9, 52, 57, 65-69, 74, 84, 138. *See also* Minority speech groups
   constitutional safeguards for, 145
Linguistic patterns (also "material"), 90, 158
   for development programs, 158
Linguistic plurality. *See* Language plurality
Linguistic regions
   four major, 4, 5
   East, 4, 53
   North-Central, 5, 47, 53, 59, 107, 109, 111, 113, 116, 168
   South, 4, 53
   West, 4, 5, 53
Linguistic reorganization of states, *1956*, 7, 68, 93, 142, 176
Linguistic relativity, 167
Linguistic skills, 131, 150, 152, 155
   hierarchical structuring of, 118
Linguistic spectrum. *See* Speech spectrum
Linguistic states, 56
Linguistic stereotypes, 49, 89. *See also* Language stereotypes
Linguistic stratification, 7, 26, 27, 32 (Table 6), 167
Linguistic Survey of India (1903-1928), 58, 84
Linguistic traits, 17n.2, 48, 49. *See also* Language traits
Linguistic usage. *See* Language usage
Linguistically heterogeneous communities, 134
Linguistics, 163-166
   centers of advanced study, 83
   formalistic studies, 157
   language materials, 28, 76, 84, 130, 158, 164, 165
   synchronic and diachronic studies, 164

Link language, 68, 134, 137, 142, 154
   formula, 142
Literacy, 60, 70, 71, 82, 125
   programs, 71, 74, 82, 125
Literary creation, 30
Literary development, trends, 68, 108
Literary elite, 147, 155
Literary identity, 68, 108
Literary standards/norms, 113, 115, 146 (Table 20)
Literary languages, 21 (Table 5), 68, 103, 112, 118, 125, 133n.5, 134, 168
Literary styles, 30, 126, 153
Literary tradition, 40, 44, 48, 111, 112
Literary and cultural periodicals in Hindi and English, 16 (Table 4)
Literate population, 53
Literature, 68, 74, 76, 113, 120, 125, 152, 155, 157
   classical, 77
   courses, 155, 157
Living languages, "organic" models, 165
"Loan proneness" of Indian languages, 37, 123
Loan translations, 37, 76
Local dialects (speech), 71, 110, 115
Loflin, Marvin D., 43
Logical formalization, 163
"Lowbrow" speech styles, 50, 113, 114

Macaulay Minute, *1835*, 20, 120-123
"MacLuhanesque" period, and mass communication, 83
Madras University, medium issue, 121, 142
madrasseh (college) system of education, 117
Mahajani script, 118
Mahatma Gandhi. *See* Gandhi
maktab (school) system of education, 117, 119, 133n.3
Malayalam characters in writings, 119
Male-female distinction in address pattern of Hindi-Urdu, 36
Marathi community, rural, 72 (Table 8)
Marquesas Islands, language use in the, 41
Mass communication, 66, 71, 72 (Table 8), 81, 113, 157, 158, 176
Mass media, 23, 126, 134, 158
Meaning, in a speech event, 31
Media/medium of instruction. *See* Instructional medium
Medium controversy, 124, 125, 139, 141-143, 146 (Table 20)

Subject Index

Medium of knowledge, English as universally developed, 141
Message, in speech communication, 166
Metalanguage, 77
"Middlebrow," speech styles in Hindi and Urdu, 113, 114
Minorities Commission, 84
Minority languages, 7, 9, 19, 21 (Table 5), 52, 65, 128, 138, 146 (Table 20), 172 (Table 21)
  as "dialects," 58, 74
Minority speech groups/communities, 3, 9, 13, 52, 53, 57, 59, 66, 68, 74, 84, 92, 103, 127, 138, 144, 145, 175. *See also* Linguistic minorities
Missionary system of education, 119, 121
Mitra, Asok, 90
Mobilization, political, 135
Mobilized (or achieved) roles in an interaction, 31
Modern/contemporary languages, 3, 37, 137, 145
Modern/modernizing societies, 82
  needs of styles of expression, 137
"Modernity" versus "tradition" in education system, 132
Modernization processes, 66, 68, 77, 123, 126, 130, 135, 159, 167, 171, 175
  characteristics, 81, 82
  four indices, 24
Monistic norms, 50
Monolingual(s), 42, 47, 58
  multilinguals declared as, 111
Monolingual behavior, psychological distinction from plurilingual, 53
Monolingualism, 169
Monosyllabicity, in Chinese languages, 24
Mother tongue, 3, 27, 51, 103, 120, 167, 168
  boundaries of, 40, 43, 56, 57, 92, 125, 152
  concept and interpretation, 17n.1, 40, 42, 43, 45, 56, 57, 63, 71, 74, 92-95, 102-105, 111, 124, 137, 144
  in-group/out-group dichotomy, 45, 111
  and linguistic minorities, 144
  narrow and broad interpretation, 56, 57, 71, 74
  versus native speech, 45-50
  and tradition, 45, 115
  UNESCO's definition, 124
Mother tongue claims (in the census), 9, 42, 49, 55 (Table 7), 56-61, 69, 90, 91 (Table 9), 92 (Table 10), 94 (Table 11), 92-95, 102-105, 107-112, 116n.1, 116n.2, 146 (Table 20), 178-181
Mother tongue identity, 45-50, 60, 103, 111
Mother tongue label, 49
Mother tongue loyalty, organization of plurality in speech, 172 (Table 21)
Mother tongue medium, 22, 69-75, 119-129, 133n.2, 136, 139, 142, 153-155
Mother tongues, 89, 90, 91 (Table 9), 92-95, 102-105, 107, 116n.1, 128
  classification of, 47, 57, 64n.5, 105, 116n.1, 178-181
  and religious affiliations, 108
  in Stable and Fluid Zones, 105, 107, 109
  trend toward "exclusiveness," 47
Mughal Court and Hindi-Urdu conflict, 135
Müller, Max, 24
Multilingual communication, 85, 111, 135
Multilingual education, 126, 127, 147
Multilingual elites, 147
Multilingual press, 15 (Table 3)
Multilingual regions, 4, 9, 81, 127
Multilingual settings, 66, 74, 165
Multilingual societies, 9, 47, 69, 89, 125, 135, 136, 152
Multilingualism, 3, 12, 25, 81, 169, 172 (Table 21)
  grass-roots, 159
Multi-modal standardization, 27
Multi-tier media system. *See* Instructional medium
"Mumbai amchi" ("Bombay is ours") protest movement, 176
"Muslim" Bengal, 175
Muslim language elite, 60, 61, 110, 119
Muslims
  traditional education, 118, 139
  and Urdu, 95, 97 (Table 13), 108, 110
Mutual intelligibility, 44, 46, 79, 118
Myrdal, Gunner, 85n.1

NCERT (National Council for Educational Research and Training), 74
Nagari writing system, 70, 119
  Bengali and Maithili variations, 119
Nagas education, 133n.4
Nagpur University Survey, *1955*, 143
Naskhi and *Nastalik* characters of Arabic writing, 118
National language, 3, 6, 21 (Table 5), 67, 134, 148, 151
Nationalism, and vernacularization, 124, 125

Nationality, in Europe, 4, 6, 172 (Table 21)
Native speakers, 46, 55 (Table 7), 109, 114, 126, 129
  elites' demand of vernacularization, 117, 124, 127
Native speech, 45, 49, 51–54, 71, 86n.3, 89, 108–114, 147, 154
  "associate," 53, 71, 111, 114
  versus mother tongue, 45, 49
Natural language, formalization of, 163
"Near-dialectized" languages, 109–112, 116n.1
Nehru, Jawaharlal, 141
Neo-classical stock (of lexicon), coining terms from, 156
"Neo-elites." See Regional elite
Neo-literates, 67, 153
Neologisms, 155
Neustupný, Jiri, 19, 24, 26, 34
Newspapers in India, 15 (Table 3)
Nonstandard Negro English (NNE), 43
Normative systems, 24, 29, 30, 32 (Table 6), 75, 115, 130, 153, 175
  dichotomy between "normative entity" and "speech process," 30, 32 (Table 6)
North Central region. See also HUP region
  assertion of monolingualism among multilinguals, 111
  as "divided joint family," 113
Novi Sad *Dogovor* (agreement) for Serbo-Croatian, 116n.3

Official language, 5, 59, 67, 69, 109, 134, 137
Official Language Commission, *1956,* 71, 84, 141, 142
"Official Language Year" in Maharashtra, 84
Optional languages, in teaching, 138
Oral-aural system of language teaching, 129
Oral communication versus written communication, 82, 110
"Ordinary" tradition in education system, 118, 119, 143
Organic pluralism. See Pluralism
"Organic unity," of Indian society, 153
Oriental languages, 34
Oriental learning, 121
Oriental and Occidental societies, 158
Orientalists' view, among British administrators, 119

Orthography, 36, 84, 156
Osmania University, 85
Out-group communication, 72 (Table 8)

Pan-Indian languages, 69, 70, 127, 129
Panjab state, bifurcation in *1966,* 97 (Table 13), 101 (Table 16)
Panjabi
  and Gurumukhi script, 54, 109
  as part of Hindi literary tradition, 111
  and Sikhs, 109
Panjabi "language" tradition, 108
Panjabi University, 85
Pan-South Asian English, 79
Parole (and langue), Saussure's dichotomy, 39n.3
Parsees, 152
Pāṭhaśālā, traditional system of education, 117, 119
Pedagogy, 82, 153, 155
Performance (distinct from expectations) in linguistic behavior, 39n.3
Performance and perception, a paradox, 45
Permissiveness in pronunciation, 86n.3, 114
Persian
  poetry, 133n.3
  vocabulary, 60
  writing system, 153
Perso-Arabic literary tradition, Urdu allegiance to, 111
Perso-Arabic script, 70, 86n.2, 109–112, 116
  modified for Sindhi, 123
  Naskhi and *Nastalik* characters of, 118
Persuasive techniques, in Oriental and Occidental societies, 158
Philippines, bilingual education programs in, 128
Philology, 38, 82, 164
Phonological features, 39n.4, 112
Pidgin (languages), 178, 180
Pidginization. See Language pidginization
Pike, Kenneth L., 39n.3
Pitt, William, 120
Plural media. See Instructional medium
Plural society (societies), 4, 25, 43, 45, 66, 67, 75, 76, 89, 122, 128, 130, 137, 155, 157, 164, 168. See also Plurilingual society, Pluralistic speech communities
  and language boundaries, 43
Pluralism, 170, 175
  cultural and linguistic expression of, 170

Subject Index

models of, organic and structural, 169, 170
types of, 172 (Table 21)
Plurality Square, 170
Plurilingual behavior, versus monolingual, 53
Plurilingual hierarchy, 50
Plurilingual situation, 71
Polarization
  of language medium issues, 145
  between oral and written transactions, 82
Polish ethnic group (nationality), 23, 62
Politicization, of language issues, 54, 56–62, 124
Politics, over language privileges, 139
"Polycentric" languages, having "composite" linguistic identity, 115, 116
Portuguese rule, 115
Post-Renaissance period, 58
"Practical" education. *See* "Ordinary" tradition
Pragmatic dimension of language activity, 34, 165
Prague School, and fostering of standard languages, 149
prayoga (usage), of newly coined terms, 155
Prescriptive code, 28
Press
  content of, in Hindi and English, 15, 16 (Table 4)
  in Indian languages, 14, 15 (Table 3)
  in metropolitan areas, 15
Press Registrar's Report, *1978* (for year *1977*), 15 (Table 3), 16 (Table 4)
Pressure groups
  Hindu and Muslim, 116
  over language, 54, 62
Pressure indices, 51–53
Primary education, 86n.5, 121, 127, 136, 145
"Primary" socialization, and education, 118
Princep, H. T., 119, 120
Printing press, 86n.4
  impact of on Indian prose, 123, 124
Privileged languages, 118, 122
Progressive differentiation in language teaching, 153
Projectional dimension of language development, 21 (Table 5), 63, 77
Pronominal system
  Gujarati, 34
  Hindi-Urdu, 35–37, 165

Pronunciation characteristics in Indian languages
  regional deviations, 78, 86n.3, 90, 114
  stereotypes, 9, 125
Propriety axis, in Hindi-Urdu pronominal system, 35–37
Propriety controls
  implicit and explicit, 28, 29, 146 (Table 20)
  situation-bound, 32 (Table 6)
Proto-language(s), chronological stages of, 164

RP (Received Pronunciation) in British English, 49, 114
Regional elite, 67
  "neo-elites," in the power structure, 147
Regional identity, 57
Regional language(s), 13, 41, 70, 75, 83, 84, 95, 105, 107, 127, 137, 138, 146 (Table 20), 147
  claimed as contact languages, 13, 14, 52, 66, 144
  in education, 127, 134, 137, 138, 142, 145, 146 (Table 20), 151
Regional speech, 125
Regional variations in Hindi-Urdu amalgam, 114
Regional varieties of speech, 71
Regional systems of writing, 70, 118, 119
Religiocultural groups, 108
Religious identity and mother tongue, 57, 108
Renaissance and Reformation, European, 19, 123
Rhetorics, 36
Role ascription and role mobility, in an interaction, 23, 31
Ross, Jennie, 50
Roy, Raja Ram Mohan, 119
Rural education, 121

Said, Abdul A., 168
Sanskrit records, 119
Sanskrit system of education, 120
Santali community, rural, 72 (Table 8)
Saraswati, Dayanand, 123
Saussure, Ferdinand, 39n.3
School/classroom language, 75, 133n.2, 147
School education system, 117, 119, 129, 130, 140 (Table 19)
School(s), 70, 72 (Table 8), 74, 79, 137, 139, 165
  in the Bellary district, *1823*, 133n.2
  bilingual, 154

Scottish census, *1931,* 57
Script(s), 13. *See also* Writing systems
  for Indian languages, 70
  controversy in Sindhi, 86n.2, 123
  of literacy, 61
  monistic demands for recognizing a single variety for each language, 82, 121
  polarization of issue, 109
  standardization of, 69, 115, 123
  for writing Sanskrit, 119
Scripts, labels
  Bhoti, 119
  Cyrillic, 116
  Devanagari, 54, 70, 86n.2, 109, 110, 112, 116, 118, 123, 133n.3
  Grantha, 119
  Gurumukhi, 54, 109, 133n.3
  Latin, 113, 116
  Mahajani, 118
  Nagari, 70, 119
  Perso-Arabic, 54, 70, 110, 153. *See also* Arabic/Persian
  regional characters, 70, 118
  Sharda, 119
  Thai, 70
Second Five-Year Plan, *1956,* and tribal languages, 145
Second-language teaching, 77, 82, 129, 132, 137, 154
Secondary education, 70, 71, 121, 127, 137
Secondary Education Commission, *1953,* 137
Segmental identities, 5-8, 118
Selection processes, in language activity, 31
Selective education
  Macaulay's policy, 123
  versus universal, 126
Semantic acrobatics, over Hindi-Urdu-Hindustani, 60, 61
Semiotics, 77
Sensibility, language performance capability, 154
Syntax and semantics. *See* Linguistic patterns
Sharda script, 119
Sikhs, and Panjabi language tradition, 108
Simmons, Luis R., 168
Sindhi
  and Gurumukhi, 54
  and Kachhi speakers, 46
  script controversy, 86n.2, 123
Situation-bound planning, 152-156
Slangs, 21 (Table 5)
Sledd, James, 43

Social borders, definition of, 50
Social elites, 78, 136
Social homogenization, valued by British rulers, 123
Social identification
  and mother tongue, 45, 59, 90
  language learning, 152
Social identity, types of, 89, 93, 114
Social justice, 169
Social mobility and language, 130
Social planning, 61-64, 156
Social sciences, 85, 157
Social stratification, 119
Social structure, stratified, 7, 8
Socialization
  "primary," 118
  processes and values, 71
Sociocultural affinities (identities), 46, 109, 175
Socioeconomic demands and bilingual media, 126
Sociolinguistics
  framework, 42
  realities, 8, 25, 67, 90, 114, 150
  studies and research, 31, 39n.3, 41, 131
  theory, 157
  variables, 132
Soviet Union, bilingual and bicultural education programs, 128
Space dimension, in linguistic studies, 164
"Specificational" meaning, in language activity, 31
Speech, 47, 59, 166
  casual, 113, 114
  characteristics of, 47, 90, 108
  diverse usage of, 114, 115, 163
  echo-pressures on, 171, 172 (Table 21)
  elite-acceptable, ideals of, 28, 53, 125
  formalistic, 113, 114
  manifestation and organization of, 170, 172 (Table 21)
  ornamental and instrumental uses of, 26
  "relativism" in, 131
  substandard, 114
  superposed, 18n.6
  time and space dimensions of, 155, 164, 172 (Table 21)
Speech act, 31, 166. *See also* Communicative act
Speech activity, 132, 158, 175
  normative patterns in, 28, 49
  plurilateral facets of, 34, 39n.3
Speech attitudes, 112
Speech area, 71, 153
Speech behavior, 28, 30, 49, 61, 63, 71, 131. *See also* Language/verbal behavior

Subject Index

contours of, 40–41, 48, 150, 158
deliberate change in, 24, 158
fluidity in, 159
patterns of, 6, 81, 112, 126, 152, 153, 164
pluralistic model of, 153
Speech communication. *See* Communication
Speech communities, 7, 25, 28, 29, 30, 41, 54, 56, 82, 123, 150
categorization process in, 47–49
homogeneous, 163
inter-urban, 110
plural, 89, 90, 92–95, 102–105, 107–116
segmented, 155
sensitivities of, 77, 158
shifts in language domain, 114, 115, 125, 126
stratificational and regional differentiation in, 25
"tradition" and "echo" systems available to, 165
traditional, 159
Speech controls
organization of plurality, 172 (Table 21)
strategy of, 30, 32 (Table 6)
Speech conventions, 115
Speech diversity, 163–165, 167
Speech event(s), 31, 111, 156, 166
Speech fluidity. *See* Fluidity
Speech functions. *See* Language functions
Speech groups, 3, 7, 43, 49, 54, 70, 86n.3, 114, 151
assertive, 98 (Table 14)
five categories claiming Hindi, 109, 110
fluid, 92, 164
heterogeneous, 28, 89, 109
"static" and "dynamic" stages of, 34
Speech habits, 47, 75, 89, 104, 109, 125
Speech heterogeneity, 32 (Table 6), 111
Speech labels, 9
parameters for distinguishing language-dialect-register, 43
Speech matrix, 29, 35, 48, 112, 115, 165
Speech message, 166, 167
Speech norms, 115
Speech patterns, 69, 70, 153
Speech process, 30, 32 (Table 6)
Speech register(s), 75, 130
Speech setting. *See* Communication matrix
Speech spectrum. *See also* Linguistic spectrum
contours of its depth and breadth, 164, 165
Speech status, organization of plurality, 172 (Table 21)

Speech stratum, identifying a variety of interactions, 71
Speech structure, 86n.3
Speech styles, 26, 27, 75
at the levels of elegance, 26, 50, 113, 114, 118, 123, 145
on the scale of formality-informality, 109, 110
spoken and written, 37, 129
standard style sheets, 32 (Table 6), 153
tatsamized, 155
Speech values. *See* Language values
Speech variation, 7, 17n.1, 18n.6, 26, 27
attitudes toward, 32 (Table 6), 40, 41, 49, 128
correlations of, 35, 172 (Table 21)
defined, 167
across dialects, 75
hierarchical patterning, 26, 115, 172 (Table 21)
as a "natural" process, 131
standardizing the unit of, 63
and territory, 172 (Table 21)
types of, 18n.6, 113, 114
Speech variety (varieties), 45, 49, 72 (Table 8), 92, 115–116, 125, 150, 167
Brahmin and non-Brahmin, 26
and language education, 72 (Table 8), 153
"privileged" versus "handicapped," 20, 21 (Table 5)
substandard, 72 (Table 8), 109, 130
supradialectal, 72 (Table 8), 153
standard, 43, 74, 77
sphoṭa (plosion) doctrine, 166
Spolsky, Bernard, 39n.1
Spontaneity, 32 (Table 6)
Sprachbund, speech area, 153
Sri Venkateswara University, 143
Stable Zone, 7, 98 (Table 14), 105, 106 (Table 17)
Stack, Captain George, 123
Standard language(s), 19, 21 (Table 5), 26, 28, 43, 49, 64n.4, 71, 130, 149, 157
Standardization
bi-modal and multimodal, 27, 116
processes, 28, 43, 76, 111, 121, 123, 125
tools of, 32 (Table 6), 115
Stanford Project, of International Language Planning Processes, 85
State languages, 5, 80, 109
State policy in education, 127
States Reorganization Commission, *1956,* 176
Steiner, George, 50, 164, 167
Štokavian, literary norm of Serbo-Croatian, 115

Stratificational hierarchy, 32 (Table 6), 171
Structural pluralism. *See* Pluralism
Stylistic variation, 28, 78, 113
Subsidiary language(s), 13, 54, 95, 129
Śuddha (pure) languages, 145
Supradialectal variants, 153
Symbols, visual, 76

tadbhava, assimilated words from Sanskrit, 39n.4
Tagore, Rabindranath, 122
Tahitianization, 41
Tamil-speaking elite, as liaison in "ordinary" tradition, 118
Tarachand Commission, *1948*, 141
tatsama, unassimilated words from Sanskrit, 39n.4, 155
Teaching matrices, and language proficiency, 128
Teaching second and third languages, compulsory versus optional, 138
Teachers
  Akhund under the *maktab* system, 133n.3
  of Barbiana, representing higher-class values of speech, 132
  Brahmin, 133n.3
  of English, 78, 157
  and language policy, 147
  linguistically oriented, 155
  multilingual, 147
Technical terms. *See* Coinage of terms
Technologization, a dimension of language development, 21 (Table 5), 114
Telugu characters, in writing, 119
Textbook language, 126, 157
Textbook preparation, 69, 77, 86n.5, 145
Thai script, for Khampti, 70
Third-language teaching, under the Three-Language Formula, 77, 82, 137, 153
Thought processes, 158
Three-Language Formula, *1956*, 51, 67, 70, 74, 137
Time dimension, temporality in linguistic studies, 164, 165
"Tradition" and "echo" systems, of a speech community, 163-165
"tradition" and "modernity," role in education of, 132
Tradition-inspired profiles of languages, 32 (Table 6)
Traditional education system
  "advanced" and "ordinary," 22, 118, 119, 120, 123, 125, 143, 144, 147
  characteristics of, 118, 119, 120
Transformationists, 164

Translations, 23, 81, 124, 146 (Table 20)
Transplanted language, 165
Trends. *See* Language trends
Tribal communities, 70, 127, 147
  identity, 89
Tribal languages, 10 (Table 2), 68, 70, 84, 103
  in education, 74, 127, 145
Trumpp, Ernest, 123
Two-tier media. *See* Instructional medium
tuu/tum, address forms in Hindi-Urdu, 36, 37

UNESCO reports, 59, 124
Unilingual character, in universities, 143
Union government and education policy, 69
United States, bilingual and bicultural education programs in, 128
Universal education, 122
Universal knowledge, 147
University(-ies)
  established by the British rulers in *1857*, 121
  establishing a vernacular university, *1876*, 22
  for maintaining traditional Muslim education, 139
  in metropolitan areas, 143
University education, 20, 121, 127, 128, 155
University Education Commission, *1949*, 71, 137, 141
University Grants Commission, 20, 142, 144
University language medium, 121, 139, 141-143
University Teachers Conference, *1952*, 147
Unwritten languages, 19
Urban elite, as language custodians, 153
Urban speakers, 113
Urban speech, 28
Urban standards, 74
Urbanization, 113
Urdu
  "associate" native speech, 111
  elites, 135
  in Fluid Zone (HUP region), 109, 112
  language teaching, 138
  linguistic features, 112-114
  literacy in, 125
  literary tradition, 111
  and Muslims, 60, 61, 95, 97 (Table 13), 108, 110, 139
  patterns of borrowing, 90, 112
  script and mother tongue, 108, 109

Subject Index

speech styles, 90, 113, 114
university medium 141
Utterances, pedantic dichotomy of, 130

Verbal behavior. *See* Speech behavior
Verbal communication. *See* Communication
Verbal hierarchy. *See* Language hierarchy
Verbal repertoire, 7, 20, 23, 89
   characteristics in, 25, 28, 30, 32 (Table 6), 109, 167
   "conditioning" and "regulative" processes in, 31, 163
   propriety, 49, 50
   and types of plurality, 170, 172 (Table 21)
"Verbalism," empty, 132
Verbalization, social, 82, 155
Vernacular(s), 18n.6, 20, 22, 94, 96 (Table 12), 122, 143, 146 (Table 20)
   diglossia functions of, 21 (Table 5), 114
   development of, 20, 103, 121, 143, 145
   versus English, 20, 122
   as mother tongue(s), 104
   as "near dialectized" languages, 27, 108–110, 116n.1
   types of, 44, 117, 119
   UNESCO definition, 59
Vernacular education, 22, 70, 121
Vernacular university at Lahore, 22
Vernacularization
   case of Awadhi and Braj, 27, 116n.1, 168

demand for cultural resurgence, 123
Illyrian movement in Yugoslavia, 115
Vidyasagar, Ishwar Chandra, 119
Vocabulary(-ies), 60, 112–114, 154
Voluntary organizations, role in language promotion, 83

Waismann, Freidrich, 156
Western Enlightenment, 122, 123
Western languages, 113
Western philologists, 25
Western theories of education. *See* Education
Westernization of Indian languages, 37, 38, 113
Westernized elite, 20, 41, 67, 136
Wider communication languages, 21 (Table 5)
Whitehead, Alfred N., 132
Winograd, Terry, 31
Wittgenstein, Ludwig, 163, 165
Wood Despatch, *1854,* 121
Working class speakers, 130
"World" languages, 21 (Table 5), 75, 134, 136
Writing systems. *See* Scripts
Written and unwritten languages, 19, 21 (Table 5), 157
Written word, in predominantly illiterate societies, 82

Yugoslav census, 56
Yugoslavia, bilingual and bicultural education programs, 128

Eileen J. Dunne, Jin Hi Lee, Nina A. McClesky, Mae M. Moriwaki, Margaret J. Obi, and Judy M. Watanabe contributed to the preparation of the index. In addition, special thanks are due Kimberly L. Kohara, Norma L. Matsukawa, and Professor Sarah K. Vann.

OHIO UNIVERSITY LIBRARY

Please return this book as soon as you

P 40.45 .I4 K5 1983

Khubchandani, Lachman Mulchand.

Plural languages, plural cultures :